The Pious Caliphs

The Pious Caliphs

By
Dr Majid Ali Khan

Edited by
Syed Athar Husain

Islamic Book Trust,
Kuala Lumpur

© Islamic Book Trust 1998

ISBN 978-983-9154-08-5

First published 1978

This Student Edition by
Islamic Book Trust
607 Mutiara Majestic
Jalan Othman
46000 Petaling Jaya
Selangor, Malaysia
ibtkl@streamyx.com
www.ibtbooks.com

First reprint 2001
Second reprint 2007

Cover
The *Hilya* of the Prophet, in traditional Turkish *nasakh* calligraphy by Ahmet Kamil Efendi, for graduation as calligrapher, 1882

Printed by
Academe Art and Printing Services

Contents

	Page
Preface	vii
Introduction	ix

Section I: Abu Bakr As-Siddiq — 1
- Chapter 1   Abu Bakr as-Siddiq: His Early Life — 3
- Chapter 2   Hadrat Abu Bakr's Caliphate — 14
- Chapter 3   Death and Review of Hadrat Abu Bakr's Achievements — 35

Section II: 'Umar Ibn al-Khattab — 53
- Chapter 4:   Umar bin al-Khattab: His Early Life — 55
- Chapter 5   Hadrat 'Umar's Caliphate — 59
- Chapter 6   Death and Review of Hadrat 'Umar's Achievements — 79
- Chapter 7   Hadrat 'Umar's Administration:
  A Picture of Islamic Democratic Rule — 87

Section III: 'Uthman Ibn 'Affan — 113
- Chapter 8   'Uthman Ibn 'Affan: His Early Life — 115
- Chapter 9   Hadrat 'Uthman's Caliphate — 119
  - A. Conquests and Miscellaneous Events — 120
  - B. Internal Disorder — 127
- Chapter 10   Hadrat 'Uthman's Martyrdom and Review of His Works — 138
  - A. Martyrdom — 138
  - B. Review of Hadrat 'Uthman's Services to Islam — 146
  - C. Administration of Hadrat 'Uthman — 152

Section IV: 'Ali Ibn Abi Talib — 157
- Chapter 11   'Ali Ibn 'Abi Talib: His Early Life — 159
- Chapter 12   Hadrat 'Ali's Caliphate — 166
  - A. Problems faced by Hadrat 'Ali as *Khalifah* — 166
  - B. Civil War — 177

Chapter 13 Hadrat 'Ali's Martyrdom and Review of His Works   198
            A. Martyrdom   198
            B. Review of Hadrat 'Ali's Service to Islam   199
            C. Administration of Hadrat 'Ali   209

Section V: The Downfall of the Pious Caliphate   215
Chapter 14 The Downfall of the Pious Caliphate   217
            A. Appraisal of the Pious Caliphate   217
            B. Islamic Democratic System observed
               by *Khulafa-i-Rashidin*   218
            C. Administration under *Khulafa-i-Rashidin*   227
            D. Social Life   232

Bibliography   235

Preface

In the name of Allah, the Beneficent, the Merciful.

There is a dire need to present Islam in its pure form in European languages, especially in English which is spoken and understood by a wide cross-section of society throughout the world. The books on Islamic history which are available in English are mostly written by European authors who have tried to taint the purity of Islamic culture and its spiritual impact on various nations.

The aim of Islam has never been to preach at the point of sword as alleged by the Orientalists. It was the charm of its sublime teachings which attracted so many of the nations, and millions of people accepted it as their way of life within a very short period of time. Islamic culture became dearer to them than their own traditions and customs. The language of Islam — Arabic — became the mother tongue of a number of non-Arab nations which rightly boast today to be Arabs. All this happened in such a short period of time that even today non-Muslim scholars wonder at the spiritual influence of Islam as a fact of history and try to cover it with the veil of their prejudiced writings. This book is written to highlight some of the facts of Islamic history and to present them in the light of original sources.

The major part of the book was written while the author was serving in Trinidad (West Indies). However, the manuscript remained incomplete due to his return from there.

Now it has been revised and a short introduction has also been added to it. May Allah accept this humble effort.

(Dr Mawlvi) Majid Ali Khan,
Dept. of Islamic Studies, Jamia Millia Islamia,
New Delhi - 110025, India.
4.9.1396 / 31.8.1976.

Introduction

Meaning of *Khalifah*

Caliph is the English version of the Arabic word *Khalifah* which means a vicegerent or viceroy or a successor. In Islamic Law a Caliph or *Khalifah* is the person who holds the delegated authority to enforce the Islamic law and religion (i.e., *Shar`ia*) in an Islamic State on the one hand and who is the sole executive authority on the other. Under the sovereignty of Allah Almighty, and the authority of His Law — the religion and law of Islam (*Shari`a*) — the *Khalifah* or Caliph is the temporal ruler of an Islamic State and defender of the Faith. Being charged with implementing *Shari`a* for its application in the everyday life of the individual and society, he secures well being in this world and bliss in the Hereafter. As far as delegated authority of the Law is concerned he is a *Khalifah*, a successor or vicegerent of the Holy Prophet (*Sallallahu `alayhi wa Sallam*) who is the "Right Vicegerent" of Allah Almighty on this earth; and as far as the execution of the law is concerned he is the *Amir* or Imam, i.e., Ruler or Leader of the Muslims in his time, and for this reason the Caliphs of Islam were commonly known as "*Amirul-Mu'minin*" ("The Ruler of the Believers").

The Pious or the Truthful Caliphs

After the Holy Prophet (*Sallallahu `alayhi wa Sallam*), the first four Caliphs — Abu Bakr, `Umar, `Uthman and `Ali (*Ridwanullah `alayhim Ajma`in*) — strictly followed his ways. Their time is the "Golden Age" of Islam when Islamic law and religion — *Shari`a* — fully flourished and were perfectly implemented. They were the ideal rulers who guided the *Ummah* (followers of the Holy Prophet) on the Right Path and discharged their duties faithfully. For this reason they are known as *Khulafa-i-Rashidin*, i.e., "The Rightly-guided Caliphs."

The Holy Qur'an on *Khilafat* (Caliphate)

Here are quoted some of the verses of the Holy Qur'an which clearly point out the institution of *Khilafat* (Caliphate) in general and the *Khilafat-i-Rashidah* (Rightly-guided Caliphate) in particular. As the political theory of Islam is not within the scope of this book, the institution of *Khilafat* is not described here in detail.

i. *"Allah has promised to those among you, who believe and work righteousness, that He will surely grant them Khilafat (i.e., inheritance of power) in the land, as He granted the Khilafat to those before them, and that He will surely establish for them their religion which He hath approved for them, and will give them in exchange, safety after their fear"* (Q. 24:55).

ii. *"And Verily We have written in the Psalms after the Message (given to the Prophet at that time): `My righteous servants will inherit the land'"* (Q. 21:105).

iii. *"(They are) those who, if We give them power in the land, establish Salat (worship), and pay Zakat (Charity), and enjoin the Right and forbid the Wrong. And Allah's is the sequel of events"* (Q. 22:41).

iv. *"O ye who believe! If any from among you turn back from his Faith, Allah will bring a people (in power) who He loveth and who love Him. (They would be) humble towards believers (but) stern towards disbelievers, (and they) will strive in the Path of Allah and will never be afraid of the blame of any blamer. Such*

INTRODUCTION

is the grace of Allah which He giveth unto whom He wills. Allah is All-Embracing, All-Knowing" (Q. 5:57).

v. *"Say to the desert Arabs who lagged behind: `Ye will be called against a folk of mighty powers, to fight them until they surrender; and if ye obey, Allah will give you a fair reward; but if ye turn away as ye did turn away before, He will punish you with a painful doom'"* (Q. 17:15).

In this verse a prophecy was made for the war with the Persian and Byzantine empires. Since only a person in power (i.e., ruler) could call people to fight against other nations, Shah Waliyullah of Delhi, has referred this verse to *Khilafat-i-Rashidah* during which this prophecy was fulfilled.

There are a number of verses in the Holy Qur'an (viz., 2:30; 7:10, 69, 74, 129; 38:26; 35:39) in which the institution of Caliphate has been defined in one way or the other. Since they do not point out directly towards *Khilafat-i-Rashidah*, they are not being mentioned here.

Traditions (*Ahadith*) on *Khilafat-i-Rashidah*

Hadrat Shah Waliyullah of Delhi has given 370 *Ahadith* in this connection in his famous book, *Izalatul Khafa*. Some *Ahadith* on this topic are mentioned here, the details can be seen in *Izalatul Khafa*.

The Holy Prophet (*Sallallahu `alayhi wa Sallam*) said, "I have put you on a way which is clear, and even its night is like an enlightened day. Nobody, will deviate from that way, after me, but a doomed person. You would come across with differences after me. But you should stick to my *Sunnah* (ways) and the *Sunnah* (ways) of my Rightly-guided *Khulafa* (successors). Hold to those ways with your teeth (i.e., be firm on them), and follow them (i.e., Muslim rulers) even though your ruler is a black slave because a believer is like a camel whose nose has been tied, therefore he is obedient to one who holds him" (*Ahmad*).

The Holy Prophet (*Sallallahu `alayhi wa Sallam*) said, "*Khilafat* (Caliphate) would continue for thirty years after *Nubuwwat* (Prophethood) then it will change into kingship" (*Hakim*).

Note — This time limit ends at Hadrat `Ali because the period of Abu Bakr's (R.A.) Caliphate is about two years, then of `Umar (R.A.) about ten years, then of `Uthman (R.A.) of twelve years and the Caliphate of Hadrat `Ali (R.A.) about six years. If the Caliphate of Hadrat Hasan (R.A.) is counted then thirty years period would be fully completed.

In another Hadith the Holy Prophet (*Sallallahu `alayhi wa Sallam*) said, "This religion has started with prophethood and Allah's Mercy. Then it would pass on to *Khilafat* and Mercy of Allah, which will be changed into a bitter kingship. Then there would prevail cruelty and injustice and the people will commit evil. They will wear silken clothes, drink liquor and will indulge in adultery. Although they would be committing sins, Allah would provide them sustenance and would continue bestowing His favours upon them until they meet Him."

Hadrat Anas (R.A.) has narrated that the people of Banu Mustaliq sent him to the Holy Prophet (*Sallallahu `alayhi wa Sallam*) to ascertain to whom should they pay *Zakat* after him. The Holy Prophet (*Sallallahu `alayhi wa Sallam*) said, "Pay to Abu Bakr." Hadrat Anas told them what the Holy Prophet said. They again sent him to enquire as to whom should they pay the *Zakat* if something happened to Abu Bakr. Then the Holy Prophet (*Sallallahu `alayhi wa Sallam*) said, "Then pay to `Umar." When Anas informed them, they again sent him back to the Holy Prophet to find out to whom should they pay *Zakat* after `Umar. The Holy Prophet (*Sallallahu `alayhi wa Sallam*) said, "Then pay to `Uthman". Hadrat Anas conveyed the reply of the Holy Prophet (*Sallallahu `alayhi wa Sallam*). They once more sent him to the Holy Prophet to ask whom should they pay *Zakat* if some thing happened to `Uthman. Then the Holy Prophet said, "There would be chaos after him" (*Hakim*).

The Holy Prophet (*Sallallahu 'alayhi wa Sallam*) said, "Last night a pious person dreamt that Abu Bakr was confided to the Prophet of Allah and 'Umar was confided to Abu Bakr, and 'Uthman was confided to 'Umar." Hadrat Jabir says, "When we departed from the Holy Prophet (*Sallallahu 'alayhi wa Sallam*) we said that the pious person (who saw the dream) was the Holy Prophet (*Sallallahu 'alayhi wa Sallam*) and confidence was the *Khilafat* (rule) after him" (*Ahmad and Hakim*).

Imam Ahmad has quoted the following Hadith from 'Abdullah bin Muhammad bin 'Aqil bin Abi Talib, who narrated from Jabir that the Holy Prophet (*Sallallahu 'alayhi wa Sallam*) said, "A man of Paradise will come soon under the shade of those trees of dates." Soon after that Abu Bakr (R.A.) came there. Again the Holy Prophet (*Sallallahu 'alayhi wa Sallam*) said, "A man of Paradise will come soon under these trees of dates." Soon after 'Umar (R.A) came there. The Holy Prophet (*Sallallahu 'alayhi wa Sallam*) further said, "A man of Paradise will come soon under these trees of dates." Then 'Uthman (R.A.) came there. The Holy Prophet (*Sallallahu 'alayhi wa Sallam*) said the fourth time, "A man of Paradise will appear soon under the shade of these trees of dates." Then the Holy Prophet prayed three times, "0 Allah let him be 'Ali if Ye desires so." When the Holy Prophet (*Sallallahu 'alayhi wa Sallam*) had finished his *Du'a* (Prayer), Hadrat 'Ali (R.A.) appeared.

In a Hadith given in *Bukhari*, Hadrat 'Abdullah bin 'Umar said, "During the time of the Prophet of Allah (*Sallallahu 'alayhi wa Sallam*) we used to make comparative assessment of the excellence of the companions, and found Abu Bakr (R.A.) the best among all, then 'Umar and then 'Uthman." This Hadith has also been given in *Abu Dawud, Musnad Ahmad, Tirmidhi* and other books with slight difference in the words.

In another Hadith mentioned by Bukhari, Hadrat `Abdullah bin `Umar (R.A.) narrated that the Holy Prophet (*Sallallahu `alayhi wa Sallam*) said, "In a dream I saw myself standing near a well. I drew from it a bucket full of water. In the meantime Abu Bakr came and took the bucket from my hand and drew from it one bucketful or two, but in his drawing there was some weakness, may Allah forgive him. Then `Umar bin Khattab came and took hold of the bucket from him. It then changed into a large bucket, and I have never seen a stronger man than `Umar drawing (water) until all the people drank it and were refreshed; then they quenched the thirst of their camels which lay down after they had enough."

Abu Said al-Khudri reported Allah's Prophet as saying, "There is no prophet who does not have two *Wazirs* (Ministers) from the inhabitants of heaven and two from the inhabitants of the earth. My two *Wazirs* (Ministers) from the inhabitants of heaven are Gabriel and Michael, and my two *Wazirs* (Ministers) from the inhabitants of the earth are Abu Bakr and `Umar" (*Tirmidhi*).

Hadrat Abu Bakr (R.A.) narrated that a man said to the Apostle of Allah, "I saw as though a scale descended from the sky. You and Abu Bakr were weighed and you (i.e., the Holy Prophet) were heavier; then Abu Bakr and `Umar were weighed and Abu Bakr was heavier; then `Umar and `Uthman were weighed and `Umar was heavier; then the scale was lifted up" (*Tirmidhi, Abu Dawud*).

In another Hadith narrated by Abdullah bin `Umar (R.A.) the Holy Prophet (*Sallallahu `alayhi wa Sallam*) said, "The most compassionate of my people is Abu Bakr, the most rigorous regarding Allah's affairs is `Umar, the most genuinely modest is `Uthman, the most learned in legal matters is `Ali, the one who knows most about obligatory duties is Zaid bin Thabit, the one who knows best how to recite the Holy Qur'an is Ubayy bin Ka`b, and the one who has greatest knowledge about what is lawful and what is prohibited is Mu`adh bin Jabal. Every people have a trustworthy guardian, and the trustworthy guardian of this community is Abu `Ubaidah bin al-Jarrah" (*Abu Ya`la* and also by *Ahmad and Tirmidhi*).

In this Hadith the qualities of the four Rightly-guided Caliphs have been mentioned in the same order as they ruled in the later periods.

The following *Ahadith* speak about the obedience of *Khulafa* in particular and Muslim rulers in general:

The Holy Prophet (*Sallallahu `alayhi wa Sallam*) said, "There will come rulers (*Khulafa* or *Umara*) after me; render them your obedience, for the ruler is like a shield where-with a man protects himself. If they are righteous and rule over you well, they shall have their reward; but if they do evil and rule over you badly, then punishment will fall upon them and you will be free from it, for they are responsible for you, but you have no responsibility towards them" (*Kanz*).

In another Hadith the Holy Prophet (*Sallallahu `alayhi wa Sallam*) said, "Obey your rulers (Caliphs) whatever may happen, for if they bid you do anything different to what I have taught you, they shall be punished for it, and you will be rewarded for your obedience; and if they bid you do anything different to what I have taught you, the responsibility is theirs and you are free from it. When you meet Allah (on the Day of Judgement) say, `O Lord, Thou didst send us prophets and we obeyed them by Thy Permission, and You set over us caliphs and we obeyed them by Thy permission, and our rulers gave us orders and we obeyed them by Thy permission, and our rulers gave us orders and we obeyed them for Thy sake', and Allah will answer, `Ye speak the truth; theirs is the responsibility and you are free from it'" (*Kanz*).

The Holy Prophet (*Sallallahu `alayhi wa Sallam*) said, "Obey every ruler (*Amir*), pray behind every Imam and insult none of my companions."

The Pious Caliphs

It was not merely the *Khalifah* but any lawfully constituted authority, that was to receive the obedience of the subjects, for in one Hadith the Holy Prophet (*Sallallahu `alayhi wa Sallam*) said, "O men, obey Allah, even though He sets over you as your ruler a mutilated Abyssinian slave" (*Kanz*).

In another Hadith the Holy Prophet (*Sallallahu `alayhi wa Sallam*) said, "When Allah wishes good for a people, He sets over them generous rulers; but when Allah wishes evil for a people, He sets over them the witless, and base and entrusts their goods to avaricious rulers" (*Kanz*).

In another Hadith narrated by Abu Hurairah (R.A.), the Holy Prophet (*Sallallahu `alayhi wa Sallam*) said, "He who obeys me has obeyed Allah, and he who disobeys me has disobeyed Allah; he who obeys the ruler (Imam or *Amir*) has obeyed me and he who disobeys the ruler has disobeyed me. The Imam is a shield behind whom fighting is engaged in and through whom protection is sought, so if he commands piety and acts righteously, he will have a reward for that but if he does otherwise he will on that account be held guilty" (*Bukhari and Muslim*).

The Holy Prophet said, "If a slave who has been mutilated is made your ruler (Imam or *Amir*) and leads you in accordance with Allah's Book, listen to him and obey."

In another Hadith the Holy Prophet (*Sallallahu `alayhi wa Sallam*) said, "Listen and obey, even if an Abyssinian slave with a head like a raisin is made ruler over you" (*Bukhari*).

Ibn `Umar (R.A.) has narrated that the Holy Prophet (*Sallallahu `alayhi wa Sallam*) said, "Hearing and obeying is the duty of a Muslim both regarding what he likes and what he dislikes, as long as he is not commanded to perform an act of disobedience to Allah in which case neither listen to him nor obey him" (*Bukhari and Muslim*).

The above-mentioned Ahadith enjoin that the Caliphs must be obeyed.

Title

After the death of the Holy Prophet (*Sallallahu `alayhi wa Sallam*) when Hadrat Abu Bakr (R.A.) was elected as the *Khalifah*, Muslims called him "*Khalifah* of Allah", but he objected to this title and said that he was only "*Khalifah* of the Apostle of Allah", therefore the title of "*Khalifah Rasul Allah*" (i.e., "Successor of the Apostle of Allah") was used with his name.

When Hadrat `Umar (R.A.) succeeded Abu Bakr (R.A.), he was given the same title, "*Khalifah Rasul Allah*" but later on he was called "*Amirul-Mu'minin*" (i.e., the ruler or the commander of the believers). Hadrat `Umar, at first, hesitated to have such a glorious title but there was a precedent. This title was given to Hadrat `Abdullah bin Jahsh (R.A.), the commander of the battalion sent by the Holy Prophet (*Sallallahu `alayhi wa Sallam*) to watch the movements of the caravan of Abu Sufyan, before the battle of Badr. Therefore, he accepted it. The same title was retained by Hadrat `Uthman and `Ali (R.A.).

SECTION I

Abu Bakr as-Siddiq
11-13 A.H. / 632-634 A.D.

1
Abu Bakr as-Siddiq: His Early Life

Name and parentage of Abu Bakr

Hadrat Abu Bakr as-Siddiq, (R.A.) was born in 573 A.D. at Mecca. Thus he was two years younger than the Holy Prophet (*Sallallahu `alayhi wa Sallam*). He belonged to a respectable and noble family, the Bani Tamim, a branch of Quraish Tribe. His lineage joins with that of the Holy Prophet (*Sallallahu `alayhi wa Sallam*) six generations before. His name was Abdullah. Abu Bakr was his patronymic name (or *Kuniyah*) which became so famous that most of the people did not know his real name. After his conversion to Islam he received the title of "As-Siddiq" (The Truthful). His father's name was `Uthman who was known by his patronymic name, Abu Qahafah. His mother's name was Salma but she was also known by her patronymic name, Ummul Khair.

Life before Islam

Since his boyhood, Hadrat Abu Bakr was a quiet and sincere man. He was very honest and truthful. Because of his sterling character he was the closest friend of the Holy Prophet (*Sallallahu `alayhi wa Sallam*) since his youth, and the friendship proved to be life-long. He was a soft-hearted man and keenly felt others' sufferings and miseries. He used to help the poor and the needy, the distressed and the downtrodden. Even before embracing Islam he did not like most of the customs of the days of ignorance and never drank any liquor.

His main profession was trade. He also accompanied the Holy Prophet (*Sallallahu `alayhi wa Sallam*) in some of his trade missions. Because of his honesty people trusted him and often kept their money as a trust with him. His nobility and truthfulness soon made him a rich trader. Actually these qualities were soon to serve the noblest cause of Allah.

First man to accept Islam

Hadrat Abu Bakr was a firm friend of the Holy Prophet and knew him better than any other man. His honesty, nobility, truthfulness and trustworthiness, had great attraction for Abu Bakr. When the Holy Prophet (*Sallallahu `alayhi wa Sallam*) disclosed to him secretly about the revelation of Allah, Abu Bakr accepted it immediately without having the slightest doubt. In this way he was the first adult free man to believe in the Holy Prophet's Mission, and became his confidant. The Holy Prophet (*Sallallahu `alayhi wa Sallam*) once spoke about this, "When I invited people towards Allah, everybody thought over it and hesitated, at least for a while, except Abu Bakr who accepted my call the moment I put it before him, and he did not hesitate even for a moment." When he accepted Islam, the Holy Prophet (*Sallallahu `alayhi wa Sallam*) was very pleased.

Da`wah (Invitation) towards Allah

As soon as he had accepted Islam he started the work of *Da`wah* (Invitation towards Allah) first secretly and then openly when it was so llowed by the Holy Prophet (*Sallallahu `alayhi wa Sallam*). First he went to `Uthman, Talha, Zubair and Said (*Ridwanullah `alayhim `Ajma`in*). They accepted Islam on his preaching. Next day he went to `Uthman bin Maz`un, Abu `Ubaidah, Abdur Rahman bin `Auf and some other prominent Quraish. They also accepted Islam at his hands. In the first instance eight prominent figures accepted Islam at the hands of Hadrat Abu Bakr as-Siddiq (R.A.). Among them was Hadrat `Uthman, the third Caliph of Islam. In this way he was the first Muslim, after the Holy Prophet, to preach Islam and to invite people towards Allah in a very fruitful way. The main reason for his success was his popularity among the Meccans because of his honesty, nobility, trustworthiness, good morals and fair dealings.

Hardships for *Da`wah* (Invitation) towards Allah

Even though he was so much respected yet he was not spared, and disbelievers of Mecca did their best to harass him.

When the number of Muslims reached 39, Abu Bakr (R.A.) asked the permission of the Holy Prophet (*Sallallahu `alayhi wa Sallam*) to invite people openly. On his persistent request the Holy Prophet (*Sallallahu `alayhi wa Sallam*) gave his consent and all of them went to the *Haram* (the Holy Mosque or Ka`bah) for *Tabligh* (Preaching). Hadrat Abu Bakr (R.A.) gave a *Khutbah* (Sermon) which was the first ever delivered in the annals of Islam. Hadrat Hamzah accepted Islam the same day. When disbelievers and idolaters from amongst Quraish heard it they fell on the Muslims from all sides. Abu Bakr (R.A.) despite the fact that he was considered to be the noblest and most respectable of all the people in Mecca, was beaten to such an extent that his nose and ears were badly mauled and his entire face was besmeared with blood. He was kicked, thrashed with shoes, trampled under feet and handled most roughly and savagely. He became unconscious and was half-dead. This is the place to observe his extreme love for the Holy Prophet (*Sallallahu `alayhi wa Sallam*) that when he gained consciousness and opened his eyes in the evening he first enquired, "How is the Prophet (*Sallallahu `alayhi wa Sallam*)?" His deep love for the Holy Prophet, really, was the main cause of his success. His love and respect for the Holy Prophet (*Sallallahu `alayhi wa Sallam*) was unbounded.

On another occasion the Holy Prophet (*Sallallahu `alayhi wa Sallam*) was offering his *Salat* in the Ka'bah. Abu Jahl came and put a sheet of cloth around his neck and twisted it hard in order to strangle the Holy Prophet to death. Seeing this, Hadrat Abu Bakr came rushing and pushed Abu Jahl aside and removed the piece of cloth from around the neck of the Holy Prophet (*Sallallahu `alayhi wa Sallam*). He then said, "Do you want to kill such a gentle person who is a Messenger of Allah and who declares Allah as the Cherisher and Sustainer?" Then Abu Jahl and other enemies of Islam fell upon Abu Bakr and beat him severely.

Miscellaneous services for the cause of Islam in Mecca

Hadrat Abu Bakr served Islam in numerous ways. The Quraish cruelly persecuted a number of slaves who had accepted Islam and made life difficult for them. Muslim slaves were the worst sufferers at the hands of non-Muslim masters. Hadrat Bilal (a Negro), one of the best known in the galaxy of Companions of the Holy Prophet, was one among such slaves. His master Umayyah bin Khalf lashed him at night and made him lie on the burning sand during the day because of Bilal's acceptance of Islam. Hadrat Abu Bakr bought him freedom and Bilal became a free Muslim. Other Muslim slaves who were bought by Hadrat Abu Bakr (R.A.) and made free were `Amir bin Fuhairah, Nazirah, Nahdiah, Jariah, Bani Momil and Bint Nahdiah (R.A.).

Before Hijrah Hadrat Abu Bakr spent lot of money on new converts.

When he found himself hard pressed by disbelievers he asked the permission of the Holy Prophet (*Sallallahu `alayhi wa Sallam*) to migrate to Abyssinia in the 5th year of the mission with other Muslims. The Holy Prophet (*Sallallahu `alayhi wa Sallam*) permitted him but in the way he met Ibn-ud-Daghna, the chief of another tribe, Qara. On his enquiry Hadrat Abu Bakr told him about the persecution of Quraish and his intention to migrate to Abyssinia. Ibn-ud-Daghna did not want him to leave Arabia and declared to the people of Mecca that Abu Bakr was under his protection. Then nobody dared to harm him.

Abu Bakr gets the title of "As-Siddiq"

The Holy Prophet (*Sallallahu `alayhi wa Sallam*) had *Mi`raj* (Ascension) in the 10th year of his Mission. He narrated his Ascension to the people in the morning. Some of them came to Abu Bakr and said, "Have you listened to your friend (the Holy Prophet)? He is claiming that he visited Jerusalem and the Sublime Throne in the heavens last night and talked with Allah Almighty. Would you believe it?" Hadrat Abu Bakr (R.A.) immediately replied. "If he said so then it is an absolute Truth". They again said, "Do you believe that he visited all these places and came back within a small part of night?" He again replied. "Of course I believe in it and I believe in the things which are farther than it, the news of Hell and Paradise". For this the Holy Prophet (*Sallallahu `alayhi wa Sallam*) named him As-Siddiq, i.e., the most Truthful and sincere person in Faith not having even the slightest doubt. Of course Abu Bakr's faith was so strong that nothing could shake it.

One of the Two in the Cave

When the Holy Prophet (*Sallallahu `alayhi wa Sallam*) decided to migrate to Medina, Abu Bakr was the only companion with him. He carried all his money, about five to six thousand Darhams, and started in the night with the Holy Prophet. They lay hidden in the cave of Thaur for three days. The Holy Qur'an describes it as follows:

> "... *When the disbelievers drove him out; he had no more than one companion. They were two in the cave. And he said to his companion: `Have no fear, for Allah is with us'. Then Allah sent down His peace upon him...* " (9:40).

Abu Bakr's slave `Amir bin Fuhairah tended the flocks of goats near the cave during the day and supplied them fresh milk in the night. After three days when Quraish stopped the search of the Holy Prophet, `Amir bin Fuhairah (Abu Bakr's slave) brought two she-camels and both started for Medina. Thus, of all the companions, Abu Bakr (R.A.) had the honour of accompanying the Holy Prophet in the most critical days of his life. He proved to be most trustworthy on all occasions.

Hadrat Abu Bakr at Medina

He reached Quba (a place near Medina) with the Holy Prophet (*Sallallahu `alayhi wa Sallam*) and stopped there. The Medinites were anxiously waiting for the Holy Prophet. At Quba there was a warm welcome. The Holy Prophet (*Sallallahu `alayhi wa Sallam*) stopped at the place of Bani `Amr bin `Auf at Quba. Multitudes of people came there to see the Holy Prophet (*Sallallahu `alayhi wa Sallam*) and most of them mistook Hadrat Abu Bakr as the Holy Prophet. On seeing this Hadrat Abu Bakr stood up and spread a sheet over the head of the Holy Prophet to protect from him the scorching rays of the hot sun. Then the Medinites recognises the Holy Prophet (*Sallallahu `alayhi wa Sallam*).

On reaching Medina he fell ill because of the change of climate and got high fever. The Holy Prophet (*Sallallahu `alayhi wa Sallam*) prayed for him and he was restored to health. At the time of establishing brotherhood bond between an immigrant from Mecca and a Medinite Muslim, the Holy Prophet (*Sallallahu `alayhi wa Sallam*) took into consideration the position in the society of the two persons. Hadrat Abu Bakr (R.A.) became the brother of Hadrat Haritha bin Zubair, a noted and respected Medinite.

Building of the Prophet's Mosque

There was an urgent need for building a mosque at Medina and a house for the Holy Prophet (*Sallallahu `alayhi wa Sallam*) and his family. The land which was selected for this belonged to two orphans. Their guardians wanted to give the land for the mosque free of charge but the Holy Prophet (*Sallallahu `alayhi wa Sallam*) did not accept their offer and asked Hadrat Abu Bakr to pay the price of the land. Thus Hadrat Abu Bakr became the first Muslim to spend most of his money for the cause of Allah at Medina. He participated in the construction of the mosque like an ordinary labourer with other Muslims.

Participation in the Holy Wars

He fought in almost all the battles along with the Holy Prophet (*Sallallahu `alayhi wa Sallam*). In the first battle of Islam at Badr he was with the Holy Prophet like a shadow. His own son, who had not embraced Islam by that time, was fighting on the side of Quraish. After he accepted Islam he said to Abu Bakr one day, "Dear father! I found you twice under my sword at Badr but I could not raise my hand because of my love for you". "If I had got a chance," Abu Bakr replied, "I would have killed you." It was Abu Bakr's suggestion on which the Holy Prophet (*Sallallahu `alayhi wa Sallam*) decided to release the prisoners of war after taking ransom.

In the battle of Uhud when some of the Muslims were running away, Abu Bakr was firm and when the Holy Prophet (*Sallallahu `alayhi wa Sallam*) was brought on the mountain after being injured, he was with him.

Hadrat Abu Bakr (R. A.) was the first companion to accept the peace plan of the Holy Prophet (*Sallallahu `alayhi wa Sallam*) without any hesitation at Hudaibiyah when all the Muslims insisted upon fighting. Even a Muslim like `Umar (R.A.) hesitated to accept the treaty with the non-believers of Mecca but Hadrat Abu Bakr fully supported the Holy Prophet's decision.

On the occasion of Tabuk expedition Hadrat Abu Bakr (R.A.) brought everything that he possessed. When the Holy Prophet (*Sallallahu `alayhi wa Sallam*) asked him, "What did you leave for your family?" Abu Bakr (R.A.) said, "I have left for them Allah and his Prophet". Even Hadrat `Umar (R.A.) admitted that he could never hope to surpass Abu Bakr (R.A.) in his sacrifice for the cause of Allah and Islam.

Amir (Chief) of *Al-Hajjul-Akbar* (9 A.H.)

It was the 9th year of Hijrah when the first Haj took place. The Holy Prophet (*Sallallahu `alayhi wa Sallam*) had then returned from Tabuk expedition but he was so busy that he could not himself attend the Hajj pilgrimage. He sent Hadrat Abu Bakr as-Siddiq as his deputy to lead the Hajj caravan to Mecca. Among others in the Hajj caravan were Hadrat Sa`d bin Abi-Waqqas, Jabir and Hadrat Abu Hurairah (R.A.). The Holy Qur'an calls this Hajj pilgrimage as *Al-Hajjul-Akbar* (the Great Hajj) because it was the first ever Hajj in the history of Islam and was the beginning of a new era of Islamic period and constitution. Hadrat Abu Bakr taught the people the Hajj rites and rituals and gave a historic sermon (*Khutbah*) on the Sacrificial Day before the congregation. Hadrat `Ali (R.A.) followed him and proclaimed severance of all connections with the heathen world. It was announced: non-believers should not approach the Ka`bah, no person should perform Hajj naked (as was observed before Islam); and all the treaties with pagan world would cease to operate after four months. The Holy Qur'an mentions it as follows:

> "*And an announcement from Allah and His Apostle, to the people (assembled) on the day of the Great Pilgrimage (al-Hajjil-Akbar), that Allah and His Apostle dissolve (treaty) obligations with the Pagans. If, then, you repent, it is better for you (O Pagan), but if you turn away then you mind it that you cannot frustrate Allah. And proclaim a grievous penalty to those who reject Faith*" (9:3).

Imam of Holy Prophet's Mosque

Since his arrival at Medina the Holy Prophet (*Sallallahu `alayhi wa Sallam*) himself led the *Salat*s at his mosque all the time, This was really a high office and was not given to anybody in the presence of the Holy Prophet (*Sallallahu `alayhi wa Sallam*). A few months after his return from the Farewell Pilgrimage (*Al-Hujjatul-Wida*) in 10 A. H., the Holy Prophet (*Sallallahu `alayhi wa Sallam*) fell ill. A time came when he was unable to move and could not go to the Mosque to lead the *Salat*. He had to appoint someone as the Imam and this honour fell to the lot of Abu Bakr. Abu Bakr's daughter, lady `A'isha (R.A.) was one of the most beloved wives of the Holy Prophet (*Sallallahu `alayhi wa Sallam*). She knew that Hadrat Abu Bakr was a soft-hearted man and it would be rather hard for him to replace the Holy Prophet (*Sallallahu `alayhi wa Sallam*) in the *Salat*. So she pleaded with the Holy Prophet (*Sallallahu `alayhi wa Sallam*) to excuse Hadrat Abu Bakr from this duty but the Holy Prophet (*Sallallahu `alayhi wa*

Sallam) did not change his decision even though he was requested three times.

During those days, once Abu Bakr was not present at the time of congregational *Salat*. Somebody asked Hadrat `Umar to lead the *Salat*. The Holy Prophet (*Sallallahu `alayhi wa Sallam*) after hearing the voice of Hadrat `Umar enquired about the Imam and when he found that Abu Bakr (R.A.) was not leading he was annoyed and said, "Nobody will lead the *Salat* besides Ibn Abu Qahafa (i.e. Hadrat Abu Bakr)." Then Abu Bakr (R.A.) was called but by that time Hadrat `Umar had completed the *Salat*. The *Salat* was repeated by the order of the Holy Prophet (*Sallallahu `alayhi wa Sallam*) and Abu Bakr (R.A.) led it.

During his sickness, the Holy Prophet (*Sallallahu `alayhi wa Sallam*) once felt some relief and went for *Zuhr Salat*, supported by Hadrat `Ali and Hadrat `Abbas (R.A.). His face beamed with joy and full satisfaction on seeing Abu Bakr leading the *Salat*. Sensing the presence of the Holy Prophet (*Sallallahu `alayhi wa Sallam*), Abu Bakr wanted to step back but the Holy Prophet stopped him and sat down by his side. After the *Salat* the Holy Prophet (*Sallallahu `alayhi wa Sallam*) gave his last address: "Allah offered one of His servants the choice of the life on this earth and a life with Him. But the servant accepted the latter." Hearing this tears came out of Abu Bakr's eyes and rolled down to his beard. He thought of the inevitable separation from his Beloved Master (the Holy Prophet). Most of the people did not understand the meaning of Holy Prophet's address and they were surprised at Abu Bakr's crying.

Early in the morning of the last day of his life, the Holy Prophet's condition became suddenly better for a while. As the apartment was just adjoining the Mosque, he raised the curtain and observed the Muslims busy in *Salat* under the *Imamat* (leadership) of Hadrat Abu Bakr (R.A.). A smile lit up the pale face of the Holy Prophet

(*Sallallahu `alayhi wa Sallam*). Seeing the sign of the Holy Prophet's recovery the people in the Mosque lost control over themselves in sheer delight. They might have fallen out of the file but the Holy Prophet (*Sallallahu `alayhi wa Sallam*) asked Hadrat Abu Bakr to lead the *Salat* and he went inside and let the curtain fall.

2
Hadrat Abu Bakr's Caliphate

News of the death of the Holy Prophet

When Hadrat Abu Bakr (R.A.) found the Holy Prophet (*Sallallahu `alayhi wa Sallam*) in a better condition in the morning of the last day of his life, he went a few miles outside Medina to meet his wife Hadrat Kharjah bint Zuhair (R.A.). After hearing the news of the death of the Holy Prophet (*Sallallahu `alayhi wa Sallam*), he immediately returned and saw great rush at the gate of the Mosque. He did not talk to anybody and went straight to Hadrat `A'isha's apartment where the Holy Corpse was lying. After taking permission he entered the apartment and kissed the Holy Face, tears rolling out of his eyes. Then he remarked, "May my parents be sacrificed for you. I swear by Allah that death will never come twice to you. You have tasted the death which was destined for you and now you will get no other." He covered the Holy Body with a sheet and came to the Mosque.

A multitude of people was crying in the Mosque. Hadrat `Umar (R.A.) was in a strong emotional state and was shouting that the Holy Prophet (*Sallallahu `alayhi wa Sallam*) had not died. Hadrat Abu Bakr (R.A.) tried to calm him but `Umar did not pay any attention to him. Noting the delicacy of the situation, Hadrat Abu Bakr stood in another corner of the Mosque and gave his most effective and historical address. All the people gathered around him. He said:

> "O People! If any one of you worshipped Muhammad (*Sallallahu `alayhi wa Sallam*) he should bear in mind that Muhammad is dead. But those who worshipped Allah should know that He is Alive and will never die. Allah says in the Holy Qur'an: `Muhammad is only a Messenger of Allah. There came down a number of Messengers before him. Then would you turn back from Islam, if he dies or is killed?'"

The address of Hadrat Abu Bakr touched the hearts of the people. Hadrat `Umar also cooled down. Hadrat `Abdullah says, "It seemed that the verse of the Holy Qur'an to which Abu Bakr referred was just revealed, although we had recited it several times in the past."

Abu Bakr chosen as the first *Khalifah*

The Holy Prophet (*Sallallahu `alayhi wa Sallam*) did not nominate his successor and left the choice of his deputy or viceroy (*Khalifah*) to his *Ummah* (followers). There were two groups of Muslims in Medina viz., *Muhajirin* (the Immigrants from Mecca), and *Ansar* (Helpers i.e., Medinites). After the death of the Holy Prophet (*Sallallahu `alayhi wa Sallam*), Ansar (Medinites) gathered in a big hall of Medina known as *Saqifah-i-Bani Sa`idah* to discuss the appointment of a *Khalifah*. Hadrat Abu Bakr and Hadrat `Umar with other prominent Muhajirin (Immigrants) were in the Mosque. When they were informed about the gathering of Ansar, Hadrat Abu Bakr and `Umar also went there accompanied by a number of eminent Muhajirin like Hadrat Abu `Ubaidah bin al-Jarrah. Since Hadrat `Ali and Hadrat Zubair (two prominent figures among Muhajirin) were not present at the spot, they could not go to the gathering.

Much discussion was going on in the gathering of the Ansar about the selection of a *Khalifah*. Some of the leading Ansar wanted a *Khalifah* from amongst the Ansar. When Hadrat Abu Bakr heard it, he said, "We acknowledge the sacrifices of Ansar for Islam. You really deserve to have a *Khalifah* from amongst yourselves, but Arabs will not agree on any *Amir* (Chief) other than a person from the Quraish." Hearing Hadrat Abu Bakr another Ansari, Khabab bin Mundhar stood up and said, "Let there be two *Amirs* (*Khalifah*s) then, one from amongst Quraish and another from amongst Ansar." On this Hadrat `Umar stood up and said, "This is not at all possible. There would be great confusion because of two *Amirs*." Hadrat Khabab bin Mundhar did not agree with `Umar and there was a hot talk between them. Hadrat Abu `Ubaidah tried to cool them down. Then another Ansari Hadrat Bashir bin an-Nu`man (R.A.) stood up and said, "The Holy Prophet belonged to the Quraish tribe. Quraishites have preference over others. All the Arabs would agree on them. Therefore a *Khalifah* must be from amongst them. We do not want any dispute with Muhajirin in the matter of *Khilafat*. We, the Medinites are Ansar (Helpers) and we would prefer to remain Helpers of Allah and His Holy Prophet (*Sallallahu `alayhi wa Sallam*)." Another Ansari Hadrat Zaid bin Thabit (R.A.) also supported this view and said, "There should be a *Khalifah* from amongst Muhajirin (Quraishis). We Medinites were Ansars (Helpers) of the Holy Prophet (*Sallallahu `alayhi wa Sallam*) and would remain Ansar of his *Khalifah* as well." A number of Ansars then supported this view, and there was general satisfaction in the council over the selection of a Muhajir (Quraishi) *Khalifah*.

Seeing this Hadrat Abu Bakr (R.A.) stood up and said, "I propose the name of `Umar and Abu `Ubaidah bin al-Jarrah for this post. Select anyone of these two men as your *Khalifah*." But both of them refused and Hadrat `Umar said, "Abu Bakr is the best of all of us because Allah has mentioned him in the Holy Qur'an saying, "The one amongst two in the cave" (9:40). He further said, Abu Bakr excelled at every occasion during the life of the Holy Prophet (*Sallallahu `alayhi wa Sallam*). He deputised the Holy Prophet (*Sallallahu `alayhi wa Sallam*) in leading *Salat*s, he was appointed the Chief of Hajj caravan. As such he is the fittest person to be the *Khalifah*." Hadrat Abu Bakr still hesitated but `Umar (R.A.) and Hadrat Zaid bin Thabit Ansari held his hand and took pledge of loyalty (*Bai`at*). Then Hadrat Abu `Ubaidah bin al-Jarrah and Hadrat Bashir bin an-Nu`man Ansari also took pledge of loyalty at his hands. Seeing this, people from all the sides rushed to pledge loyalty to Abu Bakr (R.A.) as the first successor of the Holy Prophet (*Sallallahu `alayhi wa Sallam*).

Next day a general pledge of loyalty (*Bai`at*) was taken by the Muslims in the Mosque of the Holy Prophet (*Sallallahu `alayhi wa Sallam*). Thus Hadrat Abu Bakr assumed the greatest office, after the office of prophethood, and became the first *Khalifah* of Islam. He gave his first address as a *Khalifah* in the mosque after the general *Bai`at*:

"O people! I have been selected as your Trustee although I am no better than anyone of you. If I am right, obey me. If I am misguided, set me right. Of course truth is honesty and a lie is dishonesty. The weakest among you is powerful in my eyes until I do not get him his due, *Insha-Allah* (If it should please Allah). The most powerful among you is the weakest in my eyes until I do not make him pay due rights to others *Insha-Allah*. Allah sends down disgrace on those people who give up Jihad in the path of Allah. Allah surely sends down calamities on such people who indulge in evils.

"I ask you to obey me as long as I obey Allah and His Messenger (*Sallallahu `alayhi wa Sallam*). If I disobey Allah and His Messenger you are free to disobey me. Now come and offer *Salat*."

In his short address, Hadrat Abu Bakr showed the role of an exemplary *Khalifah* of Islamic Government. No doubt Islamic Government means: "Government of Allah and His Prophet, by His obedient servants, for the benefit of the people in this world and in the Hereafter."

About thirty three thousand people took pledge of loyalty (*Bai`at*) at the hand of Hadrat Abu Bakr in the mosque. The selection (or Election) of Hadrat Abu Bakr is a pointer towards Islamic Democracy and furnishes example for selection of a Leader for *Ummat-i-Muslimah* (Muslim Community) till the Day of Judgement.

Hadrat `Ali took pledge of loyalty a few months later because he was busy in collecting various parts of the Holy Qur'an. Some other reasons have also been given for his delay in *Bai`at* which are ignored here.

Problems faced by Hadrat Abu Bakr As-Siddiq as a Caliph

After the death of the Holy Prophet (*Sallallahu `alayhi wa Sallam*), the Arabs were on all sides rising in rebellion. Apostasy and disaffection raised their heads. Christians and Jews were filled with unrest. Some Muslim tribes refused to pay *Zakat* to the Caliph for *Baitul Mal* (the Public Treasury). Some disbelievers declared themselves to be prophets. There were many problems and much confusion. Hadrat Abu Bakr (R.A.) faced all these with unparalleled courage and the highest degree of *Iman* (Faith) which is the characteristic of a "*Siddiq*". At this place I would like to point out, that *Siddiqiat* is the highest stage of *Iman* (Faith) and *Tawakkul* (Trust in Allah) after prophethood as pointed out in the following verse of the Holy Qur'an:

> "*All those who obey Allah and the Prophet are in the company of those upon whom Allah has shown favours — of the Prophets, Siddiqin (the Sincere), Shuhada (the Martyrs), and Salihin (The*

Righteous Muslims): Ah! What a beautiful company" (4:69).

In the following lines I would like to mention the main problems faced by Abu Bakr as-Siddiq (R.A.) in brief.

i. *Usamah's Expedition*

The freed slave of the Holy Prophet (*Sallallahu `alayhi wa Sallam*) and his adopted son, Hadrat Zaid bin Harith (R.A.) was martyred at the hands of Syrians (Romans) at Mautah in 8 A.H. A few weeks before his death the Holy Prophet (*Sallallahu `alayhi wa Sallam*) appointed Hadrat Usamah (R.A.), the son of Zaid to lead an expedition against Syrians in order to avenge the death of his father, Zaid. When Hadrat Usamah was about to leave, the news of the demise of the Holy Prophet (*Sallallahu `alayhi wa Sallam*) came and the departure of the army was postponed. After being chosen as Caliph, the first task before Abu Bakr (R.A.) was to send out this expedition. As a matter of fact, it was the most critical time in the history of Islam. The entire peninsula was in a state of unrest and disorder. Some of the new converts thought Islam would come to an end with the Holy Prophet's life. Many of the tribes had entered the fold of Islam only a short time before and were not firm in Islam. About this the Holy Qur'an has already predicted:

> *"The wandering Arabs (Bedouins) say: We have (firm) faith. Say (to them O Muhammad): You believe not (firmly), but rather say `We submit' for the Faith has not entered into your hearts'."* (39:14).

At the same time news came to Medina that apostates under the command of some false prophet were planning to invade the town. Hadrat Abu Bakr (R.A.) was really facing a difficult situation. In the circumstances, the companions approached him to withdraw the expedition of Hadrat Usamah bin Zaid. In their opinion it was unwise to send troops out of Medina because they were needed at home. Here was the test of Abu Bakr's (R.A.) faith in following the ways of the Holy Prophet (*Sallallahu `alayhi wa Sallam*). He got through in his test and proved to be the most firm among all of his companions including Hadrat `Umar. Abu Bakr (R.A.) said he could never alter the decision taken by his master (the Holy Prophet). He firmly replied to his companions, "How can I fold up the flag which was unfurled by the Holy Prophet (*Sallallahu `alayhi wa Sallam*) himself?" When Muslims saw that Hadrat Abu Bakr was firm they requested him to change the command of Hadrat Usamah because he was too young and inexperienced — not yet twenty, thus was not fit to lead the expedition. Hearing this Hadrat Abu Bakr was much annoyed and said, "Do you want me to dismiss a man appointed by the Messenger of Allah?"

At last the army led by Hadrat Usamah left after three weeks of Holy Prophet's death. Hadrat `Umar (R.A.) was also included in the army. Hadrat Abu Bakr sought Usamah's permission to leave him in Medina, and he agreed. Hadrat Abu Bakr himself bid him farewell and went to some distance out of Medina. The young commander of the army was riding a horse and the great Caliph was walking by his side. After forty days Hadrat Usamah returned to Medina with a great victory, the victory of Abu Bakr's (R.A.) firm Faith.

The success of Usamah's expedition also opened the eyes of those who thought Islam was dying out after the demise of the Holy Prophet (*Sallallahu `alayhi wa Sallam*). Some of the tribes again came back to Islam which they had left.

ii. *False prophets*

Some disbelievers declared their prophethood and started revolt. Four of those were main figures among such false prophets. A brief account of them is given here:

Aswad ʾAnsi

He rose in Yemen and was known as ʾAnsi, "the veiled prophet", because he put veil on his face all the time. After collecting a big army he stood up in open revolt against Islam. He was killed by Qais bin Makshuh and his followers scattered.

Tulaiha

He belonged to the tribe of Bani Asad in northern Arabia. Just after the death of the Holy Prophet (*Sallallahu ʾalayhi wa Sallam*) he rose in open revolt. Hadrat Abu Bakr sent Hadrat Khalid bin Walid to crush the rebellion. After a fierce fight Tulaiha's army was defeated and he ran away to Syria. Afterwards he again accepted Islam.

Sajah bint Al-Harith in Suwaid

She belonged to the tribe of Bani Tamim. After the death of the Holy Prophet (*Sallallahu ʾalayhi wa Sallam*) a number of chiefs of this tribe including Malik bin Nuwairah repudiated Islam and Sajah declared her prophethood. Four thousand people including some of the chiefs gathered around her to march to Medina. She also forced those who did not cooperate with her to follow. On her way to Medina she was informed about the Islamic army led by Khalid bin Walid who had crushed the rebellion of Tulaiha. Hearing the news of the Islamic army she was frightened and wrote a letter to Musailimah al-Kadhdhab (the Liar) seeking his cooperation. Musailimah had also declared his prophethood. A mutual understanding was reached in the beginning but later Sajah married Musailimah and accepted his prophethood.

In the meantime Hadrat Khalid bin Walid reached the headquarters of the tribe of Bani Tamim. After the marriage of Sajah with Musailimah most of the people belonging to Bani Tamim had already re-entered Islam. Hadrat Khalid did not say anything to such persons but fought with those who were still apostates and defeated them.

After crushing the rebellion of Bani Tamim he turned his attention to the notorious false prophet Musailimah al-Kadhdhab (the Liar).

Musailimah Al-Kadhdhab (the Liar)

Musailimah belonged to a tribe of central Arabia. His tribe did not want to follow the "Prophet of Quraish" (the Holy Prophet), so they accepted him as a prophet. According to some historians he declared his prophethood during the later period of the Holy Prophet. However he openly did so after the death of Holy Prophet (*Sallallahu `alayhi wa Sallam*). Hadrat Abu Bakr As-Siddiq (R.A.) sent Shurahbeel bin Hasnah and `Ikrimah (R.A.) to crush the rebellion. Later on Hadrat Khalid bin Walid (R.A.) also joined them.

Musailimah was commanding an army of forty thousand bedouins. Some of them joined only to support their tribe although they did not believe in Musailimah. The Islamic army of thirteen thousand men was under the command of Khalid bin Walid (R.A.). A fierce battle was fought. A number of prominent Companions were slain in the fight. In the end Musailimah's army was defeated. He himself was killed by Wahshi, (R.A.) the same person who was responsible for Hadrat Hamzah's martyrdom in the battle of Uhud at a time when he was not a Muslim.

In this battle about 800 Muslims were martyred among whom were 360 Companions of the Holy Prophet. A number of *Huffaz* (i.e., those who committed all the Holy Qur'an to memory) were also martyred.

Musailimah's defeat raised the standing of Muslims once more in the whole of Arabia. Thus in a short period the false prophets and their followers were wiped out by virtue of firm Faith and Wisdom of As-Siddiq al-Akbar. But there were still a number of problems to be solved.

iii. *Apostasy movement*

The new converts had not learnt the spirit of Islam. For centuries, the Arabian tribes knew no authority. Islam disciplined them and put them under certain moral obligations. Drinking and gambling of pre-Islamic days had been prohibited. Their wild spirit rebelled against this moral control. They wanted a chance which they got after the death of the Holy Prophet (*Sallallahu `alayhi wa Sallam*), and considered it the right time to throw off the yoke of Islam. That was the time when virtually the whole of Arabian peninsula was under the grip of civil war. It was the firm determination of As-Siddiq al-Akbar which permanently quelled the rebellions. Professor Hitti says: "The short *khilafat* of Abu Bakr was mostly occupied with the so-called *Ridda* (apostasy) wars." "The Arabs, throughout the peninsula," says another historian W. Muir, "were relapsing into apostasy". But As-Siddiq al-Akbar did not lose heart and faced the situation with utmost courage and Iman.

The rebellion started with the refusal of the tribes to deposit *Zakat* fund in the *Baitul Mal* (Public Treasury) as was done during the days of the Holy Prophet (*Sallallahu `alayhi wa Sallam*). Hadrat Abu Bakr called a meeting of his *Shura* (Advisory Council) and sought its advice. Most of the Companions did not consider it advisable to take action for the time being because of the wars against false prophets and major revolts. But Hadrat Abu Bakr was firm on taking strong and prompt action so that others may have a lesson. He therefore declared, "I swear by Allah, I will fight alone, if others do not support me, against everybody whosoever refuses a single kid due on him in *Zakat*." He launched a big campaign without delay. He collected the troops in Medina and divided them into eleven battalions, each under the command of an experienced commander, and sent them out to different parts of Arabia. His instructions for them were to call rebels to Islam first, and if they failed, to fight them. Some of the rebel tribes submitted to Islam without fighting. Wars were waged against those who remained adamant.

With the help of these battalions As-Siddiq al-Akbar crushed all the forces of rebellion, disorder and apostasy. He actually showed wonderful courage and ability in suppressing the movement. The apostasy movement which affected the whole of Arabia besides Mecca and Medina, was totally suppressed within a year and Islam was once again the only religion of the Peninsula. When the rebellion was subdued and Islam was re-established, As-Siddiq diverted his attention towards outside Arabia. Hadrat Khalid bin Walid (R.A.) was considered to be the fittest and most suitable commander for the external expeditions, which would be described later.

iv. *The rebellion of Bahrain*

Bahrain is a small state in the North-East side of the Arab Peninsula by the Persian Gulf. The people of Bahrain accepted Islam in the lifetime of the Holy Prophet (*Sallallahu 'alayhi wa Sallam*). Soon after the Holy Prophet's demise the Muslim governor of Bahrain died and there was disorder in the province. As-Siddiq al-Akbar sent a battalion under the command of 'Ala bin al-Hadrami who defeated the rebelled tribe, Banu Bakr of Bahrain. The other tribe of Bahrain, Banu 'Abdul-Qais, was loyal to Islam and helped the Muslims against the rebels.

v. *Other rebellions*

There were other rebellions as well in the adjoining small states like Oman, Mahra, Hadramaut and Yemen. All these were also suppressed and crushed.

Start of Era of Conquest

The Arabian Peninsula was surrounded by the two great Empires of that time. On its North-Eastern side was the border of Persian Empire. At that time Iraq was under the control of the Persian Empire. The Northern part of the Peninsula was bordered by the Byzantine Empire (the Eastern Roman Empire). It consisted of Syria, Palestine and Egypt. Byzantine was a Greek city on the Bosphorus and Byzantines were named after this city. It was made the capital of the Eastern Roman Empire in 330 B.C. by Constantine, the Great. The name of the city was changed later on to Constantinople after the name of Constantine the Great. (Now it is known as Istanbul in Turkey).

After suppressing the rebellions of internal tribes and adjoining small states, Abu Bakr (R.A.) turned his attention to the adjoining territories who were doing a lot of damage to Muslims and Islam and were continuously conspiring against Muslims. The aim of as-Siddiq was not only to suppress their conspiracy against Muslims but, as a matter of fact, to spread the universal message of Islam. As we will see later, each expedition was advised first to invite the enemy towards Islam in a peaceful way, if they accepted the Message of Allah, they were treated as brothers otherwise Muslims had to accept their challenge. The sword was used as a last resort for self-defense. Some of the main expeditions which took place during the time of Hadrat Abu Bakr would be discussed in the following lines in brief.

i. Expedition to Iraq (Persian Empires)

There was a lot of confusion during those days in the Persian Empire. A child, Yezdgird, was ruling over the Empire under the supervision of a lady, Puran Dukht. The Persians helped the rebels of Bahrain and had done all they could do to crush Islam. There were certain Arab tribes living near the border. Some of them accepted Islam while others were Christians. Muthanna, the chief of a border tribe (Wa'il) accepted Islam.

Since the bordering Arab tribes of Iraq (Persia at that time) were the main target of persecution by the Persians, Muthanna and his companions took advantage of the internal conflict of Persian Empire and started small fights. In order that the Persians may not wage a full scale war against Muslims Hadrat Abu Bakr (R.A.) permitted Muthanna to go ahead with his scheme. But later Muthanna came to Hadrat Abu Bakr (R.A.) and sought his permission for a regular fight. The Muslims were endangered by the Persian Empire which wanted to wipe out the increasing power and might of Muslims. Moreover they were not pleased with the help given by the Persians to the Bahrain rebels. Abu Bakr (R.A.), after consulting his *Shura* (Advisory Council) permitted him to start full scale war on the condition that first he must invite Persians to Islam peacefully. Since Muthanna was not much experienced, Hadrat Abu Bakr ordered his great general Hadrat Khalid bin Walid (R.A.) to proceed immediately to reinforce Muthanna's army. It was the first month of the year 12 A.H. (633 A.C.). Hadrat Khaild met Muthanna's army at Ubullah.

Battle of Chains

Hafir was the place where the first battle between Muslims and Persians took place. Persians were under the command of Hurmuz, a famous Persian general.

According to the Islamic practice and advice given by the Caliph, Hadrat Khalid invited the Persians to Islam and wrote to them: "We have brought for you the Message of Allah, Islam. Our aim is not to fight. Accept Islam, the peaceful way, and you will be safe. If not then clear our way to the people so that we may explain this beautiful way of life to them. If you do not accept Islam you will have to pay *Jizya*

(Defense Tax) to the Caliphate. If you do not agree to any of these conditions then the only alternative is the use of sword. Before deciding on the third alternative you should keep in your mind that I am bringing against you a people who love death more than you love your life." Hadrat Khalid (R.A.) was right in telling that Muslims loved death in the path of Allah more than life loved by non-believers. When a Muslim dies in the path of Allah he is a martyr and gets into Paradise before his blood falls on the earth.

The Persians were too proud and paid no attention to Hadrat Khalid's invitation. A battle took place at Hafir and the Persians were defeated and routed. In order not to run from the battlefield the Persians soldiers had tied themselves to one another with chains. Due to this, the battle is known as the Battle of Chains. But it proved fruitless because of the effective attack of Muslims. Even the commander of the Persian army was killed in this battle.

After the Battle of Chains at Hafir some other small skirmishes took place at Madhar, Walja and Ullis, etc. Each time the Muslims fought with a new force several times bigger than them but they defeated the Persians not because of their number and weapons but due to the power of *Iman* and trust in Allah.

The fall of Hira

Hira was a famous fort of Persians. After fighting the small battles described above Hadrat Khalid besieged the city of Hira. Persians resisted in the beginning but later on they surrendered to Muslims. Hadrat Khalid imposed *Jizya* (Defense Tax) on them. Then he captured other places including Dumatal-Jandal. Some frontier Arab chiefs also submitted to Khalid. The last battle of this expedition of Hadrat Khalid took place at Firad. A huge force of Persian Arabs (residing in Iraq) and Syrians who joined Persians in that battle crossed the river Euphrates. A fierce battle was fought on the 15th Dhul Qa'dah, 12 A. H. Hadrat Khalid routed the enemies and conquered the place. By this victory the whole of South and most of North Iraq were conquered. Then Hadrat Khalid returned to Hira.

Hadrat Khalid bin Walid, Saifullah (the Sword of Allah)

Hadrat Khalid bin Walid (R.A.) proved to be the most successful general of Islam. With a handful of troops he was able not only to overcome all internal rebellions but also to make Arabia safe for Islam. Then he proceeded to Iraq and gained victory after victory. It was for his abilities, which were foreseen by the Holy Prophet (*Sallallahu `alayhi wa Sallam*) that Khalid was given the title of "Saifullah", i.e., the "Sword of Allah".

As-Siddiq al-Akbar was quick to recognize Khalid's (R.A.) ability and he put him in charge of the Iraqi campaign. Hadrat Khalid's performance in this campaign has no parallel in history. With an army of a little more than ten thousand men, Khalid (R.A.) overcome a major part of Iraq and brought it under the banner of Islam. At many times he defeated enemies twenty times larger than his own army. Hadrat Khalid (R.A.) knew that success did not lie in the hands of majority or minority, it lies in the hands of Allah Almighty. He declared many times that they were not fighting for the sake of land or fame, their aim was to proclaim Allah's *Kalimah* (Message). When Allah was with them they did not fear any power. Once he wrote a letter to a commander of Persian army near Hira:

> "All praise is due to Allah who humbled your pride, and disunited you, and destroyed your might. Accept Islam you will be in peace; or pay *Jizya* (Defense Tax) and let us spread Allah's Message. If you do not accept any of these conditions then listen I have

brought with me such people who love death more than you love your life."

In Iraq Hadrat Khalid fought fifteen battles and won complete victory in all of them.

Hadrat Khalid was not only a great general and conqueror but also a great administrator. He appointed a deputy and a *Qadi* (Judge) at every place which he conquered. Some Muslim teachers were also left to teach Islam to the converts and to preach to non-Muslims by peaceful means. Seeing the character of these noble souls and the natural beauty of Islam, most of the time, entire population entered the folds of Islam. It is a fact that by sword or force, only tongues could be won, not the hearts. It was really the character of Muslims in those days that won the hearts of entire population where they lived. This is a clear proof that Islam never spread by sword or force. Sword was used to clear the way for preaching this truthful way of life, and when people realised its value, grandeur and significance they went all out for it. *Iman* (Faith) is the affirmation of the heart not of the tongue, and the heart could never be won by sword. Character has greater force than sword and this force was, of course, with the Muslims. Unlike most warriors Hadrat Khalid, the Saifullah (R.A.), was an extremely kind-hearted man. He had given strict orders to his army to follow all the principles of Islam. They were not allowed to do any harm to farmers and other civilians. The army treated the civilians with kindness and respect. This was a surprise for the conquered people. Instead of molesting the women they found the soldiers worshipping and crying before Allah all night. This was something new for them. This was something new for them. It was said about Muslim conquerors of the time: "They rode on the back of horse during the day (to fight in the Path of Allah) and on the back of *Mussalla* (a piece of cloth used for prayers) in the night (to worship Allah)." The word by word translation is given here to put emphasis, it actually meant that they fought in the path of Allah throughout the day and worshipped Allah throughout the night. Of course even during the day they were punctual in obligatory *Salat*s.

As mentioned above the month of Dhul-Qa`dah 12 A.H. marked the end of Hadrat Khalid's campaign in Iraq. He then returned to the headquarters at Hira. After resting for a while he took a few men with him and came to Mecca for Hajj and returned to Hira after performing the Hajj. On hearing about Khaild's presence at the Hajj, Hadrat Abu Bakr was amazed but he forbade him not to leave his army alone in future.

ii. Expedition to Syria (Byzantine Empire)

It has been stated in the life of the Holy Prophet (*Sallallahu `alayhi wa Sallam*) that the envoy of the Holy Prophet, Dihya al-Kalbi, was killed by Syrians in 6 A.H. while he was on a mission to the Roman Emperor. As a result of which there was the battle of Mu'tah. Later the Holy Prophet (*Sallallahu `alayhi wa Sallam*) himself marched with 50,000 men to Tabuk (a border post of Syria) when he heard about the invasion plan of Syrians (then known as Romans because Syria was a province of Eastern Roman Empire, the Byzantine at that time). Since Syrians did not turn up to fight, the Holy Prophet (*Sallallahu `alayhi wa Sallam*) and his Companions returned without any fight. Again there was a danger of Syrian invasion and the Holy Prophet appointed Hadrat Usamah bin Zaid as the commander of the army which was later sent by Hadrat Abu Bakr when he assumed the office of the Caliphate. It has been mentioned before that Hadrat Usamah (R.A.) returned victorious after about forty days.

Afterwards Hadrat Abu Bakr was informed about the clashes at the Syrian border and about the plan of invasion by Romans (i.e., Syrians). This was the time when Heracleus was the Emperor of

Byzantine Empire, with Constantinople (Istanbul) as the capital.

When Hadrat Abu Bakr found that the Romans (Byzantines) began to conspire against the Muslims in cooperation with the Bedouins of the Syrian frontier, he consulted the *Shura* (Advisory Council) and decided to save the frontiers. As mentioned before, the aim was never to conquer other places. The blame totally lay upon the foreign powers who always encouraged the rebels and by sending them reinforcements attempted to shatter the nascent power of Muslims. Even Western historians like Sir William Muir admit that the Muslim leaders were not responsible for the wars with Persia and Byzantium. A famous Muslim historian, M.M. Siddiqi writes in his book, *Development of Islamic State and Society*: "These (the wars) were not started by the Muslims, nor was there slightest attempt on the part of the Islamic leaders to impose their own way of life on the foreign peoples. True, Islam was a missionary religion and an expanding force. The Prophet himself had invited the ruling monarchs of the surrounding countries to accept Islam. But he had never, by word or deed, tried to trespass their domains."

To take strong action against Romans (Byzantines) was also necessary keeping in view the Arab trade with Syria as the border clashes made the trade routes dangerous. So in the year 13 A.H. he raised a big army and divided it into four battalions. Each battalion was put under the command of an experienced general. They had to march in different directions. Hadrat Abu `Ubaidah bin al-Jarrah had to march on Hims; Hadrat `Amr bin al-`As on Palestine; Yazid bin Sufyan on Damascus; and Shurahbeel bin Hasnah on Jordan (which was a part of Syria at that time). The army was divided into many companies so that the enemy may not hit with full force on any one of the battalions. The total number of men was 27,000.

At the time of departure of the army Hadrat Abu Bakr gave some valuable advice to each commander. A few of them are as under:

1. Always fear Allah because He knows what the hearts conceal.
2. Treat your subordinates well.
3. Honour the representatives of your enemies.
4. Always be truthful.
5. Keep away from untruthful men and be intimate with those who are truthful and faithful.
6. Do not be dishonest in any way.
7. Do not disturb saints and worshippers of other religions.
8. Do not destroy places of worship.
9. Do not kill women, old men and children and those who are not fighting with you (i.e., civilians).
10. Do not cut flowering trees.
11. Do not ruin any populated place.
12. Do not kill goats, camels and cattle besides what you need to eat.
13. Do not burn gardens.
14. Do not be dishonest in booty.

When Heracleus heard about the Islamic armies, he also sent four armies to face them. Each of those armies was several times bigger than the total Islamic army. The Muslim commanders informed Hadrat Abu Bakr about the situation and sought reinforcement. They also informed him about their proposal to merge the four armies under one command. Hadrat Abu Bakr approved the proposal of merger and sent the following message to Hadrat `Amr bin al-`As, one of the commanders:

"Assalamu`alaikum! (Peace be unto you!) I am in receipt of your letter in which you have mentioned about the huge Roman armies.

Listen! Allah has not given us victories because of a magnitude or scarcity of numbers when we fought in the company of the Holy Prophet *(Sallallahu `alayhi wa Sallam)*. Sometimes we fought with him in such a condition that there were not more than two horses in the whole army, and travelled on the back of one camel turn by turn . . . Muslims can never be defeated because of small numbers. O `Amr! The most righteous among us is the one who keeps away more from sins. Therefore obey Allah and ask your companions as well to obey Him (completely) . . . you would be successful" *(Quoted by Tabrani)*.

He further wrote:

"I have sent orders to Khalid bin Walid (in Iraq) to join you immediately. When he joins you give him due regard. Do not impose your superiority over him and do not try to solve your problems without consulting him, and do not oppose him" *(Quoted by Ibn Sa`d)*.

On receiving orders from the Caliph, Hadrat Khalid handed over the charge of affairs in Iraq to Muthanna bin Harith, and hastened to Syria at the head of ten thousand men. Hadrat Khalid (R.A.) faced some resistance at many places on his way to Syria and conquered many cities and forts including Irak, Rahit and Busra. Busra was a city in Syria, thus Hadrat Khalid conquered the first place in Syria before he joined the allied Islamic forces. At last he reached Ajnadayn in the month of Rabi`uth-Thani 13 A.H. (according to some historians he reached in Rabi`ul-Awwal).

The Battle of Ajnadayn: Rabi`uth-Thani, 13 A.H. (31st July 634)

When Hadrat Khalid reached Ajnadayn he called a council of all the commanders of Islamic armies whose total strength was between forty and forty five thousand. The first proposal put before them by Hadrat Khalid was to appoint a commander-in-chief. He suggested that one of them should act as the commander-in-chief turn by turn each day. The chief command for the first day was given to Hadrat Khalid (R.A.). He divided the army into several sections and put each section under the command of a commander.

The Romans were about two hundred fifty thousand in number while the Muslims were little more than forty thousand. When the Islamic and Roman armies faced each other somebody among the Muslims remarked: "How numerous is the Roman army!" Hadrat Khalid said, "The number of people does not matter. It is the final outcome which is important." At last the battle started. In the beginning the Romans put pressure upon Muslims. Seeing this Ikrimah bin Abi Jahl took pledge of some Muslims that they would not give the field to the enemy and would fight unto death. The Roman army was headed by Theodore, brother of Heracleus the Emperor but there was not that type of discipline in their army as Muslims demonstrated. A fierce battle was fought. The Roman horsemen could not bear the brunt of the Muslim attack and started to flee. Roman cavalry was totally discomfited. Then Muslim forces fell on their infantry and dispersed its ranks. Thus Romans were badly defeated and took shelter in the trench but were chased and slaughtered in large numbers. Three thousand Muslims were martyred in this battle. Defeat at the battle of Ajnadayn was a great shock to Byzantium.

After the victory at Ajnadayn the Muslim armies marched forward and laid siege to Damascus.

In the meantime Hadrat Abu Bakr (R.A.) fell sick. He received the news of the victory at Ajnadayn when he was confined to bed.

Note: There is a controversy between historians regarding the battle which took place at Ajnadayn in 13 A.H. According to some historians this was the battle of Yarmuk, while others say that the battle of Yarmuk took place after the fall of Damascus.

3
Death and Review of Hadrat Abu Bakr's Achievements

Illness of Hadrat Abu Bakr and `Umar's Nomination

It was the 7th Jamada-ul-Akhira, 13 A.H. that As-Siddiq al-Akbar fell ill. He had a severe fever. When the illness took a serious turn he called the *Shura* (Advisory Council) to consult about his successor, the second Caliph. Since he had seen some confusion after the demise of the Holy Prophet (*Sallallahu `alayhi wa Sallam*) for the selection of a Caliph, he preferred to let the Muslims decide the matter in his presence.

Following were the leading figures present in the *Shura*: `Umar, `Uthman, `Ali, `Abdur-Rahman bin `Auf, Mu`adh bin Jabal, Ubaiy bin Ka`b, Zaid bin Thabit (*Ridwanullah `alayhim Ajma`in*) and other leading Muhajirin and Ansar. According to some historians he first consulted some of the most prominent Companions before calling the meeting of the General *Shura* about this. Among these persons were 'Uthman, 'Abdur Rahman bin 'Auf and Usaid bin Hadir (R.A.). Hadrat Abu Bakr put his proposal for Hadrat `Umar to be the second Caliph. All of them agreed with the proposal except for an objection by some of the Companions about his strictness. That was the only ground on which Hadrat `Alii and Talha (R.A.) also did not agree with Hadrat

Abu Bakr. But Abu Bakr(R.A.) rejected their plea on the ground that the burden of Caliphate would make him milder. Since there was no opposition to Hadrat Abu Bakr's view, Hadrat 'Umar was declared to be the next Caliph and all the Companions, including Hadrat 'Ali and Hadrat Talha, agreed to it.

At this point I would like to point out that the decision of Hadrat Abu Bakr (R.A.) for the selection (or election) of Hadrat 'Umar in his presence during his life was purely based on his *Ijtihad* (Personal Judgment of a Jurist) as explained by him after his nomination of 'Umar (R.A.) was recorded. As a matter of fact it was the need of the time and Hadrat Abu Bakr (R.A.) was totally right in his *Ijtihad*. The proof of this is also the *Ijma'* (Agreement) of the Companions on his proposal to select a Caliph while he was still alive.

Although the appointment (election) of the Caliph did not take place in the same way as it happened with Hadrat Abu Bakr (R.A.), it was not undemocratic in the sense that the nomination of Hadrat 'Umar took place after fair consultation with the *Shura*. Hadrat Abu Bakr never wanted anything which would make Islam weak after him. He knew what had happened after the death of the Holy Prophet (*Sallallahu 'alayhi wa Sallam*) the repetition of which was to be avoided. The strength of the Muslim community lay in unity and that had to be preserved at any cost. For these reasons Hadrat Abu Bakr (R.A.) wanted an agreed person to be nominated as his successor in his presence. Therefore he took a decision by *Ijtihad* for the nomination of a Caliph after due consultation.

After the *Shura* (Advisory Council) had agreed on Hadrat 'Umar, Hadrat Abu Bakr asked Hadrat 'Uthman (R.A.) to write the will:

"*Bismillah-ir-rahmanir-Rahim* (In the name of Allah, most Gracious, most Merciful). This is the declaration which is made by Abu Bakr bin Abi Quhafah while he is about to leave for the next world. At this time even a non-believer starts to believe, and even a great sinner returns to faith, and a disbeliever begins to trust in Allah. I appoint `Umar bin Khattab as the Caliph (*Khalifah*). You must follow his orders and obey him. I have done everything good for the sake of Allah, for His Holy Prophet and for the welfare of His Religion and Muslims and for myself in appointing him (`Umar as the Caliph). I hope that he would be honest and just but if he changes his ways, and becomes unjust, I would have no responsibility, as I do not have the knowledge of the unseen. Everybody is responsible for what he does."

Afterwards he went up to his balcony with the help of some persons and addressed a big gathering of Muslims: "O my brothers! I have not appointed any of my relations or brothers as a Caliph, I have chosen the best person among you. Do you agree on this"? All of them replied in the affirmative. Then he called `Umar (R.A.) and talked with him for a long time and gave him words of parting advice. Some of them are as under:

"O `Umar, always fear Allah. An optional deed is not accepted unless the obligatory deed is done. The weight of your goodness would be heavy on the day of Judgement if you followed the Right Path in this world. The deeds of the persons who followed the wrong Path in this world will have no weight on the Day of Judgement. They will have a terrible time. Make the Holy Qur'an and Truth your guide for success. `Umar, if you follow the path I propose for you, I will surely be by your side . . ."

As-Siddiq al-Akbar passes away

After a fortnight's illness, As-Siddiq al-akbar passed away at the age of 61 on Tuesday, the 22nd of Jamadal-Akhira, 13 A.H. (23rd August 634 A.D.). Before his death he said to his daughter Lady `A'isha

(R.A.), "Do not use new cloth for my shroud. Wash the sheet in my use and wrap my corpse in it". His wish was acted upon. His next wish was to pay all the money he got as salary for Caliph from *Baitul Mal* (The Public Treasury) after selling his garden. He said, "I did not like to take anything from the *Baitul Mal* but `Umar pressed me to accept some allowance so that I would be relieved of my occupation and devote my full time to the duties of the *Khilafat* (Caliphate). I was left no choice but to accept the offer".

After his death `A'isha asked Hadrat `Umar to take over that garden as desired by her father. `Umar remarked: "May Allah bless him. He left no chance for anybody to open his lips against him."

Hadrat Abu Bakr (R.A.) was a rich merchant before his *Khilafat*. After he was selected as Caliph, Hadrat `Umar and some other Companions put pressure on him to leave his business and accept some allowance from the *Baitul Mal*. He took the least possible amount which was hardly sufficient for him and his family. Once his wife wanted to prepare some sweet dish, and somehow saved something after one month. When she brought to him the money to make purchases for the sweet dish, Hadrat Abu Bakr said, "It seems that we have been overpaid beyond our needs." He then deposited the saving in the *Baitul Mal* and she was not able to prepare the sweet dish. Not only this, he got his allowance cut down for future by the amount saved by his wife.

As-Siddiq al-Akbar left behind a noble example of selfless service. He lived and worked for the sake of Islam to his last breath, but sought no reward.

Wives and Children

Wives

His first wife was Qatilah bint 'Abdul 'Aziz who bore to him 'Abdullah and Asma (R.A.). His second wife, Umm-i-Ruman gave birth to Lady 'A'isha (R.A.), the most beloved wife of the Holy Prophet (*Sallallahu 'alayhi wa Sallam*), and 'Abdur Rahman (R.A.). Besides these two he also married Asma' and Habibah (R.A.).

Children

Daughters:

(i) *Ummul-Mu'minin* Hadrat 'A'isha (R.A.)

(ii) Asma', and

(iii) Umm-i-Kulthum, born to Habibah after his death.

Sons:

(i) 'Abdullah

(ii) 'Abdur Rahman and

(iii) Muhammad.

REVIEW OF HIS SERVICES TO ISLAM

Abu Bakr, a saviour of Islam

As-Siddiq al-Akbar took the office of Caliphate at the most crucial and critical moment of Islamic history. He gave Islam a new life after the death of the Holy Prophet (*Sallallahu 'alayhi wa Sallam*). Islam, in its infant stage, when he was entrusted with the responsibility to

Caliphate, was threatened by rebellions, rise of false prophets and apostasy movements. He crushed all the futile powers because of his unshakable faith. No amount of difficulties could make him deviate from the *Sunnah* (Path) of the Holy Master. He brought unity among the Muslims and crushed all the rebellions. In view of his great service for the cause of Islam at that critical moment when there was a lot of confusion, Abu Bakr (R.A.) may rightly be called the Saviour of Islam.

It was in the time of Abu Bakr that Islam started to cross the Arabian borders. A major part of Iraq came under his rule and Muslim armies had captured many important cities of Syria. Thus Islam, the religion of whole mankind, started to be a world religion in his period.

Collection of the Holy Qur'an

One of the greatest services rendered to Islam by Abu Bakr (R.A.) was the collection of the Holy Qur'an. There were hundreds of *Huffaz* (i.e., those who committed the whole Holy Qur'an to memory) among the Companions during the life-time of the Holy Prophet (*Sallallahu `alayhi wa Sallam*) but it had not been compiled in book form though its memorisation continued even after the death of the Holy Prophet (*Sallallahu `alayhi wa Sallam*). In various battles which took place against rebels and false prophets, a number of *Huffaz* Companions were martyred. In the battle against Musailimah al-Khadhdhab about seventy *Huffaz* had died.

It then occurred to Hadrat `Umar (R.A.) that necessary steps should be taken to preserve the Holy Qur'an intact in its original form against every kind of danger and it was not wise to depend exclusively upon those who had learnt it by heart. Therefore, he urged Hadrat Abu Bakr (R.A.) to put it in black and white in the form of a book. Other Companions also agreed with `Umar's opinion but Hadrat Abu Bakr hesitated in the beginning because it was not done by the Holy Prophet

(*Sallallahu `alayhi wa Sallam*). However after some discussion he agreed to it and appointed Hadrat Zaid bin Thabit (R.A.) for this work. He was hesitant at first but later, he changed his mind and started the work. Hadrat Zaid bin Thabit was the best qualified person for this work because he had acted as an amanuensis to the Holy Prophet (*Sallallahu `alayhi wa Sallam*), and was one of the Companions who had learnt the Holy Qur'an directly from him. Moreover, he was also present on the occasion when the Holy Prophet recited the whole of the completed Holy Qur'an to the angel Gabriel. Hadrat Zaid bin Thabit adopted the same order of the various chapters of the Holy Book as was revealed to the Holy Prophet (*Sallallahu `alayhi wa Sallam*). In the compilation of the Holy Book a number of prominent Companions assisted him. The compiled copy of the Qur'an was kept in the house of *Ummul-Mu'minin*, Hadrat Hafsah (R.A.) who was one of the wives of the Holy Prophet and daughter of Hadrat `Umar. It was proclaimed that anyone, who desired, might make a copy of it or compare with it the copy one already possessed.

The collection of the Holy Qur'an in a book form was not an act against the *Sunnah* (Ways) of the Holy Prophet (*Sallallahu `alayhi wa Sallam*), because the Holy Qur'an declares itself "A Book" at a number of places e.g., in the very beginning it says: "This is the Book . . ."(2:2).

During his caliphate Hadrat `Uthman sent copies of the same compilation of the Holy Qur'an, collected during the period of Hadrat Abu Bakr (R.A.), to various places of his caliphate.

In this way we see that Hadrat Abu Bakr (R.A.) kept doing the great work of his Holy Master (*Sallallahu `alayhi wa Sallam*). With unshakable faith and full courage he had struggled to the utmost. Islam is forever grateful to its greatest hero, the next to prophets, for the great services he rendered to it.

Hadrat Abu Bakr's caliphate lasted for only two years, three months and ten days (according to Islamic calender).

Character and Picty

Hadrat Abu Bakr as-Siddiq al-Akbar (R.A.) was the most distinguished figure of Islam after the Holy Prophet (*Sallallahu `alayhi wa Sallam*). He was mild and gentle but stern when necessary. He was the true embodiment of Islam. Being diligent, wise, full of wisdom and a great statesman, he occupies a unique place in the history of Islam. His name would remain forever in the minds of Muslims.

Hadrat Abu Bakr was the most pious Companion of the Holy Prophet (*Sallallahu `alayhi wa Sallam*). He never took unlawful meal. Once one of his slaves brought for him some food to eat. He took a morsel out of it but afterwards he learnt that the slave got it as a result of soothsaying. He then remarked, "Ah! you would have surely killed me." He tried to disgorge it and when he did not succeed he drank water and then vomited the whole thing out. He never spoke any obscene language in any situation. Once he said a harsh word to Hadrat `Umar (R.A.) which he realised later and asked him to forgive him. Hadrat `Umar delayed in excusing him. He was so much perturbed that he went to the Holy Prophet (*Sallallahu `alayhi wa Sallam*) who asked `Umar(R.A.) to excuse him.

Hadrat Abu Bakr (R.A.) used to fear Allah most of all. Once he went to a garden where he saw a bird. He sighed deeply and said, "O bird! You are lucky indeed! You eat and drink as you like and fly but do not have fear of reckoning on the Day of Judgement. I wish that I were just like you." Sometimes he said, "I wish I were a blade of grass whose life ended with the grazing of some beast; or a tree that would be cut and done away with."

He was a great worshipper. It is said that Hadrat Abu Bakr (R.A.)

used to perform *Salat* similar to that of the Holy Prophet (*Sallallahu `alayhi wa Sallam*). He was the one who spent all of his belongings for the sake of Allah and His Prophet (*Sallallahu `alayhi wa Sallam*). The Holy Prophet (*Sallallahu `alayhi wa Sallam*) gave him the glad tidings of Paradise in these words: "Abu Bakr's name shall be called out from all the gates of Paradise and he will be the first person of my *Ummah* (people) to enter it."

ADMINISTRATION OF
HADRAT ABU BAKR (R.A.)

Democratic way of his Government

Hadrat Abu Bakr (R.A.) gave the first lesson to whole mankind of "government by the people" when nobody knew about it. On every occasion he decided matters after due consultation with eminent companions. He used to say: "I am but the *Khalifah* (deputy) of the Prophet of Allah" (i.e., I have to follow only the ways of the Holy Prophet).

Many a time he told the people: "I swear by Allah, I never liked to be a *Khalifah*. I even never thought about it, nor desired it either secretly or openly. The yoke of *Khilafat* has been put on my neck by force. I wish to transfer this trust to a more suitable person." Once some Muslims complained to him about the strictness of Hadrat `Umar (R.A.) and said, "He is behaving in such a way as though he is the *Khalifah* instead of you." Hadrat Abu Bakr told them, "Of course, he is the fittest person to be the *Khalifah*. I am but a humble servant of Almighty, who has been forced to take charge of this high office."

Shura (Council of Advisors)

Hadrat Abu Bakr always decided matters of state after consultation. There was a special *Shura* (Council of Advisors) for this purpose. Although the selection or the election of such council did not take place after public voting, but the prominent figures included in the *Shura* were the most popular persons in the public. If an election, as we know it today, had taken place at that time, all of them would have won it without any exception. The membership of the *Shura* was not based upon colour, race, wealth or worldly power; it was based upon services rendered to Islam, closeness to Allah and His Prophet (of course the closeness to Allah was demonstrated by the closeness to His Prophet).

Ibn-i-Sa`d has recorded that whenever Hadrat Abu Bakr faced a problem, he called eminent *Muhajirin* and *Ansar* and the following people (i.e., the following people were the permanent members of the *Shura*): Hadrat `Umar, `Uthman, `Ali, `Abdur Rahman bin `Auf, Mu`adh bin Jabal, Ubaiy bin Ka`b and Zaid bin Thabit (R.A.)." On special occasions common consultation took place in which all the prominent *Muhajirin* and *Ansar* (i.e., Companions) were called besides the above mentioned personalities. But generally only the above mentioned Companions were called for consultation.

Appointment of Officers

For public offices Hadrat Abu Bakr did not choose his own sons or family members, but gave the chance to people of high merit.

Whenever he appointed an officer, he advised him and explained his duties. On the appointment of `Amr bin `As and Walid bin `Uqbah as the collector of the *Zakat* from the tribe of Quda`ah, he advised them as follows:

"Fear Allah openly and secretly. Whosoever fears Allah, He provides him sustenance from such source about which he never thought. Whosoever fears Allah, Allah forgives his sins and gives him double reward. No doubt to have good will for the people is great piety. You are on such a way that you may go beyond the prescribed limits very easily. Stick to the rules prescribed by the religion and that would save you from all evils."

When he appointed Yazid bin Sufyan as the governor of the conquered part of Syria he gave him the following advice:

"O Yazid! You have relations in Syria, do not try to give unlawful benefits to your kins. Of this I am afraid of my officers. The Holy Prophet said: `If a Muslim officer appoints his kins on big posts which they do not deserve, he will be cursed for that by Allah and Allah will not accept any of his excuses or apology for that but he enters Hell'."

Supervision over Officers

He was a strict administrator and never allowed any of his officers to behave in an irregular manner. Whenever he found any officer amiss, he immediately warned him. Once on some mistake he wrote to Hadrat Khalid bin Walid, "You are enjoying, and the blood of Muslims is flowing nearby your tent."

Officers of his Government

The Capital of the State was Medina where Hadrat `Umar and Hadrat `Ali (R.A.) were the *Qadis* (Judges) and Abu `Ubaidah bin Jarrah was the treasury officer. Besides performing the duties of a *Qadi* and *Mufti*

(Jurist), Hadrat `Ali also acted as the secretary to Hadrat Abu Bakr. Hadrat `Uthman (R.A.) was the chief secretary and used to write various ordinances for the *Khalifah*. The governor of Mecca was Hadrat `Utba bin Usaid. He and Hadrat Abu Bakr died the same day. Governors of other places were as under:

Ta'if: `Uthman bin al-`As.

San`a: Muhajir bin Umayyah.

Hadramaut: Zaid bin `Ubaid.

Kholan (a part of Yemen): Ya`la bin Ubaid.

South Yemen: Abu Musa al-Ash`ari.

Janad (a part of Yemen): Mu`adh bin Jabal.

Bahrain: `Ala bin al-Hadrami.

Dumatul-Jandal (Iraq): `Iyad bin Ghanam.

`Iraq: Muthanna bin Harith.

Nairan: Jarir bin `Abdullah.

Near the end of his reign, Hadrat Abu Bakr had appointed the following commanders of Islamic armies in Syria: Abu `Ubaidah bin al-Jarrah, Yazid bin Abi Sufyan, `Amr bin al-As and Shurahbeel bin Hasnah. Hadrat Khalid bin Walid (R.A.) was the commander-in-chief and the greatest general of Islam during the time of Hadrat Abu Bakr (R.A.).

Baitul Mal and revenue administration

During the time of the Holy Prophet (*Sallallahu `alayhi wa Sallam*) and also during the period of Abu Bakr there was no separate department for revenue. *Zakat, Sadaqat* and other taxes (*Kharaj*) and booty used to come to Medina for *Baitul Mal* which was under the charge of Abu `Ubaidah bin Jarrah (before his departure to Syria as the commander of an army). Whatever funds came in the *Baitul Mal* were distributed among the needy and the poor immediately.

During the later period of his *Khilafat*, Hadrat Abu Bakr built a house for *Baitul Mal* but at no time money or any other thing accumulated in it. Once somebody asked Abu Bakr to take care of the safety of *Baitul Mal*, he said that one lock was enough for that because much was not allowed to lie in it.

During the first year of his *Khilafat* he gave ten dirhams as a stipend to each adult in Medina whether he was a free person or a slave. Next year when the income had increased he distributed twenty dirhams to each person. In this way he gave the same status to a slave as that to a free person because in human needs all were equal. After the death of Abu Bakr (R.A.) when Hadrat `Umar checked the *Baitul Mal* in the presence of Hadrat `Abdur Rahman and Hadrat `Uthman (R.A.), he found only one dirham in it, he exclaimed, "May Allah bless Abu Bakr." Then he called the treasury officer and asked him, "How much money did come in revenue for *Baitul Mal*?" He replied, "Two hundred thousand dinars." (*Note*: Dirham was a silver coin in those days while dinar was a gold coin).

Following were the main sources of revenue: *Zakat*, `*Ushr* (special land tax on lands), *Jizya* (Indemnity tax) and Booty.

Army and its administration

There was no regular Islamic force during the time of the Holy Prophet (*Sallallahu `alayhi wa Sallam*). Hadrat Abu Bakr also followed his example. However, when any army departed during his time, he divided it into various battalions. Each battalion was put under the command of an officer, who was under the control of the commander of the whole army. Moreover, he also appointed commander-in-chief of various armies. The commander-in-chief of the four armies sent to Syria was Hadrat Khalid bin Walid (R.A.), who was also known as "*Amir-ul-Umara*", as mentioned in some books of history.

He took particular care for the moral training of the military personnel. When he sent armies to Syria, he gave the following instructions to them:

> "During your expedition you would find some people who devote themselves exclusively to worship of their Creator. Don't disturb them and leave them in their sanctuaries. I give you the following advice:
>
> (i)   Don't kill any woman. child or old person.
>
> (ii) Don't cut any flowering tree.
>
> (iii) Don't destroy any inhabited place.
>
> (iv) Don't kill camels or goats except when you need them for your meals.
>
> (v)   Don't burn an oasis.
>
> (vi) Don't be dishonest in booty.
>
> (vii) Don't be coward in the field."

He reserved a part of the revenue for purchase of arms and for the maintenance of forces. Special pastures were reserved for horses and camels used in the battles. One of such pastures was situated in Baqi` and another was situated at Rabadha.

He also used to inspect army camps. There were no permanent cantonments during his time. Once an Islamic army was encamped at Jarf, Hadrat Abu Bakr (R.A.) himself went to inspect the army of Banu Fazarah. Seeing him all the men stood up in his honour and he said, "God bless you." Some of them said, "O *Khalifah* (Deputy) of the Prophet of Allah! We have brought healthy horses and mares, and we are very good riders. Please give us a big standard." Hadrat Abu Bakr said, "I can't give you a big standard because it has already been taken by Banu `Abs."

Preaching of Islam

As the *Khalifah* (Deputy) of the Prophet of Allah, he paid special attention towards preaching the right way of life. Because of his efforts the whole of Arabia once more and forever re-entered Islam.

He gave strict instructions to all the armies to call, at first, the enemy to Islam. Invitation to Islam was usually given for three days before the start of a battle. A number of tribes in Iraq and other places accepted Islam without any battle when Hadrat Khalid and other commanders preached. Once a Christian bishop of Hirah accepted Islam after seeing the good conduct of the Muslims.

The Department of Jurists (*Muftis*)

Besides the Judiciary in which *Qadi*s (Judges) used to decide the cases, there was a special department of *Mufti*s (Jurists) whose duty was to solve various problems of Muslims in the light of the Holy Qur'an and the *Sunnah* (Practices) of the Holy Prophet (*Sallallahu `alayhi wa Sallam*). Following were the *Mufti*s (Jurists) in Medina: Hadrat `Umar, `Ali, `Uthman, `Abdur Rahman bin `Auf, Mu`adh bin Jabal, Ubaiy bin Ka`b, and Zaid bin Thabit. No other person besides them was entitled to give verdict or to lay down rules of Islamic Law to Muslims in the light of the Holy Qur'an and the *Sunnah*.

Judiciary

The judiciary was totally separate from the executive. The judges appointed by Hadrat Abu Bakr were Hadrat `Umar and Hadrat `Ali

(R.A.) in Medina. Being a great Jurist Hadrat Abu Bakr was also a judge and gave decisions on various cases.

Punishments

He used to give punishments as prescribed in the Holy Qur'an or told by the Holy Prophet (*Sallallahu `alayhi wa Sallam*). He did not establish any police force or any department for it. However, he appointed Hadrat `Abdullah bin Mas`ud as the Sentinel to take care of crimes. He also laid down such punishments which were given in the Holy Qur'an or the *Sunnah*. For example he fixed punishment of forty lashes for drinking liquor.

He also paid special attention to the safety of highways and various parts of the state. He gave severe punishments to robbers and persons committing breach of peace.

Division of Arabian Peninsula into various provinces

Hadrat Abu Bakr as-Siddiq divided the Peninsula into various provinces for convenience of administration. In his time, the following were the provinces of Arabia: Medina, Mecca, Ta`if, San`a (North Yemen), Yemen (i.e., South Yemen), Najran, Hadramaut, Bahrain and Dumatul-Jandal.

Every province was under the control of a governor who was the chief executive officer of that region. He did not change the governors or the officers appointed by the Holy Prophet (*Sallallahu `alayhi wa Sallam*) during his time.

He devoted his full energy to the administration of the new born Islamic state. Hadrat Abu Bakr's reign was short and full of rebellions, still his administration was very sound. He followed the footsteps of the Holy Prophet (*Sallallahu `alayhi wa Sallam*) faithfully and to the fullest possible extent and kept strict watch over the affairs of his government. Hadrat `Umar (R.A.) always helped him in administration of justice and fulfilled the promise made by him at the time of the election of Abu Bakr (R.A.).

He laid down the foundation of a true Islamic republic upon democratic principles. His strong faith and trust in Allah were reflected in his administration. A Western historian, Sir W. Muir writes, "His reign was short, but after Muhammad (*Sallallahu `alayhi wa Sallam*) himself there is none to whom the Faith was more dear."

SECTION II

`Umar Ibn al-Khattab
13-23 A.H./634-643 A.D.

4
`Umar Ibn al-Khattab: His Early Life

Life before Islam

`Umar (R.A.) belonged to the Adi family of Quraish tribe. In the 8th generation, his lineage joins with the Holy Prophet (*Sallallahu `alayhi wa Sallam*). Abu Hafs was his patronymic name and "al-Faruq" his title given by the Holy Prophet (*Sallallahu `alayhi wa Sallam*). He was born in 583 A.C., about forty years before the great Hijrah. The early life of Hadrat `Umar is not known in detail. In his youth he was a famous wrestler and orator, and a spirited person. He was one among the few people in Mecca who knew reading and writing before Islam. His main occupation was business.

When the Holy Prophet (*Sallallahu `alayhi wa Sallam*) got revelation and invited people to Islam, `Umar became the sworn enemy of Islam and the Holy Prophet (*Sallallahu `alayhi wa Sallam*) and did not hesitate to harm the Muslims and Islam at every opportunity.

`Umar's acceptance of Islam

It was the sixth year of the Holy Prophet's mission when Quraish leaders called a meeting and asked a volunteer for the assassination of the Holy Prophet (*Sallallahu `alayhi wa Sallam*). `Umar offered himself for this job and everybody in the meeting exclaimed that he was the right person for it. While he was on his way with a sword in his hand he met Sa`d bin Abi Waqqas who enquired of him about his destination. `Umar told him that he was going to murder the Holy Prophet (*Sallallahu `alayhi wa Sallam*). After some discussion Sa`d said, "You had better take care of your own family first. Your sister and brother-in-law both have accepted Islam." Hearing this `Umar changed his direction and went straight to his sister's house. When Hadrat `Umar knocked at the door, they were studying the Holy Qur'an from Hadrat Khabbab (R.A.). His sister Fatimah was frightened on hearing `Umar's voice and tried to hide the portion of the Holy Qur'an she was reciting. When `Umar entered the house he enquired about their Islam and on finding that they had accepted Islam, he first fell upon his brother-in-law and beat him severely. When his sister intervened he smote her so violently on her face that it bled profusely. On this his sister burst out: "Do whatever you like, we are determined to die as Muslims." When `Umar saw his sister bleeding, he cooled down and felt ashamed. He loved Fatimah very much but could not tolerate her conversion to Islam. However, deeply moved, `Umar asked her to show the pages on which the Holy Qur'an was written. But she was, after all, `Umar's sister and told him straight, "You cannot touch it unless you take a bath and make yourself clean." He washed his body and then read the leaves. That was the beginning of Surah *Ta Ha* (Chapter 20 of the Holy Qur'an). When he came to the verse: "*Lo! I, even I, am Allah, there is no god save Me. So serve Me and establish Salat for My remembrance*" (20:14), Umar exclaimed, "Surely this is the Word of Allah. Take me to Muhammad (*Sallallahu `alayhi wa Sallam*).

On hearing this Hadrat Khabbab (R.A.), who had hidden himself in the house, came out from inside and said, "O `Umar! Glad tidings for you. It seems that the prayer of the Holy Prophet (*Sallallahu `alayhi wa Sallam*) which he said last night has been answered in your favour. He had prayed to Allah: "O Allah, strengthen Islam with either

'Umar bin Khattab or 'Umar bin Hisham whomsoever Thou pleaseth."

'Umar then went to the Holy Prophet (*Sallallahu 'alayhi wa Sallam*). On seeing him, the Holy Prophet (*Sallallahu 'alayhi wa Sallam*) asked him, "Umar! What brings you here?" He said, "I am here to accept Islam." Hearing this the Muslims shouted with joy, "*Allahu Akbar!*" (Allah is the Greatest) and the sound rent the air of Mecca. As a matter of fact, 'Umar's conversion to Islam was a terrible blow to the morale of the disbelievers. 'Abdullah bin Mas'ud, a great Companion, says, "Umar's conversion to Islam was a great triumph, his emigration to Medina a tremendous reinforcement and his accession to Caliphate a great blessing for the Muslims." In some history books there are more details in this connection. I have followed the version of Shaikh Muhammad Zakariya (Damat Barakatuhu) given in his book *Hikayat-i-Sahabah*.

'Umar (R.A.) gets the title of "*Al-Faruq*"

Conversion of Hadrat 'Umar (R.A.) strengthened Islam. Hitherto, Muslims had lived in constant fear of disbelievers, and most of them were concealing their faith. The Muslims were now able to offer their *Salat* publicly. When Hadrat 'Umar (R.A.) became a Muslim he declared his faith openly before the Quraish Chiefs. Though they stared at him but could not do any harm to him. Then he requested the Holy Prophet (*Sallallahu 'alayhi wa Sallam*) to offer *Salat* in the Ka'bah. On getting the consent of the Holy Prophet (*Sallallahu 'alayhi wa Sallam*), Hadrat 'Umar led a party of the Muslims to that place. Hadrat Hamzah, who had accepted Islam a few days before 'Umar (R.A.), carried another party of the Muslims to Ka'bah. When all the Muslims gathered in the Ka'bah they offered their *Salat* in congregation. The Holy Prophet (*Sallallahu 'alayhi wa Sallam*) led this first public *Salat* in the history of Islam. For this courageous and bold action of Hadrat 'Umar (R.A.), the Holy Prophet (*Sallallahu 'alayhi wa Sallam*) gave him the title of "*al-Faruq*", i.e., the one who makes a distinction between the "Right" (*Haqq*) and the "Wrong" (*Batil*).

Migration to Medina

When the Muslims were ordered to migrate to Medina, most of them left Mecca quietly and secretly, but Hadrat `Umar (R.A.) declared it openly. He put on his arms and first went to the Ka`bah. After performing the *Salat* he announced loudly: "I am migrating to Medina. If anyone wants to check me, let him come out. I am sure that his mother would cry for his life." There was no man in Mecca to accept the challenge of Hadrat `Umar (R.A.). Then he migrated to Medina boldly.

`Umar's services to Islam before his *Khilafat*

Hadrat `Umar (R.A.) had great love for Allah and the Holy Prophet (*Sallallahu `alayhi wa Sallam*). He participated in almost all the big battles: Badr, Uhud, Ahzab, Khaibar, Hunain, etc. In the expedition to Tabuk he gave half of his wealth in the path of Allah. He was next to Hadrat Abu Bakr (R.A.) to sacrifice his belongings for the cause of Allah.

The Holy Prophet (*Sallallahu `alayhi wa Sallam*) also had a deep love for him. Once he remarked, "Were a prophet to come after me, he would have been `Umar." In another Hadith mentioned in Bukhari, Hadrat Abu Hurairah (R.A.) narrated that the Holy Prophet (*Sallallahu `alayhi wa Sallam*) said, "In Bani Isra'il (Israelites) there were people who were not prophets but talked to Allah. Were anyone in my *Ummah* (people) like those persons, he would be `Umar."

The death of the Holy Prophet (*Sallallahu `alayhi wa Sallam*) was a great shock to him, and he could not believe it until Hadrat Abu Bakr (R.A.) reminded him of a clear verse of the Holy Qur'an on the subject. He then went to the Council Hall along with Hadrat Abu Bakr (R.A.) where the people of Medina had assembled to select the first Caliph. Hadrat `Umar (R.A.) was the first person to pledge loyalty (*Bai`at*) at the hand of Hadrat Abu Bakr (R.A.), and then helped him throughout the duration of his rule.

5
Hadrat `Umar's Caliphate

Hadrat `Umar (R.A.) as the second Caliph of Islam

As described in connection with the life of Hadrat Abu Bakr, during his illness he consulted the *Shura* about the next *Khalifah* and then gave his decision in favour of Hadrat `Umar (R.A.) who took the charge of Caliphate after the death of Hadrat Abu Bakr (R.A.) on the 22nd of Jamadi-uth-Thani, 13 A.H. (23rd August, 634 A.C.). `Umar (R.A.) followed fully the ways of the Holy Prophet (*Sallallahu `alayhi wa Sallam*) and the policy of his predecessor with his characteristic zeal and vigour. It was his strict adherence to the *Sunnah* of the Holy Prophet (*Sallallahu `alayhi wa Sallam*) which helped him to subdue the mighty empires of Persia and Byzantine. His caliphate marked the "Golden Age" of Islam. I would like to discuss only the main events which took place during the Caliphate of Hadrat `Umar (R.A.) in brief.

FALL OF PERSIAN EMPIRE

During the time of Hadrat Abu Bakr (R.A.), Hadrat Khalid bin Walid conquered part of the Persian Empire, known as the Kingdom of Hira. Then he was ordered by Hadrat Abu Bakr (R.A.) to join the expedition to Syria. At the time of his departure, he appointed Muthanna bin Harith as the commander of the Islamic army. The Persians became furious at the loss of the kingdom of Hira and the Emperor sent a large army under the command of a very famous General, Rustam, the Commander-in-Chief of Persian armies. In view of the growing pressure of Persians, Muthanna requested Hadrat 'Umar (R.A.) for reinforcement. At that time there was a large gathering of Muslims in Medina to take pledge of loyalty (*Bai'at*) at the hand of the new Caliph (Hadrat 'Umar). He put the matter before the Muslims but did not get any response in the beginning. Then Hadrat 'Umar (R.A.), in his sermons stressed the importance of Jihad and a large number of Muslims volunteered to help Muthanna against the Persians. Abu 'Ubaid ath-Thaqafi was appointed as the commander of the Islamic army comprising five thousand men.

In the meantime Persians attacked the places conquered by Muslims and they lost some of them. In the early stage of the battles Rustam sent his subordinates to face Muslims.

The Battle of Namariq

When Abu 'Ubaid had reached there a battle took place at Namariq and the Muslims won it. A number of famous generals of the Persian army including Jaban, right hand of Rustam, were killed in the battle. Then some small battles also took place at Kaskar, etc.

The Battle of the Bridge

The defeat of Persians startled Rustam and he gathered a huge army to face the Muslims. The army met the Muslims on the other bank of the Euphrates under the command of Bahman, a famous Persian warrior. Bahman asked Hadrat Abu 'Ubaid whether Persians should cross the river or the Muslims. Hadrat Abu `Ubaid was over-confident and chose to cross the river, although some of the Muslim generals like Muthanna did not like to cross the river, and preferred to let the Persians come. The Islamic army crossed the river but lost the battle. Hadrat Abu `Ubaid was also martyred and Muslims fell one after the other. Muthanna took over the command and ordered rebuilding of the bridge which had been destroyed. The elephants of the Persian army caused considerable damage to the Muslim army. However Muthanna could save only 3000 men out of an army of 9000.

The Battle of Buwaib

Hadrat `Umar (R.A.) was shocked at the defeat of the Muslim army. He sent special messengers to various tribes and exhorted the Muslims to prepare for the Holy War against Persians. A new reinforcement was sent to Muthanna's army. In this army a number of Christian Arabs were also included.

The Persians also gathered a huge army. This time Rustam, the Commander-in-Chief of the Persian armies, appointed Mehran Hamdani as the Commander because he had travelled Arabia and knew the Arabian way of fighting. The Muslim army, under the command of Muthanna, met the Persians at a place called Buwaib (where Kufa is situated). The Muslims invited the Persians to cross the river and they accepted it. The number of Muslim army was a little more than 20,000 while the Persians, several times larger in number, were estimated as two hundred thousands. A fierce battle took place. Muslims fought desperately and after a grim fight, the Persians were defeated. They could not find the way to cross the river Euphrates because the bridge built by them was destroyed by the Muslims. There was a total disorder in the Persian army. The commander of the army, Mehran was slain in this battle and not less than a hundred thousand men lost their lives in

THE PIOUS CALIPHS

the field. As a result of this victory the whole of western part of the Persian Empire (now Iraq) fell into Muslim hands.

Change of Persian Ruler

The great defeat at Buwaib shocked the Persian Empire. It was not only a cause of great disturbance to the rulers but to the public as well. For the first time they realised the strength of Muslims. The news of loss of one hundred thousand Persians and only few hundred Muslims was received with great surprise. At that time a woman, Puran Dukht was the Empress. The Persians replaced the Empress by a young twenty-one year old Emperor, Yezdgird. The new Emperor reorganised the army and strengthened the frontier defences. There arose a number of rebellions in the places conquered by Muslims as a result of which Muslims again lost some of the parts which they had conquered.

When Hadrat `Umar heard this news he asked Muthanna to call the border tribes and to return within safer borders till reinforcement reached him. He himself declared Jihad all over the land and sent emissaries to collect an army for the Holy War. An army of 20.000 Muslims was collected. Hadrat `Umar (R.A.) himself wanted to lead the army this time but the *Shura* (Advisory Council) did not agree to it. The name of Hadrat Sa`d bin Abi Waqqas (R.A.), a great warrior and one of the uncles of the Holy Prophet (*Sallallahu `alayhi wa Sallam*) was proposed to lead the army to which Hadrat `Umar (R.A.) agreed. The army was having seventy of those Companions who had participated in the first battle of Islam at Badr. When the army was leaving Medina, Hadrat `Umar (R.A.) gave instructions to Hadrat Sa`d bin Abi Waqqas (R.A.). Some of those are as under:

"Allah does not repel evil with evil but he repels evil with good. All men high and low are equal before Him. One can win Allah's favour only through devotion to His service. Remember that the

Sunnah (the Way) of the Holy Prophet is the only correct way of doing things. You are going on a heavy mission which you can discharge only by following the Truth. Inculcate good habits in yourselves and in your companions."

This advice clearly shows that the aim of Muslims was to proclaim Allah's message — Islam —, rather than to fight. The sword was used to clear the barriers in the way.

In the meantime Muthanna died and has brother Bashir joined Hadrat Sa`d (R.A.) with an army of eight thousand. Hadrat Sa`d was in direct contact with Hadrat `Umar all the time who was constantly giving instructions about the movement of the army from place to place. Finally Hadrat `Umar (R.A.) sent instructions to it to encamp at Qadisiya and to send an envoy to the Persian Emperor, Yezdgird, with the message of Islam and peace.

Islamic emissaries

Following the instructions of the Caliph, Hadrat Sa`d encamped at Qadisiya. The Muslims had to wait there for about two months for the Persian armies. In the meantime Hadrat Sa`d sent an envoy to the Emperor Yezdgird.

Yezdgird held his court to receive Muslim envoys. The court was a mirror of the worldly pomp and glory of the Persians. Hadrat Nu`man bin Maqram invited the Persians and the Emperor to Islam and told them about the Holy Prophet (*Sallallahu `alayhi wa Sallam*). He said:

> "O Persians, we call you towards the path of peace, Islam. If you accept it, you are our brothers and we will leave Allah's Book, the Holy Qur'an, for your guidance to follow His commandments. If you reject this sacred message, pay us the *Jizya* (Defense Tax). The third alternative is the sword in case you reject the first two

offers, so that we may take our own course to spread this message."

Yezdgird who was very proud of his power and army, lost his temper on hearing this and insulted the envoys. He got a basket full of earth and put it on the head of the leader, Hadrat `Asim (R.A.). When Hadrat `Asim carried the earth to Hadrat Sa`d (R.A.), he took it as a sign for victory. The illtreatment of the Persian Emperor hastened the war.

The Emperor sent an army of one hundred thousand men. This time Rustam, the Commander-in-Chief, was himself leading the Persian army. Other famous commanders of the army were Jalinus, Mahran bin Bahram Razi and Harmuzan. Rustam was afraid of Muslims and hesitated to face them. He took six months to reach Qadisiya from Mada'in (Ctesiphon), the capital. He wanted to negotiate with the Muslims in the first instance. Therefore he asked them to send a delegation. The Muslim delegation went to Rustam's camp at the head of Hadrat Rabi` bin `Amir (R.A.) There took place much discussion but no decision was reached. Hadrat Rabi` (R.A.) gave the message of Islam boldly and put the same three conditions which were put before the Emperor by Hadrat Nu`man. On the second day Rustam again asked Hadrat Sa`d (R.A.) to send the delegation. This time he sent Hadrat Hudhaifah (R.A.) who also put the same three conditions and told him if he did not accept them within three days, the third alternative i.e., the use of sword would remain and would be acted upon.

On the third day Rustam again requested Muslims to send an emissary and this time Hadrat Mughirah bin Shu`bah (R.A.) went. Rustam tried to negotiate in terms of money by saying, "I think you are poor and hungry. We would give you so much of wealth that would be sufficient for the whole of your life." Hearing this Hadrat Mughirah (R.A.) angrily replied, "Of course we were hungry and poor but Allah sent His Messenger to us because of whom our fate changed and Allah nourished us. He asked us to obey only One God and to spread His message. If you follow His message (Islam) you are our brothers, we will never fight with you. If you don't, then let us spread His *Kalimah* and you pay to us *Jizya* (Defense Tax) otherwise the sword will give the final decision."

Hearing this Rustam got furious and vowed to kill all the Muslims as soon as the sun rose the next day. Hadrat Mughirah (R.A.) returned to the Muslim camp saying, "*La haula wala quwwata illa billahil `Azim* (There is neither any power nor any might besides Allah, the High)."

The Battle of Qadisiya

As soon as Hadrat Mughirah left the Persian Camp, Rustam asked his army to prepare for the attack in the morning. There was a canal between the two armies. He ordered building of a bridge over it. Next day in the morning he crossed the canal to attack the Muslims. When both the armies were ready to fight, Hadrat Sa`d bin Abi Waqqas (R.A.) told Rustam through an epistle, "Rustam! There are people with me to whom death (in the Path of Allah) is more attractive than is wine to the people in your army."

At last the battle started at Qadisiya in the month of Muharram, 14 A.H. (June, 637). Hadrat Sa`d was sick and directed the operations from the sick bed. This battle was hotly contested and lasted for three days. Muslims were about 28,000 in number while the Persian army was estimated at 120,000 (four times bigger than Islamic army). Rustam displayed great skill in arraying his troops. On the first day the battle started amidst loud cries of "*Allahu Akbar*" (Allah is the

Greatest). Though the Muslims displayed great valour and skill but the Persian elephants played havoc with the Muslim cavalry. The Arab horses were not trained to fight in a battle having elephants. However Muslim archers and lancers rained arrows and spheres and knocked down many elephant riders. The battle ended without reaching a final decision on the first day.

The following day the battle again ended without a victory for any of the two armies. On the third day Muslims wrapped pieces of cloth round the bodies of their camels to frighten the Persian elephants. The plan worked out successfully. Moreover a number of Muslim archers pierced the eyes of the elephants and cut their trunks. The blind elephants ran towards the Persian army and destroyed their ranks.

The battle continued to the fourth day. Now the blind elephants played a havoc with the Persians themselves. Then some of the Muslim warriors from among the chief of the clans rushed towards Rustam and destroyed the special battalion around him. The canopy of Rustam was blown in the air and he himself tried to flee. He was detected by the Muslims and was slain. Seeing their slain Commander, the Persians started fleeing for their lives. Thousands of Persians were slain. There were about six thousand Muslim casualties while the number of the Persians killed was thirty thousand.

The battle of Qadisiya proved to be decisive in the history of Islam. It shattered the strength of the Persian Empire. Hadrat 'Umar (R.A.) received the news with great joy. The Muslims gained immense booty which was distributed among the troops according to the Islamic law and a fifth portion was despatched to the *Baitul Mal*.

Following the victory at Qadisiya, Muslims chased the Persians. They captured Babal and Kutha and then laid siege to Bahrah Sher, a very important and strong fort at the outskirt of the Persian capital, Mada'in (Ctesiphon). The siege went on for two months and ultimately

Muslims captured the fort. The next step was to conquer Mada'in, the capital itself.

Fall of Mada'in (Ctesiphon), the capital of Persian Empire

The City of Mada'in was situated on the east bank of river Tigris and was almost surrounded by it. After a rest of few months, Hadrat Sa'd took permission from Hadrat 'Umar (R.A.) to invade the Capital. When Hadrat Sa'd (R.A.) marched, the Persians destroyed the bridge on the river. The river was deep and turbulent but the determination of Muslims was not affected. They were having full faith in Allah Almighty, the Creator of the Universe. It has been recorded in some books of history that on finding the destruction of the bridge by the Persians Hadrat Sa'd said, "Allah made a way in the Red Sea for Moses and his followers, He will surely help us who are following His Last Prophet, Hadrat Muhammad (*Sallallahu 'alayhi wa Sallam*)."

He consulted the generals of his army and then ordered the Muslims to go across. First of all sixty horsemen plunged themselves in the river and crossed it. Then the whole army crossed the river as if it was walking on the ground. Seeing the Muslims crossing the river the Persian archers rained arrows on the Muslims. Hadrat Sa'd had already appointed six hundred archers on a nearby hill. They assaulted the Persians who ran away saying, "*Dev amdand, Dev amdand* (i.e., 'The giants have come! The giants have come!')." The Muslims crossed the Tigris without any severe loss. Yezdgird and his ministers had already fled and the capital was captured without any opposition. With this victory the whole of the territory between the Euphrates and the Tigris came under the possession of the Muslims. The prophecy of the Holy Prophet (*Sallallahu 'alayhi wa Sallam*) came true, "A group of Muslims will capture the White Palace of the Persian Emperor."

Both Hadrat 'Umar and Hadrat Sa'd (R.A.) thanked Allah for this great victory. When the rich booty from the White Palace of Yezdgird reached Medina, tears came out in the eyes of Hadrat `Umar (R.A.) and he remarked, "I am weeping because riches are often the cause of enmity and mutual bitterness. Those people who have such evils, ultimately lose respect."

The Battle of Jalula

The Persian Emperor took shelter in Hulwan and started preparation for a big assault on the Muslims. Now Kharzad, brother of Rustam was the Commander-in-Chief. He gathered a huge army to avenge the past defeats. After consultations with Hadrat `Umar (R.A.) Hadrat Sa'd bin Abi Waqqas (R.A.) sent an army under the command of Hashim and Qa`qas to face the Persian army at Jalula. Again a fierce battle was fought and ultimately the Persians were defeated and fled further north.

The Muslims advanced ahead and captured Qaka and finally Hulwan where Yezdgird, the Emperor, was staying. He fled to Khurasan and settled down in Mery. The last big battle was fought in the month of Muharram, 19 A.H. (642 A.C.) at Nihawand in which the Persians were completely defeated. Then a number of small battles took place and the Muslims conquered Hamdan, Azerbaijan and Armenia by the year 21 A.H.

Muslim rule over the Persian Empire

The Persian Emperor fled to Isphan, then to Kirman and from there to Balkh. The Muslims chased him everywhere. Ultimately the whole of Persia came under the sway of Islam, by the year 23 A.H. The Muslims marched as east as Sind (the Indian territory, now Pakistan). They captured Makran and Baluch. But Hadrat `Umar (R.A.) stopped them — who were under the command of Hakam at that time. He did not want to extend his frontiers at the price of Muslim blood. Thus Makran was the last place in the east under the rule of Muslims during the caliphate of Hadrat `Umar (R.A.).

After the capture of Persian Empire, Hadrat `Umar (R.A.) remarked, "Allah has destroyed the Persian Empire, now they cannot harm the Muslims. O Muslims, if you do not follow the Straight Path, Allah would take this power from you and hand it over to whom He likes."

It must be clarified here that at no place Muslims forced non-Muslims to accept Islam. Islam spread because of its teachings and because of the practical life of Muslims. Some western scholars have accepted this fact. R.A. Nicholson writes in *A Literary History of the Arabs*, "It must not be supposed that the followers of Zoroaster and Christ in these countries were forcibly converted to Islam. Thousands embraced it voluntarily."

The conquest of the Persian Empire provided the Muslims with unlimited resources. At the same time it also brought Muslims into touch with luxuries and as time passed they gave up their simple living and fell prey to some vices prevailing in those days Hadrat `Umar had feared.

The cities of Basra and Kufa

Muslims established two military cantonments, one at Basra and the other at Kufa in 638 A.C. Later on these cantonments became big cities. Basra was established at the Shatt-ul-Arab and was important because it guarded the passage from the Persian Gulf to Mesopotamia. Kufa was founded at the bank of the Euphrates. Afterwards these cities became important centres of Islamic culture and civilization.

THE EASTERN ROMAN EMPIRE (BYZANTIUM)

Conquest of Syria

The causes of the war between the Muslims and the Byzantines (commonly called as Romans) have already been discussed. During the time of Hadrat Abu Bakr (R.A.) the Muslims had defeated Romans on the Syrian front and captured a number of cities like Busra and Ajnadain. They laid siege to Damascus when Hadrat Abu Bakr (R.A.) passed away. After his death they captured Damascus, Hims and Qansrin. In all the three battles Hadrat Khalid bin Walid played an important role. Hadrat `Umar (R.A.) recognised Khalid's merits and said, "May Allah bless the soul of Abu Bakr, he put Khalid in the right place." The fall of these important cities made the Byzantine Emperor, Heraclius, furious and he sent a huge army to fight with the Muslims. In order to face this big army, Muslims left some of the places, occupied by them and returned to safer border.

When the Islamic armies were leaving the conquered places they paid back the *Jizya* (the Defense Tax) received from the non-Muslim inhabitants of those places saying, "Since we cannot protect you, we are returning it." This was a unique example in history. The people of those places were greatly impressed by the Muslims' treatment. It is given in some books that the people of those places cried when Muslims left their places.

The Battle of Yarmuk (Rajab 15 A.H./636 A.C.)

After the fall of Damascus, Hims and other places, the Romans fled to Antioch where Heraclius was staying and was thinking of moving to Constantinople, his permanent capital. They appealed to Heraclius to help them against the Muslim armies. He held this court at Antioch and began raising a huge army against the Muslims to wipe them out of Syria.

The Muslims had already gathered at Yarmuk to face the Roman Byzantine army. The Romans were several times larger in number than the Muslims. In the beginning the command was in the hand of Khalid bin Walid (R.A.) but during the battle he received the letter of Hadrat `Umar deposing him from the post of Commander-in-Chief. Hadrat `Umar (R.A.) appointed Abu `Ubaidah bin Jarrah (R.A.) as the Commander-in-Chief.

A fierce battle was fought on the 20th August, 636, and at the end the Romans lost the field. The cavalry fled and the infantry was put to sword. Theodorus, the Commander of Roman army himself fell and his entire army was turned into a fleeing, panic-stricken mob. According to Tabari, about one hundred thousand Romans were killed in this battle. Muslim casualties were three thousand.

The battle of Yarmuk was a turning point in the history of Byzantine Empire. The power of Byzantine was crushed in the battle. The fate of Syria was decided and it fell in the hands of Muslims for ever. Hearing the defeat at Yarmuk, Heraclius left Antioch and fled to Constantinople saying, "Farewell, 0 Syria! and what an excellent country this is for the enemy." (*Note*: According to some historians it was the second battle of Ajnadan and not the battle of Yarmuk which took place in 15 A.H.).

Removal of Hadrat Khalid (R.A.) from the command

Hadrat Khalid bin Walid (R.A.) was a successful and powerful general of Islam. He occupied a unique position in the history of heroism, and devoted his whole life to the cause of Islam. Hadrat `Umar (R.A.) always appreciated his services. But there were certain complaints against him, especially for being extravagant, when he awarded 10,000 dinars to a poet. Hadrat Khaild could not give satisfactory explanation to Hadrat `Umar (R.A.) hence he was removed from the command. But Hadrat Khaild proved to be a very true Muslim and fought alongside ordinary soldiers in the army.

As narrated above, he was deposed when the battle of Yarmuk was going on. The Caliph's order was delivered to Khalid but it had no effect on him. He went on fighting as fiercely as before. After the battle was over, his dismissal became known. When somebody asked him why the news did not damp his spirit at all, he said, "I was fighting for the cause of Allah."

According to those historians who hold the opinion that the Battle of Yarmuk took place before the fall of Damascus, Hadrat Khalid was deposed in the early part of `Umar's (R.A.) caliphate, while some think it took place around 17 A.H. because according to them the battle of Yarmuk took place after the fall of Damascus.

Regarding the removal of Hadrat Khalid some of the Muslim historians say, "He (Hadrat `Umar) had deposed Khalid from the government, not because of tyranny or fraud, but because he deemed it essential to admonish the people, who were inclined to put their trust in an arm of flesh, instead of looking to the Giver of all victory."

Fall of Jerusalem

Hadrat `Amr bin al-`As was in the beginning leading the army in front of Jerusalem. After the capture of Antioch and other key cities of Byzantium, Hadrat Abu `Ubaidah also joined him along with Hadrat Khalid bin Walid (R.A.). They laid siege to the great city of Jerusalem, surrounded by a huge wall. Since the people of Jerusalem had already seen the defeat of Byzantine forces they offered a peaceful truce provided the *Khalifah* came in person to sign the treaty in their presence. The proposal was passed over to Hadrat `Umar (R.A.) at

Medina and after consultation with the *Shura* he accepted the offer.

Hadrat `Umar at Jerusalem

Hadrat `Umar (R.A.) appointed Hadrat `Ali (R.A.) as his deputy and went to Jerusalem with his slave. They were having one camel on which each of them rode by turn.

When Hadrat `Umar (R.A.) was entering Jerusalem it happened to be the slave's turn to ride on the camel. Though the slave offered his turn to the *Khalifah* but Hadrat `Umar refused and remarked, "The honour of Islam (i.e., being Muslim) is enough for all of us." He entered Jerusalem holding the rope of the camel on which was riding his slave. His clothes were dirty and there were several patches on them. Hadrat Abu `Ubaidah, Khalid bin Walid and other commanders came some distance to receive him. They were wearing costly garments. This made Hadrat `Umar (R.A.) angry. He threw some pebbles at his generals (to show his anger) and said, "Have you changed so much in just two years? The only way for the success is the way of the Holy Prophet (*Sallallahu `alayhi wa Sallam*)."

Then Hadrat `Umar (R.A.) signed the treaty under which the inhabitants of Jerusalem were granted complete security of their life and property. Their places of worship were secured and remained intact. All the people were allowed to follow their religion freely.

The gates of the city were then opened and the Muslims entered Jerusalem in the year 16 A.H. (635 A.C.) According to some history books the date given on the treaty signed by Hadrat `Umar (R.A.) falls in the 17th year A.H. It is possible therefore that the Muslims conquered it early in 17th year A.H.

Hadrat `Umar (R.A.) visited the city. The time of the *Salat* had reached. The Christians allowed the Muslims to perform *Salat* in the big Church but Hadrat `Umar declined to do so that it might not be an excuse for the future generations to take over the Church from them. He offered the *Salat* with the Muslims on the steps of the Church. Even then he gave in writing to the Bishop that the steps would never be used for congregational prayers or for the *Adhan* in future.

`Umar's Mosque at Jerusalem

Hadrat `Umar (R.A.) laid the foundation of a mosque at a place known as Sakhra proposed by the Bishop, where Allah sent revelation to Prophet Yaqub (Jacob or Israel, *'alayhis-Salam*) and where the great temple of Solomon was built. He himself worked like a labourer for building the mosque. That mosque is known as "`Umar's Mosque."

Conquest of Jazirah Mesopotamia

After the conquest of Jerusalem the Romans (Byzantines) tried to regain Syria. The Muslims did not want territorial expansion, they were fighting either to protect the birth-place of Islam, Arabia or in self-defense. Their aim was only to proclaim Allah's message and to preach Islam freely. Whenever they were allowed a free passage to show the right path no fighting took place as it could be noticed in the case of Jerusalem. Never in the history of Islam any nation was forced to forsake its religion and to accept Islam.

The people of Jazirah (now north-western part of Iraq) plotted to oust the Muslims from Syria. Heraclius, the Emperor of Byzantine sent his army to help the people of Jazirah. They invaded Hims, a fort which had been conquered by the Muslims under the command of Hadrat Abu `Ubaidah (R.A.). The Muslims fell upon the enemies and beat them off. Under such conditions Hadrat `Umar (R.A.) ordered the Muslim forces to occupy Jazirah.

After its conquest Jazirah (Mesopotamia) was put under the Governor of Homs (Home). Jazirah was conquered under the command of `Ayad bin Ghanam (R.A.).

The severe famine and plague

In the year 17-18 A.H., Hijaz (Northern Arabia) and Syria were faced by a severe famine and drought. Hadrat `Umar (R.A.) took steps to get food supplies from Egypt, part of which had been conquered by Hadrat `Amr bin al-`As (R.A.). He sent three big ships of grains to Medina which were unloaded in the presence of Hadrat `Umar (R.A.). He himself distributed the grains among the needy. Hadrat `Umar (R.A.) did not take any delicacy (butter, etc.) during the famine period. When he was requested to take care of his health he said, "If I don't taste suffering, how can I know the sufferings of others?"

When the famine became intolerable he prayed to Allah in a big gathering of Muslims. It has been narrated that the prayers had not even finished when rains started to pour down.

About the same time plague spread in most parts of Iraq, Syria and Egypt and it caused great havoc not only to civilians but also to the Muslim armies. After the plague, Hadrat `Umar went to Syria to inspect the losses caused by the plague. Three important figures — Abu `Ubaidah, Mu`adh bin Jabal and Yazid bin Abu Sufyan (R.A.) — had passed away. He appointed Mu`awiyah bin Abi Sufyan as the Governor of Damascus in place of his brother Yazid bin Abi Sufyan.

The conquest of Egypt

Being a powerful province of Byzantine Empire and having the strong base of Byzantine navy at Alexandria, Egypt was a great danger to the security of Hijaz (Northern Arabia). The Romans were busy in plotting against the Muslims to regain the territories conquered by the Muslims and to attack them through Egypt. Obviously it was necessary from the point of view of defense to drive back the Romans (Byzantines) from Egypt. Therefore, towards the close of 17 A.H. (638 A.C.), Hadrat `Amr bin al-`As (R.A.) who had collaborated in the conquest of Palestine, repeatedly urged the Caliph to authorize him to lead a campaign against the valley of the Nile. He got the necessary permission from the Caliph and set out from Palestine for Egypt at the head of four thousand men. (*Note:* According to a number of historians it took place in the 18th year A.H. i.e., 639 A.D. All of them agree that a part of Egypt had been conquered before the great famine which happened in 17-18 A.H. If it is true, the date of invasion by `Amr bin al-`As must be before 18 A.H.).

Hadrat `Amr bin al-`As entered Egypt by the route of Wadi al-Arish and after attacking some small towns laid siege to one of the strongest forts of Romans in Egypt at Fustat (which later became Cairo). The fort was conquered after some time.

The fall of Fustat gave a severe blow to Roman might in Egypt. Constantine II, the Byzantine Emperor, hearing the news of the fall of the fort near Fustat, got furious and sent a big army to Alexandria. Hadrat `Amr bin al-`As therefore set out for Alexandria from Fustat. He got reinforcement from the Caliph. Alexandria was the strong hold of the Romans in Egypt. They could easily send reinforcement and supplies to Alexandria by sea. It was really a difficult task to conquer it. Hadrat `Amr bin al-`As laid siege to the city but no result came out for six months. Seeing this condition Hadrat `Umar (R.A.) wrote to Hadrat `Amr bin al-`As (R.A.), "I am afraid that the Muslims have not been acting fully upon the teachings of the Holy Qur'an and the *Sunnah* (ways) of the Holy Prophet (*Sallallahu `alayhi wa Sallam*). The only way to get victory is to follow strictly the ways of the Holy Prophet (*Sallallahu `alayhi wa Sallam*). They should therefore be more and more strict on it... Then try to give the final blow to the enemy."

Hadrat `Amr (R.A.) read the letter before the Muslims. `Umar's orders were at once carried out and at last Alexandria was conquered after a heavy engagement. According to some Western historians it was conquered in 642 A.D. while some of the Muslim historians say that Alexandria was conquered in 640 A.D. (20 A.H.). After the conquest of this great city — once a glory for the Romans — Hadrat `Amr wrote to the Caliph, "I have captured a city from the description of which I shall refrain. Suffice it to say I have seized therein 4,000 villas with 4,000 baths, 40,000 poll-tax-paying Jews and 400 places of entertainment for royalty." Philip Hitti writes, "The Caliph entertained his general's messenger with bread and dates; they all joined in a Thanksgiving service in the Prophet's mosque."

Afterwards Hadrat 'Amr (R.A.) captured the remaining fortresses in Egypt and it came under the full sway of Islam. Local Christians and Jews were given freedom of religion; various taxes imposed by the Romans were abolished and the general condition of the country improved. The Egyptians had never enjoyed such a period of prosperity and peace before.

A very inhuman custom was prevailing in Egypt at that time. The Egyptians used to sacrifice a beautiful maiden every year to please the river Nile so that it may bring more water. After the victory the matter was reported to Hadrat `Umar (R.A.) who prohibited this. By chance the same year the Nile had very little water and a condition of drought seemed to prevail over there. Hadrat `Amr (R.A.) wrote to Hadrat `Umar (R.A.) to seek his advice. He wrote the following letter and asked Hadrat `Amr to throw it in the Nile:

"From `Umar, the servant of Allah and *Amir* (Leader) of the Muslims to the River Nile of Egypt. O Nile! If you flow of your own desire, we do not need you. If you flow by the order of Allah, we pray to Him to keep you flowing."

The letter was thrown into the Nile and it over-flowed that year. In this way Egyptians were stopped from an un-Islamic practice. This had a very good effect. The Egyptians realised the spiritual power of Islam, and entered its folds.

6
Death and Review of Hadrat Umar's Achievements

Martyrdom of Hadrat `Umar (R.A.)

The glorious rule of Hadrat `Umar (R.A.) came to an end with his death on Wednesday, the 27th of Dhil-Hijjah, the year 23 A.H. (643 A.C.) when he was 61 years old. There was a Persian slave of Hadrat Mughirah bin Shu`bah, named Abu Lu'Lu' Firoze. One day he complained about the burden his master had imposed upon him. The complaint was not genuine, hence Hadrat `Umar (R.A.) ignored it. Next day, early in the morning when Hadrat `Umar (R.A.) went to *Masjid* to perform the *Fajr Salat*, the slave who was hiding in a corner, attacked him with a danger and stabbed him six times. People overpowered the assassin but he slew himself with the same dagger. The injuries were so serious that the Caliph died the next morning.

Before his death the Muslims asked him about his successor. He appointed a panel of six persons — Hadrat `Uthman, `Ali, Zubair, Talha, Sa`d bin Waqqas and `Abdur Rahman bin `Auf (R.A.) — to select a *Khalifah* from amongst them within three days after him.

He requested Hadrat `A'isha (R.A.) for permission for his burial by the side of the Holy Prophet (*Sallallahu `alayhi wa Sallam*). Though she had reserved that place for herself but on `Umar's request she gave it to him where he was buried.

Review of Hadrat `Umar's service to Islam

The period of Hadrat `Umar's caliphate undoubtedly is the "Golden Age" of Islam in every respect. He was a man of extraordinary genius who not only moulded the destiny of the nation but made history of his own. He followed the footsteps of the Holy Prophet (*Sallallahu `alayhi wa Sallam*) to the fullest extent. It was `Umar under whose rule Islam became a world power and the mighty empires of Persia and Byzantine (Eastern Roman) crumbled before the arm of Islam. Within ten years of his glorious rule, the whole of the Persian Empire, Syria, Palestine, Egypt and a part of Turkey came under the banner of Islam and the nations entered the fold of Islam. He was not only a conqueror but also an exemplary administrator who originated an efficient system of administration, and thus he was the real founder of political system of Islam (to be discussed in brief in the next chapter). He enforced Divine Law (*Shari`ah*) as the code of a newly formed international Islamic State; he safeguarded the internal safety by introducing the police force; he gave stipends to the poor; he constructed cantonments and forts for the safety of Islamic armies; he founded new cities for the growth of Islamic culture and civilization; he improved agriculture and economics of the Islamic State; he founded the educational system in an Islamic State; in brief he was the founder of a great Islamic State.

We would discuss his achievements more elaborately in the next chapter.

Character

He was a very pious Muslim. His success lay in two things: fear of Allah and his love for the Holy Prophet (*Sallallahu `alayhi wa*

Sallam). He never used even oil from the *Baitul-Mal* (Public Treasury) to burn a lamp at night for his personal needs. Whenever he finished the official work he put off the lamp. He used to patrol in the city at night to find out the needs and requirements, and conditions of the people. He did not hesitate to take his wife to work as a midwife for a poor woman. The salary he got from the *Baitul-Mal* was so low that it was hardly enough for him and his family's needs. When some of the eminent Muslims requested him to increase the amount he said, "The Holy Prophet (*Sallallahu `alayhi wa Sallam*) has left a standard by his personal example. I must follow him."

Hadrat `Umar was the most just ruler in the history of Islam. All the citizens, including the Caliph himself, were equal before law. Once he appeared before a court at Medina to clarify his position against a complaint. The *Qadi* (Judge) wanted to stand in his honour, but he did not allow him to do so, so that there would be no distinction between him and an ordinary person before the Law. He was really the founder of modern democratic system.

In short he was the best example of an ideal character and was the greatest *Khalifah* of Islam after Abu Bakr (R.A.). He selflessly devoted his whole energy for the cause of Islam. Muslims will always be indebted to him for his great achievements. As a matter of fact a separate book is required to describe his character and his services to Islam.

Piety

His dress, meals and general behaviour were similar to those of the Holy Prophet (*Sallallahu `alayhi wa Sallam*). There were usually a number of patches on his dress. He always took very ordinary meals. Once Yazid bin Abi Sufyan invited him to a feast and when special dishes were brought before him, he stopped eating and said, "I swear by Allah, in Whose hand is the life of `Umar, if you would not follow the ways of the Holy Prophet (*Sallallahu `alayhi wa Sallam*), Allah would cause you to be away from the *Siratul-Mustaqim* (the Straight Path)." He did not leave his characteristic simplicity even though he was ruling over a vast empire from Iran to Tripoli. He used to sit on a mat made of grass leaves.

Hadrat `Umar feared Allah and was wholly devoted to Him. It was his usual practice to cry and weep during *Salat*. Sometimes he passed whole of the night performing *Salat* and crying before Allah; and because of tears his beard used to get wet. It was his usual practice to weep during the *Fajr Salat*. On hearing or reading the verses of the Holy Qur'an containing description of the Day of Judgement and the Hell, he used to weep so much so that his whole beard would get wet. Once he was leading the *Fajr Salat* when he recited a verse from Surah Yusuf, "I expose my distress and anguish only to Allah (12:16)", he started to weep and his voice was heard in the back row of the congregation. Because of excessive weeping due to fear of Allah, his eyes were swollen.

He was fearful of the account to be taken on the Day of Judgement. Once he took hold of a straw and said, "I wish I was a straw (to be saved from the account on the Day of Judgement)."

Hadrat `Umar (R.A.) sacrificed almost all of his wealth for the sake of Allah and for His Holy Prophet (*Sallallahu `alayhi wa Sallam*). Once he said, "I love the Holy Prophet (*Sallallahu `alayhi wa Sallam*) more than anything besides my life." Hearing this the Holy Prophet (*Sallallahu `alayhi wa Sallam*) remarked, "Nobody is (a true) Muslim unless he loves me more than everything of the world including his own life." On this Hadrat `Umar (R.A.) said, "Now I love you, 0 Prophet of Allah, more than my life."

His belief in the Unity of God was unshakable. Once he went to

Hajj during his *Khilafat* and while kissing the Black Stone (an act included in the rites of Hajj), he remarked, "I know that you are a stone. Neither can you harm anybody nor can do good to anybody. If I had not seen the Prophet of Allah kiss you I would have never kissed." He was a strict follower of the Holy Prophet (*Sallallahu `alayhi wa Sallam*).

Hadrat `Umar (R.A.) as a great scholar

Before the advent of Islam there was no tradition in Arabia of reading or writing. There were only seventeen people among Quraish who could read or write at the time when the Holy Prophet (*Sallallahu `alayhi wa Sallam*) started to receive divine revelations. Hadrat `Umar was one of those seventeen persons. His writing and lectures are still found in some old books. The first address he gave as a Caliph is as under:

> "O Allah, I am strict, make me soft. I am weak, give me power. The Arabs are like refractory camels, I will endeavour to bring them to the straight path."

He was also interested in poetry and sometimes he composed verses. `Umar (R.A.) was one of the most fluent Quraish. Arabic knowing persons can appreciate the fluency of his writings and addresses. Many of his sayings became aphorisms of literature.

He was a great jurist and theologian of Islam. Because of the fear of making any mistake he did not quote many *Ahadith* (Sayings of the Holy Prophet) even though he was fully conversant with them. He never allowed a person (companion) to quote any Hadith which was not well known without producing an attestator in support of it. If somebody quoted a Hadith before him which he had never heard, he at once asked him to bring a witness failing which he would be punished. He was expert in deriving laws from the Holy Qur'an and the Hadith. A full volume could be compiled out of the verdicts and Judgements given by Hadrat 'Umar (R.A.). As a matter of fact he opened a new door of *Ijtihad* (disciplined judgement of a Jurist) in the history of Islamic Law and Jurisprudence, and settled a number of disputable cases during his caliphate.

Preaching of Islam

As the viceroy of the Holy Prophet (*Sallallahu 'alayhi wa Sallam*) his foremost duty was to spread and preach Islam. As mentioned above, the aim of various battles and wars was to clear the way for the Muslims for preaching Islam. Whenever any army had to attack a place it had to call the inhabitants of the place to Islam. Hadrat 'Umar was very strict in this respect and he had given standing orders to the commanders not to start war unless they had first invited the people to Islam. If they accepted it, there was no question of war and if they did not, then the war was fought only with those who were not giving a free hand to Muslims to preach the Right Path. No person was ever forced to forsake his own faith and accept Islam.

The method adopted to preach Islam was demonstrated by actual practice. For this purpose he ordered Muslims to establish their own quarters and present the practical shape of Islam before the population. Seeing the truthful way, the inhabitants of the place were attracted towards Islam. No soldier was allowed to take any property or anything by force from the conquered people.

Because of fair treatment by the Muslims sometimes the whole army of the enemy accepted Islam. After the battle of Qadisiya a battalion of four thousand Persians accepted Islam. After the victory of Jalula, the chiefs of the place entered the folds of Islam along with the inhabitants. A commander of the army of Yadzgird named Siyah accepted Islam with his battalion during a battle in Persia. All the inhabitants of the town of Bulhat in Egypt accepted Islam at once without the use of any force only by seeing the piety of Muslims. A rich merchant and the chief of a place in Egypt, named Shata, accepted Islam with all the inhabitants of the place only after hearing about the character and piety of Muslims at the time when Muslims had not even reached that place. These are only a few examples to show that Islam spread because of the character of Muslims at that time.

'Umar (R.A.) was very strict in ensuring that no Muslims forced any non-Muslim to accept Islam. Through his advice, letters and addresses he made it clear to all the Muslims that they had to adhere to the ways of the Holy Prophet (*Sallallahu 'alayhi wa Sallam*) which was the only method to preach Islam.

Wives and children

Hadrat 'Umar (R.A.) married the following women during his lifetime:

1. Zainab (R.A.), she accepted Islam but died in Mecca. She was the sister of 'Uthman bin Maz'un. 'Abdur Rahman, 'Abdullah and lady Hafsah (wife of the Holy Prophet) were the children she bore to Hadrat 'Umar.
2. Malkiah bint Jarwal, she did not accept Islam and was divorced in 6 A.H. according to Islamic law. She gave birth to 'Ubaidullah.
3. Quraibah bint Abi Ummiyah, she also did not accept Islam and was divorced in 6 A.H.

The above three marriages had taken place before 'Umar (R.A.) accepted Islam. After accepting Islam he contracted marriages with the following:

4. Ummi Hakim bint-ul-Harith, she gave birth to a girl named Fatimah.
5. Jamilah bint 'Asim, she gave birth to a son who was named 'Asim. Though she was a Muslim she was divorced because of some other reason.
6. Umm Kulthum bint Hadrat 'Ali (R.A.), she was married in the year 17 A.H. She gave birth to Ruqayyah and Zaid.
7. 'Atikah (R.A.).

Children:

1. *Ummul-Mu'minin* Hadrat Hafsah (R.A.), the wife of the Holy Prophet (*Sallallahu 'alayhi wa Sallam*).
2. Ruqayyah, she was the youngest daughter of Hadrat 'Umar.
3. 'Abdullah, son.
4. 'Ubaidullah, son.
5. 'Asim, son.
6. Abu Shahmah, son.
7. 'Abdur-Rahman, son.
8. Zaid, son.
9. Mujir, son.

7
Hadrat `Umar's Administration: A Picture of Islamic Democratic Rule

i. `Umar the pioneer of the Islamic democracy

Hadrat `Umar (R.A.) was the pioneer of modern civilization to form a state based upon the Islamic democratic system, the system which was incorporated in the West as late as 19th and 20th centuries. He was the greatest democratic administrator whose example is unparalleled not only in the history of Islam but also in the history of modern civilization. A vast part of the Middle East, Persian Empire and Byzantium, was conquered during the ten years of his *Khilafat* (Caliphate) which he consolidated into a state governed by Islam i.e. laws. "As an administrator," says Prof. K. Ali, a Muslim writer, "he remained a model for all great Muslim rulers during the whole Islamic history." Another famous historian, Amir Ali says, "During the thirty years that the Republic lasted, the policy derived its character chiefly from `Umar both during his life-time and after his death."

The constitution of Islamic caliphate during the time of Hadrat `Umar (R.A.) was based entirely on the Islamic democratic system. All matters were decided after consultation with the *Shura* (the Council of Advisors) the details of which would be given in the following pages.

He remarked, "It is essential for a *Khalifah* to consult his *Shura*." Once he said, "I do not desire that you may follow anything that arises from my caprice." Hadrat `Umar had clearly stated on various occasions that he should be obeyed as long as he was obeying Allah and the Holy Prophet (*Sallallahu `alayhi wa Sallam*).

Muslims and non-Muslims were treated alike. Although the Arab peninsula was declared to be purely an Islamic State, his attitude towards the non-Muslims was very tolerant. He allowed the Jews and the Christians, living in the Peninsula, to stay there if they so wished and nobody would interfere in their religious affairs. To those who desired to migrate he ensured safe journey up to the borders. Hadrat `Umar (R.A.) also gave compensation for their properties and other facilities.

ii. Islamic Republic based upon *Shura*

As stated before all matters were decided after consultations with the *Shura*, the Advisory Council during his time. There were three main types of *Shura*. The first *Shura* consisted of very prominent and popular Companions like Hadrat `Uthman, `Ali, `Abdur Rahman bin `Auf, Mu`adh bin Jabal, Ubayy bin Ka`b, Zaid bin Thabit, Talha and Zubair (R.A.). They were permanent members of the *Shura*. All the important matters were decided in consultation with these persons. This *Shura* could be named as the Higher Advisory Council.

The second *Shura* was the General Advisory Council which consisted of many companions from amongst the Ansar and Muhajirin (R.A.). The Companions who participated in the battle of Badr were given, priority in this *Shura*. All matters of general interest were discussed with this *Shura*. In this *Shura* were also included the chiefs of various clans and tribes.

The third type of *Shura* ranked in between the Higher and the

General Advisory Councils. It consisted of some selected Companions among the Muhajirin and Ansar. Matters of special interest were put before the *Shura*.

Whenever a *Shura* was called everyone of its members was fully allowed to give his opinion without any fear or hesitation. On various occasions Hadrat `Umar said, "I am but an ordinary person like you. I can only request you to cooperate in the work with which I have been entrusted by you."

iii. The way to call the General *Shura*

Since the Special *Shura* comprised only few members there was no special way to call it. The way to call the General Council of Advisors was that a man used to call the following words loudly — "*As-Salatu Jamiah*," — in the Prophet's Mosque from a high place. Hearing this call the people would know that a meeting of the *Shura* has been called and assembled in the mosque. Hadrat `Umar first of all offered two *raka'at* of *Nafl* (optional) *Salat* and then put the matter before the *Shura*. Every person was allowed to give his opinion. Decisions were usually taken on the basis of unanimity or sometimes by majority. But the *Khalifah* was not bound to accept the decision of majority. In the interest of Islam and Muslims he could use power of veto if he considered it proper.

iv. Freedom of opinion

Freedom of opinion was not only allowed at the time of meeting of the *Shura* but on all occasions. As a matter of fact Hadrat `Umar's period was an exemplary period as far as this principle of the democratic way of government is concerned. There is no other example in history when people gave their opinion so freely, and criticised the ruler (i.e., the

Government) so openly.

The Caliph had himself introduced this principle, novel in those days, through his addresses. A part of one of his addresses is quoted as under:

> "O people! I am but a trustee of your property and wealth, like a person who is trustee of the property and wealth of an orphan child. Had I been rich I would not have taken any allowance for my services. In case I needed I would have accepted only to the extent of the need. Friends! you have certain rights over me and you are fully allowed to claim your rights anytime. One of such rights is: don't allow me to misappropriate the Indemnity Tax and the Booty. You have the right to check that the poor, the needy and disabled person amongst you should get allowances for their livelihood. You have the right to make sure that the borders of the State are safe and that you are not in danger."

The above address clearly shows his liberal principles and the basic foundation of his government. Once some cloth came to Medina as a part of booty. It was distributed among Muslims in accordance with the Islamic Law. The piece of cloth given to each of the Muslims was not enough to make a *Kurta* (Arabian shirt). On the following Friday Hadrat ʻUmar (R.A.) came to deliver the *Khutbah* (Sermon) of the *Salat* wearing the *Kurta* of the same cloth. As soon as he stepped on the *Mimbar* (pulpit) one man stood up and asked him to account for the *Kurta*. Without being annoyed Hadrat ʻUmar stepped down the *Mimbar* and asked his son to give explanation on his behalf. His son told the congregation that he gave his share to his father and he was able to get his *Kurta* prepared out of that cloth. Hearing this the man was satisfied.

Once Hadrat ʻUmar asked in a gathering to test them, "If I do not obey the *Shari`ah* (Divine Law), what would you do?" A Bedouin immediately stood up and replied in a harsh tone, "O `Umar! we will straighten you (i.e., put you on the straight path) as we straighten our arrows to put in the bow." Hadrat `Umar (R.A.) was very pleased to hear it.

Once a person in a public meeting stood up and said, "O `Umar, fear Allah." The audience tried to stop him but Hadrat `Umar said, "Let him say, he is free to give his opinion. If people do not give their opinions they are useless and if we (the rulers) do not listen to them, we are useless."

Not only the men but women too enjoyed the freedom of opinion. Once Hadrat `Umar (R.A.) was suggesting the quantity of dowry to be fixed at the time of *Nikah* (Marriage) which was not in accordance with Islamic principle. A veiled lady immediately stood up and said, "O `Umar, fear Allah." Hearing this Hadrat `Umar (R.A.) realised his mistake and accepted her objection.

It was this freedom of thought and opinion which paved the way to Hadrat `Umar's (R.A.) success. He was a stern ruler as far as for implementation of law was concerned but at the same time he was just, and democratic, a true follower of Islamic democracy in which every person has freedom of opinion within the limits of *Shari`ah* (Divine Law), i.e., under the Sovereignty of Allah and the authority of His Law. He acted upon the principle of equality and brotherhood of mankind on one side and justice and truthfulness on the other. Not only the Muslims but the non-Muslims were also free to express their opinion. He made no discrimination between Muslims and non-Muslims in matters of justice, human rights and fair play.

v. Provincial administration

Hadrat `Umar was an outstanding model for the succeeding Muslim rulers in administration. "During the thirty years that the Republic lasted," says Amir Ali, "the policy derived its character chiefly from `Umar both during his life time and after his death."

Hadrat `Umar (R.A.) divided the whole Islamic *Khilafat* (i.e. Islamic State) into various provinces each with a capital. The following were, the provinces and their governors in 23 A.H., i.e., near the end of Hadrat `Umar's Caliphate.

1. **Hijaz** with Mecca as its capital; Governor — Nafi` bin Abu Harith.
2. **Syria** with Damascus as its capital; Governor — Mu`awiyah bin Abu Sufyan.
3. **Iran** with Basrah as its capital; Governor — Abu Musa al-Ash`ari.
4. **Iraq** with Kufa as its capital; Governor — Mughirah bin Shu`bah.
5. **Egypt** with Fustat as its capital; Governor — `Amr bin al-`As.
6. **Palestine** with Jerusalem as its capital; Governor — `Alqamah bin Majaz.
7. **Jazirah** (i.e., Mesopotamia) with Hims (Homs) as its controlling capital; Governor — `Umair bin Sa`d.
8. **The central province of Arabia** with Medina as its capital.

The Capital of the State was also Medina. The title of a Provincial Governor was *Wali*, who was the chief administrator and generally the supreme commander of the armed forces of that province. In each province there were usually following officers besides the Governor:

the Treasury Officer (*Sahib-i-Baitul-Mal*);

the Revenue Collector (*Sahib-i-Kharaj*);

the Chief Police Officer (*Sahib-i-Ahdath*); and

the Judge (*al-Qadi*).

In those provinces where the governor was not holding the office of the commander of armed forces, a separate commander was appointed. For example, in the beginning in Kufa, Hadrat `Amar ibn Yasir (R.A.) was the *Wali* (the Governor), `Uthman ibn Hanif (R.A.) was the Revenue Collector, `Abdullah ibn Mas`ud (R.A.) was the Treasury Officer, Hadrat Shuraih (R.A.) was the Judge and `Abdullah ibn Khaza`i (R.A.) was the Secretary of Defense (i.e., *Diwan*). Usually the officers were appointed after consultation with the *Shura* (the Advisory Council).

The provinces were divided into districts. Each district was administered by an officer called `*Amil*. All the governors and the high officers of the province were called to Mecca every year on the occasion of Hajj when Muslims from the entire area gathered there. Complaints against them were recorded by the *Khalifah*. Enquires were made and grievances were removed.

All the officers were paid high salaries so that they may not indulge in bribery and corruption.

vi. The *Khalifah* was the religious head of the State

Not only the *Khalifah* the Governors were also great scholars of Islam. They were all administrative officers, theologians, jurists and pious.

The *Khalifah* himself was the overall religious head of the State. He used to lead five times compulsory *Salat*s and the *Jumu`a* (Friday) *Salat* in the Holy Prophet's Mosque at Medina, and also the *'Id Salat*s at the "*Musalla* for `*Id*" (`*Idgah*) in Medina. At the time of Hajj he was the leader of the Hajj and in his absence a person was appointed by him as his deputy. In religious matters he used to give his verdict based

THE PIOUS CALIPHS

upon the *Shari`ah* (Divine Law). In case of a question of law he usually consulted a special committee for that purpose working under a department known as *Shu`ba-i-Ifta* (the Department of Jurists) or sometimes he sent the matter directly to the committee. Hadrat `Ali, `Uthman, Mu`adh bin Jabal, `Abdur Rahman bin `Auf, Ubayy bin Ka`b, Zaid bin Thabit, Abu Hurairah and Abu Darda (R.A.) were the main *Muftis* (Jurists) at Medina. The *Khalifah* did not hesitate to enquire about a Hadith which he did not know. At the same time he did not allow others to narrate *Ahadith* (sayings of the Holy Prophet) not known to him without a witness.

Besides performing the duty of administration each governor was also the religious head of the province. He had to lead five *Salat*s in the nearest mosque, the *Jumu`a Salat* in the Masjid al-Jami` (the main mosque of the Capital), and also the *`Id Salat*s in "*`Id Musalla*s."

vii. Judiciary

The judicial functions were entrusted to *Qadi*s (Judges). A *Qadi* was completely free of the executive administration. On a number of occasions the *Khalifah* (Hadrat `Umar) himself appeared before a *Qadi* to defend himself in some cases. The provincial *Qadi*s were completely independent of the provincial governors. The *Qadi*s were paid good salaries so that there might not be even a slightest chance of bribery. The monthly salary of *Qadi*s like Hadrat Salman, Rabi`ah and Shuraih (R.A.) were 500 Dirhams. The monthly salary of Hadrat Amir Mu`awiyah (R.A.) was 1000 dirhams. "Umar was the first ruler in Islam," says Amir Ali, "to fix salaries for judges and to make their offices distinct from the executive officers."

In a number of books like *Tabaqatul Fuqaha*, and *Mawardi* an ordinance sent by `Umar (R.A.) to various *Qadi*s is quoted:

"It is essential for a *Qadi* to be just in his decisions and should not give any preference to the persons considered eminent in the society. The complainants should produce proof in support of their case while the defendants are allowed to take an oath (depending upon the nature of the case). Agreement between the two parties is permissible except when such agreement makes unlawful act lawful or a lawful act unlawful. If truth is known after a decision has been given, you are allowed to reconsider the case and change the decision.

"When you do not find guidance in the Holy Qur'an or in the *Ahadith* (i.e., practices and the sayings of the Holy Prophet) for decision of a case, ponder over it (on the basis of the broader principles of *Shari'ah* i.e., Divine Law) and search for its solution in the light of past decisions given by the righteous predecessors. (In case you do not get the solution in past decisions), then apply your own mind (i.e., do *Ijtihad* or *Qiyas* based upon the Holy Qur'an and the *Sunnah*, i.e., the practices of the Holy Prophet)."

In another ordinance, given in *Kanzul 'Ummal*, Hadrat 'Umar told the *Qadis*:

"Decide cases according to the Holy Qur'an. If you do not find any solution in it base your decision upon the *Sunnah*. In case you do not find an appropriate Hadith, search in the unanimity of the righteous predecessors (i.e., *Ijma'*), in the absence of *Ijma'*, give your own verdict based upon the Holy Qur'an and the *Sunnah* (i.e., do *Ijtihad* or *Qiyas*)."

The *Qadis* appointed by Hadrat 'Umar were among the most pious, truthful and trustworthy Muslims of his period. Besides being pious, they were also great jurists and scholars. The *Qadi* of Medina was Hadrat Zaid bin Thabit (the "Scribe of *Wahy*" — Revelation). There were two *Qadi*s at Kufa, Hadrat 'Abdullah bin Mas'ud and Hadrat Shuraih (R.A.) Other *Qadi*s during the caliphate of Hadrat 'Umar were: Salman bin Rabi', 'Abdur Rahman bin Rabi', 'Imran bin Hasin, Abu Maryam, and Jamil bin al-'Umar (R.A.), etc.

The *Qadi*s were instructed to be impartial and totally free from the executive. In a dispute between Hadrat 'Umar (the *Khalifah*) and Hadrat Ubayy bin Ka'b, Hadrat 'Umar went to the court of Hadrat Zaid bin Thabit at Medina. Hadrat Zaid wanted to stand up to show respect to the *Khalifah*, on which 'Umar (R.A.) remarked, "This is your first unjust behaviour." Then Hadrat 'Umar sat with Hadrat Ubayy, the complainant like an ordinary person. In the same case Hadrat Ubayy wanted Hadrat 'Umar to take oath, but Zaid wanted to spare him because of the dignity of his office. Seeing this 'Umar (R.A.) admonished him, "You cannot be a just *Qadi* until a common man is equal to 'Umar before you."

Since Hadrat'Umar was also a jurist, he also held courts, and sometimes as the Court of Appeal in a position which could be described as the Chief Justice nowadays. Once he inflicted the *Shari'ah* punishment of eighty lashes for drinking on his own son Abu Sahmah which resulted in his death on the spot. There are a number of other examples which show the Islamic justice prevailing at the time. Muslims and non-Muslims both were equal before his justice. Once a Muslim killed a Christian, Hadrat 'Umar inflicted capital punishment upon him.

viii. Department of Education

Hadrat 'Umar took special interest in imparting Islamic knowledge to the Muslims. The Holy Qur'an was compiled in a book form during the period of Hadrat Abu Bakr on 'Umar's (R.A.) insistence. He established schools for teaching the Holy Qur'an in all the conquered territories. Such schools were located in the *Masjid*s. A number of writers like Ibn-i-Jauzi (see *Sirat `Umar*) have mentioned that the teachers of such schools received good salaries. Besides teaching the Holy Qur'an they also trained the people in reading and writing. The *Huffaz* (i.e., the Muslims who commit whole of the Holy Qur'an to their memory) were specially honoured.

In the provinces of Syria and Palestine, the following teachers were appointed: `Ubadah bin Samit, Mu`adh bin Jabal and Abu Darda (R.A.). They established schools in Hims, Palestine (Jerusalem) and Damascus.

Hadrat Abu Sufyan was appointed to teach Bedouins. He was asked to test the knowledge of the Muslims learning the Holy Qur'an. It was compulsory for every Muslim to memorise sufficient part of the Holy Qur'an especially Surahs al-Baqarah, an-Nisa, al-Ma'idah, al-Hajj and an-Nur (Chapters 2, 4, 5, 22 and 24 of the Holy Qur'an). In these Surahs Islamic laws and principles are described elaborately. To know basic Islamic laws was compulsory. Thus the concept of compulsory education was introduced at a time when nobody knew about it. The students memorising whole of the Qur'an by heart were given scholarships and other facilities.

He also appointed teachers to teach Hadith and Islamic Law. Hadrat `Abdullah bin Mas`ud (R.A.) was sent to Kufa; Ma`qal bin Yair (R.A.), and `Imran bin Hasin (R.A.) to Basra; Hadrat `Ubadah bin Samit used to teach Hadith and Islamic Law as well in Syria besides the Holy Qur'an.

ix. Police department and institution of prisons

To keep order inside the State, a police force was necessary. Hadrat `Umar (R.A.) was the first Muslim head of State who established the police department. The police force at that time was known as *"Ahdath"* and the police officer as the *Sahibul Ahdath*. Hadrat Abu Hurairah (R.A.) was appointed as the *Sahibul Ahdath* for Bahrain. When he was going to take charge of his duty, Hadrat `Umar (R.A.) gave him the following instructions:

> "Keep peace in the area. Let not the people contravene law. They should not measure or weigh incorrectly. Nobody should build any house on roads so as to hinder the passage. No one should overload an animal. Nobody is allowed to sell or buy liquor."

There was no jail in Arabia before Hadrat `Umar (R.A.). He bought five houses in Mecca and used them as prisons. He also set up jails in some districts of various provinces. The punishment of exile was for the first time introduced by Hadrat `Umar (R.A.). He exiled Abu Mihjan Thaqafi to an island as punishment for drinking liquor.

x. The *Baitul-Mal* (Public Treasury) and revenue administration

A Public Treasury (*Baitul-Mal*) was for the first time established by the Holy Prophet (*Sallallahu `alayhi wa Sallam*) in the form of a common fund for the benefit of the general public. During the time of Hadrat Abu Bakr (R.A.), a house was purchased for the purpose but there were no savings beside one Dirham when he passed away. During the caliphate of Hadrat `Umar (R.A.) the *Baitul-Mal* was immensely enlarged.

He reorganised the entire system on a very sound and just basis. The officer in charge of the Public Treasury (*Baitul-Mal*) was known as *Sahib-i-Baitul-Mal*. There were Treasury officers in each province. Guards were also appointed for the *Baitul-Mal*. In Medina there was the central Treasury and regular accounts were kept.

Following were the main sources of revenue:

i. *Jizya* (Indemnity or Defense Tax);

ii. *Zakat* (Poor Tax);

iii. *Khiraj* (Land Tax);

iv. *'Ushr* (Special Land Tax);

v. Booty (income from the conquered places);

vi. Tax on non-Muslim merchants or traders (because they did not pay *Zakat*).

The tax on non-Muslim traders was introduced by Hadrat 'Umar (R.A.) for the first time. The reason was obvious — they did not pay *Zakat* while Muslim merchants had to pay *Zakat*. *'Ushr*, the special land tax equal to one tenth of the produce was taken from large holdings.

The *Zakat* fund was kept in special account books and was spent in accordance with the Islamic laws as given in the Holy Qur'an. From the rest of the fund, expenditure on general administration and warfare was met. The surplus was distributed among Muslims which was determined by three main principles — the relationship and the closeness with the Holy Prophet; priority of conversion to Islam and sacrifices for its cause; and military service to Islam. For example, the *Badriyin* (the participants of the Badr battle) received 5,000 Dirhams each, those who participated in the battle of Uhud or participated in the Treaty of Hudaibiya received 4,000 each. The Muslims who accepted Islam before the conquest of Mecca but after the Treaty of Hudaibiya received 3,000 each. Those who fought in Syria or Iraq received 2,000 each and those who took part in the battles after this received 1,000 each. An ordinary soldier who fought during the time of Hadrat 'Umar (R.A.) received 500 to 600 Dirhams. The stipend was given to every

THE PIOUS CALIPHS

Muslim whether male or female, young or old. Even newborn babies also received stipends. Sir William Muir in his book *Caliphate* comments on it:

> "A people dividing amongst them the whole revenues, spoil and conquests of the state, on the basis of an equal brotherhood is a spectacle probably without parallel in the world."

Hadrat `Umar (R.A.) was very cautious in spending the Public Fund. There are a number of instances which could be presented here.

Once his daughter, *Ummul Mu'minin* Lady Hafsa (the widow of the Holy Prophet, *Sallallahu `alayhi wa Sallam*) came to him and demanded some share in the booty, that came from a battlefield, saying, "Give me some because your relatives have certain rights over you." He replied, "Of course my relatives have certain rights in my personal property but not in the property of Muslims."

Once Hadrat `Umar fell sick and the physician advised him to take honey. There was plenty of honey in the *Baitul-Mal*. He went to the Prophet's Mosque and called general *Shura*. When people assembled he said, "I need some honey, I would be thankful if you allow me to take some honey from the *Baitul-Mal*."

Once he saw a fat camel being sold in the market. He enquired about it and found out that the camel belonged to a man who allowed it to graze in the public pasture. Hadrat `Umar (R.A.) told the man, "You are entitled to get as much as the camel would have fetched before it grazed in the official pasture. The balance must go to the *Baitul-Mal*."

He took personal care of the *Baitul-Mal* properties. Once a camel belonging to the *Baitul-Mal* ran away. He himself went in search of it. In the meantime a chief of a clan came to meet him. Hadrat `Umar said to him, "Please help me in my work. I am searching a camel of the *Baitul-Mal*."

Such examples are unparalleled in the history of whole civilization and they show extreme vigilance by Hadrat `Umar (R.A.) of Public Funds. At this place I would like to mention two more things in connection with the Revenue Administration of Hadrat `Umar: (a) Survey of lands in Iraq; and (b) Indemnity Tax.

a. *Survey of lands in Iraq*

Before Islam there was no administration in Arabia. Hadrat `Umar (R.A.) introduced a full administrative system based upon Islam. When Iraq was conquered he did not allow the conquered land to be distributed as estate among the warriors. He granted it to the people as State property. There were many objections raised by some of the Companions. After consultation with the *Shura* Hadrat `Umar's plan was formulated. Then he ordered survey of the conquered land in Iraq. Land tax has assessed according to the income of the farmers. No tax was levied on lands which were trusts for places of worship or which were owned by orphans. Forests were considered as State property. Big estates, owned individually by people were not taken away from them.

In other places like Syria and Egypt more or less the same system remained enforced as was before Islam as far as the ownership of estates was concerned. However he took those estates which were owned by Imperial Officers of the Roman Empire and distributed them among the farmers. No Muslim was allowed to take over any piece of land. However purchase of lands was allowed.

He constructed a number of canals for irrigation purposes. In Egypt alone one hundred twenty thousand labourers worked to construct various canals from the river Nile. All these labourers were paid by the State.

b. *Jizya (Indemnity or Defense Tax)*

Some western writers have objected to realisation of Indemnity Tax (*Jizya*) from the non-Muslims of the State. But this tax was taken for their safety against any invasion from outside. There are instances that when Muslims left a conquered place due to some reasons, they returned the *Jizya* taken from non-Muslims of that place. In many agreements signed by Muslims during the wars, it was clarified that *Jizya* would be paid to the State by the non-Muslims for their protection and in case the State (i.e., Muslim Government) took any help from them for their protection they would not have to pay the *Jizya*. The following agreement was signed with the inhabitants of Jarjan:

> "It is our responsibility to protect you and your property against any invasion and you would pay annual tax (*Jizya*) in lieu thereof. If we seek your help for protecting you, we would not charge any tax (*Jizya*)."

In the agreement signed at Adharbijan, the tax was as under:

> ". . . *Jizya* would not be taken from those who serve in the army, for the year of services."

Hadrat 'Umar (R.A.) had issued orders to various commanders during the battles with Persians:

> "Do not charge any *Jizya* from those who have helped the Muslim cavalry (i.e., army)."

Hadrat Abu 'Ubaidah (R.A.), the commander at the Syrian front returned all the Indemnity Tax, he had received, when he left the conquered places for the time being to return to safer borders in order to prepare against the Romans at Yarmuk.

Moreover utmost care was exercised in levying the *Jizya*. The poor and orphans were never charged. There was no Indemnity Tax on old persons who could not work. In the agreement which was signed at Hirah this can very well be seen: "If any old man is unable to earn, or if a rich man becomes poor, of if a person meets an accident, then no *Jizya* would be charged from him. Muslims are responsible to take care of such persons and to pay them for their needs from the *Baitul-Mal*."

Once Hadrat `Umar (R.A.) saw an old non-Muslim begging. He asked him the reason for begging. The old man said that he had to pay *Jizya*. Hadrat `Umar immediately brought him home and gave some money to him. Then he ordered the officers not to charge *Jizya* from such persons. He was so solicitous about non-Muslims that he left a will, "Take care of the *Dhimmis* i.e., the non-Muslims. Do not break any agreement signed with them. Do not take that work from them which they cannot do. Fight for their protection (if somebody attacks them)."

This is an exemplary treatment, a nation could give to conquered people.

xi. Personal care of the public and stipends to disabled persons and the poor

Hadrat `Umar used to take personal care of the public. A number of instances could be cited in this connection. I would quote only a few.

Once a caravan came to Medina and alighted outside the city. He himself guarded the caravan during the night and saw to their needs. He was going round one night when he saw a woman with some children just on the outskirt of the city. The children were crying due to hunger. He himself brought some flour and butter, etc., from the *Baitul-Mal* and personally prepared meals for the children. His slave, Aslam offered his services but he said, "You cannot help `Umar on the

Day of Judgement. He is himself responsible for it."

Once he saw a Bedouin staying outside the city and his wife was in the throes of child birth. He immediately called his wife who worked as a midwife.

Every day after the congregational *Salat*s he used to sit in the *Masjid* in order to listen to the complaints of the people. Any person having any need reported to `Umar (R.A.) and he helped him.

Besides the allowances described above he also gave stipends to the poor and disabled persons regardless of their faith and creed. To find out the needs of the people he used to go out during night time.

xii. Construction of *Masjid*s and establishment of schools

He founded a number of schools. *Masjid*s were used for giving religious instructions. A number of *Masjid*s were built by Hadrat `Umar (R.A.). He asked the governors of various provinces, especially of Syria, to build at least one mosque in each city or town. In Kufa a separate *Masjid* was built for every clan. According to some historians he built four thousand *Masjid*s.

The *Haram* (*Masjid-ul-Haram*) in Mecca was too small for the increasing Muslim population. He extended it and built a wall around it in order to separate it from the township. He covered the Ka`bah with very costly Egyptian cloth instead of ordinary cloth.

The *Masjid* of the Holy Prophet was also extended. He bought all the houses and properties surrounding the *Masjid* besides the houses of the chaste widows of the Holy Prophet (*Sallallahu `alayhi wa Sallam*), and extended the *Masjid*. A big platform was constructed in the yard of the *Masjid* to impart Islamic knowledge.

xiii. Construction of office buildings and erection of new cities

Hadrat 'Umar (R.A.) built a number of offices for various needs. The construction of prison in Mecca and *Baitul-Mal* in Medina has been mentioned before. The Treasury houses were also built in various provinces. The construction of the building of the Treasury House (*Baitul-Mal*) was supervised by a Persian engineer Rozbah who used the same type of cement in the building as was used in the palaces of the Persian emperors.

A number of rest-houses for travellers were also built. Hadrat 'Umar (R.A.) also built many new roads and bridges. The road between Mecca and Medina was broadened and a number of rest-houses and police posts were built on this road.

As described above a number of canals were constructed for irrigation and for supply of fresh water. A nine mile long canal was constructed in Basrah which brought water from the river Tigris. Some governors also built canals. Hadrat Sa'd bin Waqqas built a canal in Kufa.

A number of new cities were founded. The aim of the construction of these new cities would be discussed in the following pages. Here are names of some of the important cities:

Basrah:

It was built in Iraq in 14 A.H., near the border of present day Iran. In the beginning the population of the city was only 800 but soon it increased to about 100,000. During the time of Umayyads it was a big city of 120,000 inhabitants.

Kufa:

It was built in the central part of Iraq. In the beginning residences for

40,000 people were built there. Hadrat `Umar took personal interest in its construction and sent the maps and a plan for the city which he himself had prepared. The streets of the city were 60 feet wide. Al-Masjid-ul-Jami` could accommodate 40,000 people i.e., the total population of the city. This city was often called by Hadrat `Umar as "*Rasul-ul-Islam*" (the head of Islam). The famous Imams (Great Scholars) namely Nakh`i, Hammad, Abu Hanifah and Shubi lived in the same city. Thus it became the centre of Islamic knowledge and learning in later centuries, proving the prophecy of Hadrat `Umar.

Fustat: It was built in Egypt by Hadrat `Amr bin al-`As on the orders of `Umar (R.A.)and became a big city in the later period of Islamic history. In the 4th century A.H., it was the most beautiful city of Islamic state after Baghdad.

Mosul and Jizah were other cities built by Hadrat `Umar (R.A.). Mosul was a small village but Hadrat `Umar converted it into a city. This was in the centre of Eastern and Western part of Islamic state. Jizah was built after the victory of Alexandria in Egypt.

xiv. Special care of agriculture

Agronomy was the main source of income during those days. Hadrat `Umar (R.A.) took special care of the welfare of agriculture and the farmers. As stated before he dug a number of canals for irrigation. A number of gardens were planted on his order. He made a law under which no Muslim could acquire land from the natives of the soil in the conquered territories. However land could be purchased. He supported both Muslim and non-Muslim farmers.

Besides the construction of canals a number of barrages, and big pools were constructed for supply of water in various parts of the State. Hadrat `Umar also issued an ordinance under which uncultivated lands could be acquired by the permission of the government. Such lands were treated as the estates of those persons who cultivated them within three years of acquiring them, otherwise land would vest in the government. Large areas of land were thus cultivated because of this ordinance.

xv. Introduction of Islamic calendar

For the first time in the history of Islam, Islamic calendar was introduced in the present form by Hadrat `Umar (R.A.). The date of start of this calendar was fixed as the date of the *Hijrah* (Migration) of the Holy Prophet (*Sallallahu `alayhi wa Sallam*). Thus the calendar is also known as the *Hijrah* calendar.

xvi. Regular army

One of the biggest achievements of Hadrat `Umar (R.A.) was to keep regular armies of the State. He encouraged Muslims to join the regular forces whenever the need arose. For the first time in the history of Islam all irregular armies or mercenaries were divided into clear-cut classes of regular and irregular armies. The army personnel was well paid and their families also got allowances. Separate registers for regular and irregular armies were maintained.

In order to keep military tradition of the Muslims, Hadrat `Umar (R.A.) did not allow the army personnel to hold land in the conquered territories, which might have impaired military prowess of Muslim soldiers.

Cantonments were built for soldiers where they lived in accordance with Islamic practices. It would be discussed in the following pages how these cantonments turned into centres of Islamic culture and knowledge, thus became the Muslim quarters to preserve Islamic culture and practice. Central cantonments were built in the following places: Medina, Kufa, Basrah, Mosul, Fustat, Damascus, Hims (Homs), Jordan, Palestine (Jerusalem) and Ramla.

Besides the Commanding Officer, the army had Translators, Doctors, Surgeons and Detectives. Each Corps of soldiers was headed by an officer known as "Arief" whose duty was to distribute the salary, dress and other necessities. The non-commissioned officer on every ten soldiers was known as "*Amirul A`shar*". The minimum salary of a soldier was 200 to 300 Dirhams annually besides his personal necessities and allowances given to his family in his absence. Some officers got salaries ranging from 7,000 to 10,000 Dirhams annually. No regular military personnel was allowed to do business or agriculture. It was compulsory for every soldier to be trained in swimming, riding, and walking bare-footed besides other military training. The army was generally divided into cavalry and infantry.

Each central cantonment had at least four thousand horses for the cavalry. Stables were provided with big pastures. Special care was taken of the horses. There were big granneries in cantonments to supply food to the military personnel.

Special arrangements were made to protect the frontiers. Hadrat `Abdullah bin Qaish was the officer in charge of this branch. He built a number of fortresses in the frontier region.

Once the number of soldiers in all the Islamic armies was counted and it was found that about one million equipped soldiers were present in all the regular and irregular armies. This was done after the Muslims had conquered the Persian Empire and a major part of Byzantium, otherwise in the beginning the number was far less as mentioned in connection with the various battles that took place during the time of

Hadrat 'Umar. As a matter of fact 'Umar made every Muslim a soldier and everyone was anxious to fight in the path of Allah. Non-Muslims were also included in the army. It is wrong to say that only Arabs were in the army because among Muslims themselves there were a number of non-Arab races commonly known as "*Ajamis*" who accepted Islam during the time of Hadrat Abu Bakr and Hadrat 'Umar (R.A.) and took part in Jihad (Holy War).

Special care was taken for the health of army personnel. In 17 A.H., when Mada'in was conquered, the climate was not suitable for the soldiers. When Hadrat 'Umar heard about it he wrote to 'Utbah bin Ghazwan that soldiers should be permitted to go to suitable places during autumn. Cantonments were constructed at places suitable from the point of view of climate.

The mail system was very efficient. Suitable persons were appointed to carry mail from the army to Medina and vice versa. The caliph (Hadrat 'Umar) used to direct the army from Medina.

The *Khalifah*, was the commander-in-chief of the armed forces. He delegated his powers to a nominated commander-in-chief of each army or province. These commanders were always in touch with the *Khalifah* and took instructions from him.

The most important thing which could be noted during the time of Hadrat 'Umar (R.A.) was a regular military code. No soldier, whose family was not residing in the cantonment, was allowed to be away from his family for more than four months. After four months they could visit their homes on holidays. The same code was also applied to those civil servants whose families were away from them.

xvii. Preservation of Islamic practice and culture by establishing Muslim quarters

As stated above the Muslim army was required to live in the cantonments. Later these cantonments were annexed to the civil quarters which ultimately resulted in the establishment of new cities.

These Muslim quarters or small colonies were established in the conquered territories in the form of Model Islamic Towns in order to preserve Islamic practices and culture. The purpose of such quarters was to save Muslims from the effect of non-Islamic culture and to show local non-Muslims the practical shape of Islamic society. These Muslim quarters attracted the local public towards Islam. It was the charm of Islam which ultimately caused them to accept it and to change their non-Islamic beliefs, traditions, culture and in many instances the language as well. All this cannot be done by force. Hearts and languages cannot be changed at the point of sword. If Muslim quarters had not been set up at that time it would have been difficult for Islamic ways to prevail in the countries which are now proud to call themselves as Muslim States.

Seeing the practical lives of Muslims, their sense of equality and high morals, the local population was so attracted that they changed even their languages. Arabic was not the local languages of Syria, Egypt and Iraq when these places were conquered by Muslims. The love for Allah, His Holy Prophet and His Last Book (the Holy Qur'an) caused the inhabitants of these places, who accepted Islam, to change their languages and treat the beautiful Arabic, the heavenly language, as their own language rather their mother tongue. In this way Hadrat 'Umar's (R.A.) act of setting up Muslim quarters, ultimately became the cause of the spread of Islam. Separation of Muslim quarters is positive proof that Islam never spread at the point of sword. Another purpose of separate localities was that the Muslims might not interfere with the local population in observing their own religion and customs. Their churches and places of worship were safe. Their worshippers, religious leaders and saints were left undisturbed. There is not even a single example of any Muslim civilian or military personnel who ever forced a non-Muslim to leave his faith or to accept Islam.

The purpose of wars was to remove the barriers set up by these powers who did not allow Muslims to show the practical shape of Islamic society and to preach the *truth* and the right way of life — *Islam*. When these powers did not allow the Muslims to do so their intransigence was met by sword. The way was cleared and the local populace saw the *truth* and left the *wrong way*. This is the proof that Islam is the most peaceful and the *right* way of life.

xviii. `Umar's (R.A.) period as the "Golden Age" of Islamic history

Thus we see that Hadrat `Umar's period was the "Golden Age" of the Islamic history when Islam was practised in its true form. Hadrat `Umar (R.A.) initiated 41 good practices during his period, which were based upon the Holy Qur'an and the *Sunnah* of the Holy Prophet (*Sallallahu `alayhi wa Sallam*). These are known as "*Awliat-i-`Umar*" (the "Initiations of `Umar"). The details can be seen in the books of Islamic history like *Tabari*, *Ibn-I-Athir*, and *Tarikh-i-Khulafa*, etc. Most of these initiations have been mentioned in the preceding pages in brief. Actually Hadrat `Umar (R.A.) was the founder of Islamic democracy based upon the Holy Qur'an and the *Sunnah* of the Holy Prophet (*Sallallahu `alayhi wa Sallam*). The words of the Holy Prophet are very true:

> "If there were to be a prophet after me he would have been `Umar ibn al-Khattab" (*Tirmidhi*); and

> "Among the nations before your time there have been inspired people (who were not prophets), and if there is one among my people he is `Umar" (*Bukhari and Muslim*).

SECTION III

`Uthman Ibn `Affan
24-36 A.H./644-656 A.D.

8
`Uthman Ibn `Affan: His Early Life

Life before acceptance of Islam

Hadrat `Uthman (R.A.) belonged to a noble family of Quraish in Mecca. His ancestral pedigree joins with that of the Holy Prophet (*Sallallahu `alayhi wa Sallam*) in the fifth generation. He was from the Umayyah family of Quraish, which was a well reputed and honourable family of Mecca during the pre-Islamic days. In the famous battle of Fajar the Commander-in-Chief of the Quraish army, Harb bin Umayyah was from the same family. The descendants of this family are known as Banu Umayyah or Umawwin.

Hadrat Uthman (R.A.) was born in 573 A.C. His patronymic name was Abu Amr and his father's name was Affan bin Abul-As. He was known by the name `Uthman ibn `Affan. Hadrat `Uthman was one of the few persons of Mecca who knew reading and writing. When he grew up, he started business in cloth which made him very rich. He used his money in good ways and always helped the poor. `Uthman (R.A.) was a soft natured and kind-hearted man. He did not hesitate to spend any amount of money on seeing a man in trouble in order to remove his misery. For his noble qualities the Meccans had great respect for him.

Acceptance of Islam

Hadrat 'Uthman (R.A.) accepted Islam when Abu Bakr (R.A.) preached to him. He was one of those Muslims who accepted Islam in its very early days. Though Banu Hashim (the Holy Prophet's family) was rival to Banu Umayyah (Hadrat 'Uthman's family), and the latter was in power at that time, yet 'Uthman (R.A.) did not hesitate to acknowledge the prophethood of Hadrat Muhammad (*Sallallahu 'alayhi wa Sallam*) which meant authority and supremacy over Banu Umayyah. This was one of the reasons why Quraish leaders, belonging to Banu Umayyah (like Abu Sufyan) were opposing the Holy Prophet (*Sallallahu 'alayhi wa Sallam*). Thus acceptance of Islam in such a position shows the clear-mindedness of Hadrat 'Uthman (R.A.). When he accepted Islam, the Quraish who once loved 'Uthman became his enemies. Even his relatives like Hakam (one of his uncles) began to rebuke him and chastised him severely.

One of the daughters of the Holy Prophet (*Sallallahu 'alayhi wa Sallam*), Hadrat Ruqayyah (R.A.) was married to one of the sons of Abu Lahb (an arch-enemy of Islam). When the Holy Prophet (*Sallallahu 'alayhi wa Sallam*) started to preach Islam, Abu Lahb asked his son 'Utbah to divorce her. Then the Holy Prophet married her to Hadrat 'Uthman (R.A.).

Emigration to Abyssinia

When life in Mecca became hard for the Muslims, he went to the Holy Prophet (*Sallallahu 'alayhi wa Sallam*) and sought permission to take refuge in Abyssinia along with other Muslims. The permission was granted. Hadrat 'Uthman and his wife crossed the Red Sea with other Muslims and migrated to Abyssinia. At the time of his migration the Holy Prophet (*Sallallahu 'alayhi wa Sallam*) remarked, "'Uthman is the first man of my *Ummah* to migrate (for the sake of Allah) with his family." He stayed there for a couple of months and came back to Mecca when he was wrongly informed by somebody that the Quraish had accepted Islam.

`Uthman (R.A.) gets the title of "*Dhun-nurain*"

Hadrat `Uthman (R.A.) migrated the second time with the other Muslims to Medina. He could not participate in the first battle of Islam against non-believers of Mecca at Badr, because his wife was very ill. She died before the Muslims returned from Badr after the victory. The Holy Prophet (*Sallallahu `alayhi wa Sallam*) gave him glad tidings that he would get the same reward as though he had participated in the battle. After the death of Hadrat Ruqayyah (R.A.), the Holy Prophet (*Sallallahu `alayhi wa Sallam*) married his next daughter, Umm Kulthum with him and he was given the title of "*Dhun-nurain*" ie., "the man with two lights."

His other services for the cause of Islam before Caliphate

He was a very prominent Muslim to serve Islam by all means. He participated in almost all the battles with the non-believers in which the Holy Prophet (*Sallallahu `alayhi wa Sallam*) had also taken part, except Badr. At the time of the Treaty of Hudaibiya he was sent to Mecca to negotiate with the non-believers. Then the Muslims were wrongly informed about his murder by the non-believers of Mecca. It is for this reason that the Holy Prophet (*Sallallahu `alayhi wa Sallam*) sought a pledge by the Muslims to fight with the non-believers in revenge of his murder. That pledge is known as "Bai`at al-Ridwan" (the Pledge of Ridwan). For `Uthman's pledge, the Holy Prophet (*Sallallahu `alayhi wa Sallam*) put his left hand (representing `Uthman's hand) on his right hand.

The Pious Caliphs

When the Muhajirin (Emigrants) from Mecca came to Medina, they had great difficulty in getting drinking water. Hadrat 'Uthman (R.A.) bought a well named *Bi'r-i-Rumah* from a Jew for twenty thousand dirhams for free use of Muslims. That was the first trust ever made in the history of Islam. The Holy Prophet (*Sallallahu 'alayhi wa Sallam*) gave him the glad tidings of Paradise for this act.

When the number of Muslims increased, the Prophet's mosque became too small to accommodate the increasing population, it was 'Uthman (R.A.) who responded to the Prophet's call and bought land for its extension. When the Holy Prophet (*Sallallahu 'alayhi wa Sallam*) went to the expedition of Tabuk, Hadrat 'Uthman bore the expenses for one third of the Islamic army (i.e., about 10,000 men). He also gave one thousand camels, fifty horses and one thousand Dinars (gold coins) to support the rest of the army. The Holy Prophet (*Sallallahu 'alayhi wa Sallam*) remarked on this, "Nothing will do any harm to 'Uthman from this day, whatever he does."

Hadrat 'Uthman (R.A.) was one of the scribes of the *Wahy* (Revelation) and also used to write other documents (letters and messages, etc.) of the Holy Prophet (*Sallallahu 'alayhi wa Sallam*).

At the time of the election of Hadrat Abu Bakr (R.A.) Hadrat 'Uthman (R.A.) was present in the Assembly Hall of Medina. During the caliphate of Abu Bakr and 'Umar (R.A.), he was a member of the *Shura* (Advisory Council). He occupied a prominent position in the affairs of the Islamic State during that time.

9

Hadrat `Uthman's Caliphate

Hadrat `Uthman (R.A.) elected as the third *Khalifah*

Before his death, Hadrat `Umar (R.A.) appointed a panel of six men to select a *Khalifah* from amongst themselves and then sought his approval through *Bai`at* (pledge of loyalty) by the Muslim public. He also instructed them to make the nomination within three days. The panel included `Uthman, `Ali, Sa`d bin Abi Waqqas, Talha, Zubair and `Abdur Rahman bin `Auf (R.A.) as the members.

The panel could not arrive at any decision even after long meetings. Then, Hadrat `Abdur Rahman bin `Auf proposed somebody to withdraw his name in order to decide the matter. When he got no response, he withdrew his own name. The remaining members agreed that he could take a decision. He consulted each member individually except Hadrat Talha (R.A.) who was not present at Medina. It so happened that Hadrat `Uthman proposed `Ali's name and Hadrat `Ali proposed `Uthman's name for the post of *Khalifah*. But Zubair and Sa`d (R.A.) were more in favour of Hadrat `Uthman than Hadrat `Ali. After more consultations with other companions and thinking over the problem during the third night, Hadrat `Abdur Rahman bin `Auf (R.A.) gave his decision in the morning of the fourth day in favour of Hadrat `Uthman (R.A.).

First of all Hadrat `Abdur Rahman bin `Auf (R.A.) took *Bai`at* at the hands of Hadrat `Uthman and then all the Muslims present in the mosque followed suit and took *Bai`at* at the hands of Hadrat `Uthman (R.A.). In this way, Hadrat `Uthman (R.A.) was declared to be the third *Khalifah*. When Hadrat Talha (R.A.) returned to Medina, `Uthman (R.A.) requested him either to accept the post of *Khalifah* (as he was among the persons proposed by Hadrat `Umar for the post) or to acknowledge him as *Khalifah* by taking *Bai`at*. Hadrat Talha declined to be the *Khalifah* and took pledge of loyalty at his hand, saying, "How can I object to your being the *Khalifah* when all the Muslims have agreed upon you."

A. CONQUESTS AND MISCELLANEOUS EVENTS

Administration of Syria

During the time of Hadrat `Umar (R.A.), Amir Mu`awiya (R.A.) was the governor of Damascus controlling a part of Syria. Hadrat `Uthman after combining three provinces viz. Syria, Palestine and Jordan into one, appointed Amir Mu`awiya (R.A.) as the governor of the whole Syria. During the late period of Hadrat `Umar (R.A.), Heraclius, the Emperor of Byzantium died at Constantinople in 641 (A.C.). His son, Constans (641-668) after some confusion, became the Emperor of Byzantine Empire which was reduced to Antalya (now a part of Turkey) and Asia Minor besides some states in the Eastern Europe, with Constantinople as its capital.

The Romans (Byzantines) were having a covetous eye on the parts conquered by the Muslims, specially Syria and Alexandria (in Egypt). They again started raising a big army against Muslims and incited the people to rebel against the Islamic Government after the death of Hadrat `Umar (R.A.).

Roman invasion of Alexandria

In the year 25 A.H. (645 A.C.) there was a big rebellion in Alexandria, and in 26 A.H., the Roman army took possession of the city after a fight with the Muslims. Hearing this Hadrat `Uthman (R.A.) directed `Amr bin al-`As (R.A.) to crush the rebellion and beat back the Roman invasion. Hadrat `Amr (R.A.) again attacked the city and drove the Romans out and recovered the port city of Alexandria.

Administration of Egypt

During the time of Hadrat `Umar there was no full pledged governor in Egypt. The powers of the governor were divided. Hadrat `Amr bin al-`As was the Commander-in-Chief of the forces and Hadrat `Abdullah bin Sarah (R.A.) was in charge of Revenue. But Hadrat `Amr (R.A.) had more say in the matters of administration. There arose a dispute between Hadrat `Amr and Hadrat Sarah in the year 27 A.H. Hadrat `Uthman investigated the case and found that Hadrat `Amr was not right; so he recalled him to Medina and Hadrat `Abdullah bin Sarah was appointed as governor of Egypt. Hadrat `Amr was not pleased with the decision. During the time of Hadrat `Amr (R.A.) the annual amount of taxes was two million dinars. Hadrat `Abdullah raised it to four million dinars annually.

Conquest of Antalya and Cyprus

Constan II, the Byzantine Emperor tried to take over Syria and ordered his army to march on the Muslims. Seeing the Roman invasion, Hadrat Amir Mu`awiya (R.A.) led an army to Asia Minor where the Romans were gathered. He defeated the Romans and took over the city of Amuria. Within a short period of time he conquered a vast part of Asia Minor. Following these victories Hadrat Amir Mu`awiya (R.A.) turned his attention to Mediterranean. The island of Cyprus was very important from the defense point of view. He sought `Uthman's (R.A.) permission for sea-fighting. The *Khalifah* approved his plan. For the first time in the history of Islam, a naval force was built and in the year 28 A.H. Hadrat Mu`awiya sent a fleet of 500 ships under the command of Hadrat `Abdullah bin Qais Harthi. After some fighting, the island of Cyprus was occupied and the inhabitants of the island agreed to pay the same tribute to Muslims as they did to the Romans.

Later on in the year 33 A.H. (653 A.C.), Hadrat Amir Mu`awiya also conquered the great fort of Antalya (also known as Anatolia). He also attacked Constantinople (now Istanbul), the capital of Byzantium in the year 34 A.H. (654 A.C.) but was not successful in conquering it. (It was really in the lot of Sultan Muhammad Fatih who conquered it on 20 Jumadil Awwal 857 A.H. (29 May 1453 A.C.).

Administration of Iraq

During the time of Hadrat `Umar (R.A.) Iraq was governed by the governor at Kufa. Hadrat Sa`d was the governor whom Hadrat `Umar (R.A.) recalled to Medina on some minor complaints. But at his death bed Hadrat `Umar desired reinstatement of Hadrat Sa`d (R.A.). Hadrat `Uthman fulfilled his desire and appointed Hadrat Sa`d as the governor of Iraq. In the year 26 A.H., there arose a dispute between Hadrat Sa`d and Ibn Mas`ud (R.A.) who was the Treasury officer of Kufa. Ibn Mas`ud complained to the *Khalifah*. Hadrat `Uthman enquired into the matter and found that Hadrat Sa`d was not right, therefore Hadrat Sa`d was again deprived of the governorship and Hadrat Walid bin `Uqbah was appointed as the new governor. In 30 A.H. Hadrat Walid bin `Uqbah was accused of drinking liquor for which he was not only dismissed but was also whipped in accordance with Islamic law. According to some historians Hadrat Walid bin `Uqbah was wrongly accused by some conspirators but Hadrat `Uthman had to punish him because of the evidence given against him. Then Hadrat `Uthman appointed Hadrat Sa`d bin al-`As as the governor of Kufa.

Again rowdy elements of Kufa plotted against their governor in the year 34 A.H. When Hadrat `Uthman received a number of complaints against Sa`d bin al-`As he replaced him by Hadrat Abu Musa Ash`ari (R.A.).

Rebellion of Azerbaijan and Armenia

Azerbaijan and Armenia were conquered during Hadrat `Umar's time. There arose a rebellion against Islamic Government after his death. Hadrat `Uthman ordered Hadrat Walid bin `Uqbah (who was the governor of Kufa at that time) to crush the rebellion. He sent Islamic forces and regained the territory taken over by the rebels. This happened in the year 26 A.H.

During the same period, Hadrat Amir Mu`awiyah (R.A.) sent an army to Armenia to face the Romans. The Islamic army was under the command of Habib bin Muslimah. He occupied some of the forts but Constans II sent a huge army of 80,000 men to face the Muslims. Seeing the situation, Amir Mu`awiya (R.A.) wrote to Hadrat `Uthman for reinforcement. He ordered Walid bin `Uqbah. He received the Khalifah's order when he was returning from Azerbaijan after taking it over from the rebels. He immediately sent an army of eight thousand men under the command of Salman bin Rabi`ah to Armenia. The two armies conquered the whole region of Armenia after defeating the Roman forces. They also conquered more parts of Asia Minor including Aran and Garjastan. Thus by the end of the 26 A.H. the territory up to Caucasus Mountains (now in the former USSR) came under the sway of Islam.

Administration of Iran and conquest of Afghanistan

Iran was under the administrative control of the governor of Basrah. Hadrat Abu Musa Ash`ari (R.A.) was the governor of Basrah when Hadrat `Umar (R.A.) died. The people of Basrah complained against him and wrongly accused him of partiality for the Quraish. At last Hadrat `Uthman (R.A.) recalled him to Medina and appointed Hadrat `Abdullah bin `Amir (R.A.) as the governor of Basrah.

As stated before, the whole of the Persian Empire was conquered during the time of Hadrat `Umar (R.A.) and the Persian Emperor, Yedzgird had ultimately fled to Balkh (a place in Afghanistan). After the death of Hadrat `Umar (R.A.), the exiled Emperor tried to instigate a rebellion in the frontier region of the Empire against the Islamic rule. To crush this rebellion Hadrat `Uthman (R.A.) appointed Hadrat `Ubaidullah bin Ma'mar but he was not successful and was martyred in a battle. Then Hadrat `Uthman asked `Abdullah bin `Amir, the newly appointed governor to deal with the rebels. He crushed the rebellion and conquered some more parts viz. Hisraf, Gazna, Herat and Kabul. He also took over Balkh, thus the whole of Afghanistan was conquered. Then he took over Samarkand, Tashkent, Sajestan, Arghiyan and Turkmenistan.

Conquest of Khurasan and Tabrastan

In the year 30 A.H. Hadrat Sa` bin `As, newly appointed governor of Kufa, marched towards Khurasan with an army in which some prominent figures who had returned from North African expedition like Hadrat Hasan, Husain, `Abdullah bin `Abbas, `Abdullah bin `Umar, etc. (R.A.) were also included. At the same time Hadrat `Abdullah bin `Amir (the governor of Basrah) also marched there. Before Hadrat `Abdullah bin `Amir reached, Sa`d bin `As conquered a number of places including Tabrastan and Jarjan.

In the year 31 A.H. Hadrat `Abdullah bin `Amir again marched there after hearing the news of rebellion. Then he conquered the remaining part of Khurasan.

In the meantime, Yedzgird, the exiled Persian Emperor reached the north in Turkmenistan and tried to collect an army but was again defeated by the Muslims at Sistan and fled. Thereupon one of the Turk chiefs, Naizak Khan invited him. While he was going to meet him he stayed in a village. There some body killed him while he was asleep for his precious garments and cash. In this way the last Emperor of the vast Persian Empire passed away.

Conquest of North Africa

For the defense of Egypt it was necessary to drive away the Byzantines from North Africa. Tripoli (now the capital of Libya) was a stronghold of Byzantium. When Hadrat `Abdullah bin Sarah was appointed as a full-rank governor of Egypt, he took permission from the *Khalifah* to advance into the northern territory. During Hadrat `Umar's time, `Amr bin al-`As (R.A.) had penetrated into the coastal part of North Africa for some distance.

After his appointment as a governor of Egypt, Hadrat `Abdullah bin Sarah (R.A.) received permission from the *Khalifah* to penetrate deep into North Africa. In 27 A.H. he went with an army to conquer Tripoli, the main Byzantine fort of North Africa at that time. Hadrat `Uthman (R.A.) also sent a reinforcement from Medina which included men like Hadrat Hasan, Husain, `Abdullah bin `Umar, `Abdullah bin Zubair, `Abdullah bin `Amr bin al-`As, and `Abdur Rahman bin Abu Bakr (R.A.). After some fight the inhabitants of Tripoli agreed to enter into a settlement and promised to pay *Jizya* equal to two-and-a-half million Dinars annually.

After the conquest of Tripoli, Hadrat `Abdullah bin Sarah spread his armies around Tripoli. Near a city named Yaquba he faced a huge Byzantine army, under the command of a famous Byzantine general named Jarjir. The battle began and the Byzantine commander announced a reward of one hundred thousand Dinars (gold coins) and the hand of his beautiful daughter, to the person who struck off the head of Hadrat `Abdullah bin Sarah, the Muslim Commander.

Hearing this Hadrat `Abdullah bin Zubair requested Hadrat `Abdullah bin Sarah to announce a reward of one hundred Dinars and the hand of Byzantine Commander's daughter (the princess) for the person who brought the commander's head. The reward was announced and the same day the commander was slain but nobody claimed the reward. However the princess recognized the man who had slain her father. He was no other than `Abdullah bin Zubair (R.A.). The princess was married with him and he also got the reward of one hundred thousand Dinars.

This victory cleared the way for advance of Muslims in North Africa and soon they captured Tunisia and Morocco and a part of Algeria.

Second invasion of Alexandria by Romans

In the year 31 A.H. (651 A.C.) Constantine sent a fleet of 500 ships to invade Alexandria. The Muslims got ready to beat back the enemy. Hadrat Mu`awiya (R.A.) the governor of Syria, also ordered his fleet to sail from there to face the Romans. Hadrat `Abdullah bin Sarah advanced with his fleet and faced the Romans in the mid sea. That was the first big naval battle in the history of Islam. Though the Muslims were not experienced in naval battles, yet they did not find it difficult to beat back the enemy. The retreating Romans took refuge in the island of Sicily and the Muslims returned victorious.

Invasion of Spain

After the conquest of North Africa, Hadrat `Uthman gave orders for the invasion of Spain. He appointed `Abdullah bin Nafai` as the Commander of Muslim army under the chief command of `Abdullah bin Sarah, the governor of Egypt. `Abdullah bin Nafai` conquered some part of Spain but soon returned and was not successful in his mission. (Spain was, as a matter of fact, in the lot of Tariq bin Ziyad who conquered it in the year 92 A.D., i.e. 711 A.C.).

A brief review of the conquests during Hadrat `Uthman's caliphate

Thus we see that during the caliphate of Hadrat `Uthman (R.A.) the Muslims conquered a number of new areas. They took over Antalya and Asia Minor in the west including Cyprus. Afghanistan, Samarkand, Tashkent, Turkmenistan, Khurasan and Tabrastan in the East and North

East; and Libya, Algeria, Tunisia and Morocco in North Africa. In this way Muslims were ruling over a vast part of Asia and Africa viz. Afghanistan, Turkmenistan, Uzbekistan, Persia or Iran, Iraq, Armenia, Azerbaijan, Turkey, Cyprus, Syria, Palestine, Jordan, Egypt, Libya, Algeria, Tunisia, Morocco and of course Arabia (now Saudi Arabia) and Yemen including the Gulf states. All these countries and places were under one flag, and the Islamic state was far bigger than any one of the past mighty Byzantine or Persian Empires. Islam as a religion was also prevailing in Abyssinia (now Ethiopia) and in some parts of East and Central Africa though these places were not under the direct control of the Caliphate.

B. INTERNAL DISORDER

Introductory note

The first half of Hadrat `Uthman's caliphate was very peaceful. During this time the Muslims gained many victories as described above, and the caliphate extended to a vast area of the then known world. But the later part of Hadrat `Uthman's caliphate was marred by a terrible civil war which ultimately led to the murder of the caliph himself. Hadrat `Uthman (R.A.) was a very gentle and soft-hearted person. The people who wanted to create chaos among the Muslims took advantage of his soft nature. Hadrat `Umar's stern hand had kept away the undemocratic and non-Islamic customs, and the practices that prevailed in the courts of Persian and Byzantine Empires. But Hadrat `Uthman (R.A.) sometimes overlooked the faults of the governors and other officers in various provinces, though he himself totally and completely followed the ways of the Holy Prophet (*Sallallahu `alayhi wa Sallam*) and the first two caliphs. His compassionate nature made the provincial governors bold as a result of which unrest in the provincial capitals grew and ultimately it engulfed the whole Islamic State.

The enemies of Islam were in search of a suitable occasion to work against Islam and the Muslims. They got the desired opportunity for this and sent out their men to disturb the peace and to spread false news. Only the main events that happened during that time would be discussed in the following lines.

Conspiracy of 'Abdullah bin Saba

'Abdullah bin Saba, a clever Yemenite Jew who had accepted Islam only for self interest and to destroy peace of the Islamic state, took the leading part in the agitation against Hadrat 'Uthman (R.A.). He was having a number of followers who had accepted Islam only to create disharmony among the Muslims.

He invented quite a few beliefs and started to preach them. He based his beliefs upon the love of the Holy Prophet (*Sallallahu 'alayhi wa Sallam*) and his family (*Ahli-Bait*). Some of the beliefs invented by 'Abdullah bin Saba were:

1. Every prophet left a *Wasi* (administrator) behind him, and the *Wasi* was his relative. For example Prophet Musa (Moses) made Harun his *Wasi* (administrator). Consequently the Holy Prophet (*Sallallahu 'alayhi wa Sallam*) must have a *Wasi*, and his *Wasi* was Hadrat 'Ali (R.A.). Being the *Wasi*, Hadrat 'Ali (R.A.) was the only rightful man to be the *Khalifah*. He went to the extent of declaration that the caliphate of Hadrat Abu Bakr, 'Umar and 'Uthman (R.A.) was unlawful. The only way to redress matters was to remove the then Caliph, Hadrat 'Uthman (R.A.).

2. He said that it was strange for the Muslims to believe that Jesus (*'Alayhis Salam*) would descend from the heaven to follow Islam and to fight for Muslims against non-believers, and not to believe that the Holy Prophet (*Sallallahu 'alayhi wa Sallam*) would not come back. So he believed that the Holy Prophet (*Sallallahu 'alayhi wa Sallam*) being superior to Jesus as the Last Prophet and the Leader of all prophets, would also come back.

3. He started to give wrong commentaries of various verses of the

Holy Qur'an and twisted their meaning in favour of his beliefs.

He preached his false self-coined beliefs secretly and selected the main headquarters of Muslim military power — Kufa, Basrah, Syria and Egypt — as centres of his activities. He picked up a number of newly converted Muslims who lent an easy ear to what he said. Some simple Muslims who were having certain complaints against various governors also joined him. It was the real cause of all the troubles.

First of all he visited Medina to note the internal conditions of the capital. He pretended to be a very pious Muslim but could not get much followers over there. Then he came to Basrah and started to preach his beliefs and incite the public against Muslim officers. At that time Hadrat `Abdullah bin `Amir was the Governor. Hearing about his activities, he called him and made certain enquiries because of which he was frightened and left Basrah leaving his followers and workers over there under the supervision of Hakim bin Hublah, one of the opponents of the governor.

From Basrah, `Abdullah bin Saba moved to Kufa and found it more suitable for his destructive activities. He pretended to be a very pious Muslim and because of his show of piety, a number of simple Muslims started to respect him. Then he preached his beliefs. Soon the governor of Kufa, Hadrat Sa`d bin al-`As was informed about him. He called him and warned him against his false beliefs and the damage he wanted to cause to the Muslim community. For this reason he left Kufa as well but made Ashtar as his deputy with instructions that the mission should be carried on secretly. From there he also went to Damascus but was not successful because of the strict control of Amir Mu`awiya (R.A.).

At last he selected Egypt and went there. The governor of Egypt, Hadrat `Abdullah bin Sarah was busy in the battles against Byzantine forces in North Africa and could not pay much attention to Ibn Saba's activities. He continued correspondence with his followers in Basrah, Kufa and other places from Egypt, and gave them directions for creating disorder and rivalry among the Muslims.

His followers, most of whom were pretending to be Muslims, used various techniques to increase their strength. They made a great show of piety and posed to be very pious worshippers. They incited people to forge complaints against the governors, various officers and the *Khalifah* as well. A new campaign against most of the officers was started by calling them irreligious, non-practical and bad Muslims. They sent forged letters from place to place which talked of injustice and unrest in the place from where they were posted. Such letters were usually sent to Sabaites (the followers of `Abdullah bin Saba) who read them out to as many people as possible. These forged letters also showed that Hadrat `Ali, Talha, and Zubair (R.A.) had full sympathy with them and with their mission and they disliked the *Khalifah*, Hadrat `Uthman (R.A.). These were the three leading Companions in Medina at that time. Thus the people of various places began to believe that there was a widespread unrest and that the leading Companions wanted to remove the *Khalifah*.

The Sabaites also worked throughout the state against various governors. They were the real cause of their removal from time to time. Sabaites were the main figures behind the removal of Hadrat Abu Musa Ash`ari from the governorship of Basrah at the time when their mission was not so popular. They spread rumours against Hadrat Walid bin `Uqbah, governor of Kufa, and wrongly accused him of drinking liquor, and provided false witnesses against him because of which the *Khalifah* punished him. When he was punished they accused the *Khalifah* of punishing innocent Muslims. When Hadrat `Abdullah bin `Amir (R.A.) was appointed as the governor of Basrah to replace Hadrat Abu Musa Ash`ari they incited the public against him and against the *Khalifah* that he was related to the *Khalifah* because of which he was given the governorship in his young age.

On one side they incited the people against the governors and on the other they accused the *Khalifah*. On the basis of complaints when Hadrat `Uthman (R.A.) removed the governors they criticised him to be unduly kind to his relatives by appointing them to big posts.

Allegations against Hadrat `Uthman

1. Hadrat `Uthman belonged to the family Banu Umayyah of Quraish. Before Islam there was rivalry between Banu Umayyah and Banu Hashim, the family of the Quraish to which the Holy Prophet (*Sallallahu `alayhi wa Sallam*) and Hadrat `Ali (R.A.) belonged. In Medina the Sabaites incited Banu Hashim against Banu Umayyah, actually against Hadrat `Uthman, by saying that he was removing Hashimites from the big offices in order to support Umayyads and that he was unduly considerate to his family.

2. They alleged that Hadrat `Uthman (R.A.) was extravagant and gave away money to his relatives, thus squandered the *Baitul Mal*. The allegation was absolutely false. Hadrat `Uthman (R.A.) was one of the wealthiest merchants in Arabia due to which people called him *Ghani* (the wealthy man). His liberal contributions towards the cause of Islam during the life of the Holy Prophet (*Sallallahu `alayhi wa Sallam*) have been mentioned in the preceding pages. His generosity continued in the same way during his caliphate. He spent his own money to help the poor, and also his relatives but never took anything wrongfully from the *Baitul Mal*. Not only this he did not accept any allowance from the *Baitul Mal* for his services as Caliph. Through his addresses and speeches he clarified his position several times and gave satisfactorily explanations to the false accusations against him. Once he promised to give one fifth of the booty of Tripoli, the state share, to Hadrat `Abdullah bin Sarah, the then Governor of Egypt, for his invaluable services and the bravery he showed in the battles that took place between the Muslims and the Byzantine forces in North African territories. But the general public disapproved his view and he asked `Abdullah to return that share.

3. One of the allegations, levelled by Sabaites against Hadrat Uthman was that he had burnt some copies of the Holy Qur'an. The fact was that Hadrat `Uthman (R.A.) sent copies of the Holy Qur'an, written by Hadrat Zaid bin Thabit by the order of Hadrat

Abu Bakr during his caliphate, to various places of the state and asked the governors and other officers to burn all those copies of the Holy Qur'an which were incomplete and were not in accordance with the Holy Qur'an compiled by Hadrat Zaid bin Thabit. This was done in order to avoid confusion between the Muslims because there were some copies of the Holy Qur'an at that time in which the order of the Surahs (Chapters) was not like that which was proposed by the Holy Prophet (*Sallallahu `alayhi wa Sallam*) in accordance to Hadrat Gabriel's instructions as commanded by Allah. Moreover, some of the copies existing at that time at various places other than Medina were lacking in some chapters, and were incomplete. For this reason Hadrat `Uthman (R.A.) got copies made from the standard Book compiled during the time of Abu Bakr (R.A.) and sent them to various places. Differences had also arisen due to differences in handwritings so he also standardised the way of writing the Holy Qur'an. This has been considered as one of the greatest services Hadrat `Uthman (R.A.) rendered to Islam for which he has been given the title of "*Jami`ul-Qur'an*" (the Compiler of the Qur'an) although the Holy Qur'an was compiled in a book form by Hadrat Abu Bakr (R.A.) on the insistence of Hadrat `Umar (R.A.).

4. At this place I would like to mention something about Hadrat Abu Dharr Ghifari (R.A.) because this allegation is concerned with him. He was a well-known and pious Companion of the Holy Prophet (*Sallallahu `alayhi wa Sallam*) who always kept aloof from the world and its riches. He was not in favour of accumulation of money and saving it. As regards the *Baitul Mal* (Public Treasury), he held the view that all the money should be spent for the welfare of Muslims as soon as it came through taxes, etc. In Syria he started to publicise his opinion and a number of people followed him. Seeing this Hadrat Amir Mu`awiya wrote to Hadrat `Uthman who recalled Hadrat Abu Dharr to Medina and then he retired to a village named Rabdhah near Medina. `Abdullah bin Saba tried to gain favour of Hadrat Abu Dharr

(R.A.) when he was in Syria but he rebuked Ibn Saba and told him that the beliefs he was preaching were foreign to Islam and that his aim was to create chaos among the Muslims.

When Hadrat Abu Dhar (R.A.) had retired they started accusing Hadrat `Uthman that he forced him to live in a village. Not only this but they also accused him of ill treatment of other recognised Companions like Hadrat `Ammar bin Yasir and Hadrat `Abdullah bin Mas`ud (R.A.). But all of these accusations were false.

5. One of the allegations against Hadrat `Uthman was that he called Hakam bin `As, who was exiled by the Holy Prophet (*Sallallahu `alayhi wa Sallam*), to Medina. However this step of Hadrat `Uthman was not too wise. Not only this but he also appointed Hakam's son Marwan as his chief secretary which was not liked by some prominent Companions and also by the Muslim public.

The forthcoming discussion on this point would reveal that Marwan became the main cause of insurgents' existence who ultimately assassinated the *Khalifah*. It is alleged that he wrote to Egypt's governor Hadrat `Abdullah to kill Muhammad bin Abi Bakr whom Hadrat `Uthman had appointed the governor of Egypt in place of Muhammad bin Abi Bakr when the insurgents pressed Hadrat `Uthman to do so but this, too, was false. The letter was sheer forgery. There are some other false allegations which were levelled by Sabaites to defame the *Khalifah*. Since most of them are purely theological in nature and not political, they are not being mentioned here.

Conference of the Governors

When the unrest caused by Sabaites went on growing in all parts of the State, the news began to pour in Medina. The leading Companions asked Hadrat `Uthman to take steps against them. So he called a conference of the governors in Medina in the year 34 A.H., just after the Hajj. All the governors attended the meeting. Hadrat `Uthman

(R.A.) enquired from them about the growing unrest in the State. They told him that it was due to some mischief mongers who wanted to overthrow the government. They suggested that such persons must be punished and those who were the leaders must be put to sword. But Hadrat `Uthman disliked the suggestion and told them that without just cause he would never shed even a single drop of Muslim blood. Hadrat `Uthman (R.A.) was not willing to take stern action against such persons because he did not want that hundreds of men should be massacred for his interest. Instead, he sent a mission of four persons: Muhammad bin Muslimah, Usamah bin Zaid, `Ammar bin Yasir and `Abdullah bin `Umar (R.A.) to tour the provinces.

After the governors' conference was over Hadrat Amir Mu`awiya (R.A.) suggested that he should leave Medina and should pass some time in Damascus but he said, "I would not leave Medina even though people kill me." Then Amir Mu`awiya (R.A.) requested Hadrat `Uthman (R.A.) to allow him to send an army to Medina for his protection but Hadrat `Uthman did not agree to even that.

Tour of the mission

The mission sent by Hadrat `Uthman toured various places and talked with the people. Three of them returned to Medina and reported to Hadrat `Uthman that the conditions were normal. The fourth member of the mission Hadrat `Ammar bin Yasir (R.A.) did not return. He was sent to Egypt where `Abdullah bin Saba and his followers coaxed him and he started to live with them instead of returning to Medina.

Saba gets friends

`Abdullah bin Saba was in search of some important men who were having some influence over the Muslims. At last he won over three important figures. One among them was Hadrat `Ammar bin Yasir, described above. The other two joined Ibn Saba before Hadrat `Ammar. They were Muhammad bin Abi Hudhaifah and Muhammad bin Abi Bakr. Muhammad bin Abi Hudhaifah was an orphan and was brought up by Hadrat `Uthman along with some other orphans. When he grew up he desired some big post. Hadrat `Uthman (R.A.) did not consider him fit for that. So he left Medina and went to Egypt and ultimately joined Ibn Saba. Muhammad bin Abi Bakr (R.A.) was in debt. The creditor complained to the *Khalifah* who decided the case impartially in favour of the creditor as a result of which Muhammad bin Abi Bakr left Medina and came to Egypt and ultimately joined Ibn Saba.

Plan of the Sabaites

The Sabaites were planning to cause a general rising when the Governors were away to attend the conference. However the plot could not be carried out.

Kufa was the main centre of the Sabaites besides their headquarters in Egypt. The hooligans of Kufa tried to carry out the plan and did not allow the governor to enter the city when he returned from the conference. They demanded that Hadrat Musa Ash`ari should be appointed as the governor in place of Sa`d bin `As. Their request was granted and Hadrat `Uthman (R.A.) sent Hadrat Musa Ash`ari to Kufa.

Then they chalked out another plan and decided that their ring leaders should meet at Medina. This plan had to serve double purpose. On the one hand they wanted to study the situation for future course of action, and on the other hand they wanted to show to the public that they put their grievances before the *Khalifah* but he did not pay any attention to them.

According to the plan three delegations came, one from Egypt, the second from Kufa and the third from Basrah. Hadrat `Uthman was informed about their plan but he accepted it quietly. When these Sabaites entered Medina some Companions suggested to `Uthman (R.A.) to kill them but he told that without sufficient legal grounds no man can be executed, and that he would try to remove the misunderstandings. He told them, "I would be kind to them and if kindness failed to work I would rather sacrifice myself for Allah's Will."

Hadrat `Uthman (R.A.) listened to them and gave a long address in which he replied to all the charges which were put against him. Some parts of his historical address are quoted here:

"I have been accused of loving my kinsmen and to be unduly kind to them. It is not a sin to love one's relatives but I have never been unjust to other people because of my love of my relatives. Whatever I give them that is from my own pocket. I never spent anything on my relatives and kinsmen from public funds . . .

"It has been said that I have appointed comparatively young men as officers. I did it only because I found them abler for the cause of Islam. Nobody could deny their honesty and the work they rendered for the cause of Islam and the Muslims. The appointment of Usamah as the commander of the army by the Holy Prophet is proof that youth is no disqualification.

". . . It has been alleged that I gave the whole booty of North Africa as reward to the governor of Egypt. It is true but when I learnt the public objection to it, I took back the money from the governor and deposited it in the *Baitul Mal* . . .

"It is said that I have reserved the public pastures for my personal use. I swear by Allah that I never did it. In public pastures only those animals graze which are the property of the *Baitul Mal*. All of you know that when I was entrusted with this office (i.e., caliphate) I had more animals than any one in the whole of Arabia but now I have only two camels that are to serve me at the time of Hajj. How could I reserve the public pastures for my personal use?

"People accuse me of sending copies of the Holy Qur'an. The Holy Qur'an is Allah's book sent down to His Prophet. The Companions who wrote it under the direct supervision of the Holy Prophet are still alive. I have sent only that copy of the Holy Qur'an which was compiled by those Companions.

". . . It is said that I called Hakam to Medina who was exiled by the Holy Prophet. Actually the Holy Prophet exiled him from Mecca to Taif. Then the Holy Prophet had allowed him to live at Medina on my request. I only put into force the permission granted by the Holy Prophet himself . . ."

In this way Hadrat `Uthman gave satisfactory explanation to all the allegations put against him by the Sabaites. In the end of his address he asked the audience, "Tell me if all what I have said is not correct."

But the aim of these ring leaders was to create mischief. They returned to their places and instead of telling the truth told them that the *Khalifah* was not ready to set things right. Then they planned to send strong contingents from places like Basrah, Kufa and Egypt for the forthcoming Hajj. The parties were to leave their places pretending to perform Hajj but there aim was to go to Medina and decide the matter with the sword, i.e., to change the *Khalifah* by force. Though the *Khalifah* knew about this plan from before hand, he did not want to use force. He was determined to win over his enemies with love and compassion.

10
Hadrat `Uthman's Martyrdom and Review of His Works

A. MARTYRDOM

Insurgents (Sabaites) enter Medina

As the time of Hajj in the year 35 A. H. (656 A.C.) came near they started to put their plans into action. In the month of Shawwal 35 A.H., they started coming in small groups from various places. In all, about three thousand Sabaites came, one thousand from each place viz. Basrah, Kufa and Egypt. The groups from Basrah stayed at Dhi-Khashab, and those from Kufa stayed at A`was while the Egyptians stayed at Dhi-Murwah. All the three places are near Medina. All of them wanted Hadrat `Uthman to step down but there were some differences of opinion regarding the next *Khalifah*. Because of Ibn Saba, the Egyptians wanted Hadrat `Ali (R.A.), but Kufites preferred Hadrat Zubair while Basrites were in favour of Hadrat Talha. The Egyptians came to Hadrat `Ali and requested him to accept the *Khilafat*. Hadrat `Ali replied, "The Holy Prophet (*Sallallahu `alayhi wa Sallam*) has told us that the parties of Dhi-Khashab, Dhi-Murwah and A`was are cursed. Every pious Muslim knows about it. I can't cooperate with you. Go back to your places."

The insurgents from Kufa made the same request to Hadrat Zubair who also gave the same reply. The Basrites approached Hadrat Talha who also refused.

When Hadrat `Uthman heard about the insurgents he sent some of the leading Companions including Hadrat `Ali to them. Hadrat `Ali assured the insurgents that their complaints would be listened to. They put certain demands including the dismissal of the governor of Egypt and appointment of Muhammad bin Abi Bakr as the new governor. Hadrat `Uthman acceded to their demand without any question. Then he gave a short address in which he said, "By Allah, for the cause of truth, I am ready to obey even a slave. I promise to fulfil your demands." Saying this tears rolled down the eyes of Hadrat `Uthman, and the audience also wept.

Hadrat `Ali (R.A.) then again assured the insurgents and they seemed to be satisfied and started to go back. All the Muslims in Medina thought that the trouble had ended.

The siege of *Khalifah*'s house

A few days later the Medinites were surprised to hear shouts of "Revenge! Revenge!" in the streets of Medina. Hearing the shouts Hadrat `Ali came out to enquire about the matter. The insurgents showed a letter to him under the seal of *Khalifah* and signed by Marwan bin Hakam, the chief secretary of Hadrat `Uthman (R.A.). The letter was being carried to the Governor of Egypt by a special messenger whom they intercepted on the way. The letter said, "Uqtul Muhammad bin Abu Bakr"* (i.e. "kill Muhammad bin Abu Bakr")

---

*It seems that the *nuqtah* (dot) of the Arabic letter *Ba* was wrongly placed at the top giving it a letter similar to another letter *Ta* due to which the meaning was totally changed. But according to most of the historians the letter was intentionally written by Marwan about which Hadrat `Uthman did not know. While some others say that it was a plot of insurgents and they instead of "Iqbil Muhammad bin Abu Bakr" (i.e. "accept Muhammad bin Abu Bakr as governor").

Hadrat `Ali tried to pacify them but they did not listen to him and went straight to `Uthman, saying, "We do not want `Uthman (R.A.) to be the *Khalifah*. Allah has made his blood lawful for us. You should also help us." Hadrat `Ali said, "By Allah, I have nothing to do with you. It seems that you have hatched a plot and are trying to carry it out."

When the insurgents went to Hadrat `Uthman (R.A.) he took a solemn oath that he knew nothing about the letter. But they did not believe him and said, "Whether you wrote it or not, you are unfit to be the *Khalifah* and you must abdicate." They threatened to kill him on which Hadrat `Uthman (R.A.) replied, "I do not fear death, but I do not want to shed Muslim blood."

When Hadrat `Ali saw that the insurgents were not in control and Hadrat `Uthman did not want to use force against them, he left for Ahjar, a place few miles away from Medina, because his position was becoming difficult as the insurgents wanted to drag him in the dispute.

The insurgents demanded Hadrat `Uthman (R.A.) to give up the *Khilafat*. He rejected their demand and said, "I can't take off the robe of honour with my own hands that Allah has bestowed upon me." Consequently the insurgents laid a siege to his house and did not allow him to come out except for offering *Salat*s in the *Masjid*. But later on they did not allow him to come out even for the *Salat*s. The siege went on for forty days. During the last few days they also stopped supply of water. Some brave Muslim youths like Hadrat Hasan, Husain, Muhammad bin Talha and `Abdullah bin Zubair (R.A.) were guarding

---

produced a forged letter. The reason given in *The Glorious Caliphate* by Athar Husain was the letter "was a clean forgery."

the gate of the house so that nobody among the insurgents could enter the house. Beside Hadrat 'Uthman and his wife, Nailah, Marwan bin Hakam was also in the house. He did not allow any person to fight with the insurgents although a fight took place between Hadrat Hasan, Husain and Marwan and the insurgents when they did not allow *Ummul Mu'minin* Hadrat Habibah (R.A.) to supply meals to Hadrat 'Uthman. Hadrat Hasan received minor injuries but Marwan was seriously hurt. However the insurgents did not fight with Hadrat Hasan and Husain because of the fear of Hashimites. During the siege Hadrat 'Uthman sent 'Abdullah bin 'Abbas to Mecca to lead the Hajj and also to inform people about the insurgents. He also sent messengers to provincial governors.

When hardship grew, some eminent Companions like Hadrat Mughirah bin Shu'bah requested the *Khalifah* to take action against the insurgents and said that all the people of Medina were ready to fight for him but he did not agree to shedding the blood of Muslims. Then they proposed that he should leave the house through the back door and either go to Mecca or to Damascus where he would be safer but he accepted neither of the proposals. Things got worse day by day, and at last the crisis arrived.

Martyrdom of Hadrat 'Uthman (R.A.)

The only weapon with Hadrat 'Uthman was his kindness and soft nature. He addressed several times the insurgents from the roof of his house and reminded them about his family relations with the Holy Prophet (*Sallallahu 'alayhi wa Sallam*), and the services he had rendered to Islam but they never listened to him.

The insurgents were afraid that the Hajj was coming to an end and after the Hajj a number of supporters of the *Khalifah* would come to Medina. They decided therefore to assassinate him without delay. As stated before, they did not want to fight with Hashimites like Hadrat Hasan, Husain and `Abdullah bin Zubair who were standing guard at the main gate of Hadrat `Uthman's big residence. The reason not to fight with Hashimites was that they had incited a number of people against Banu Umayyah (Hadrat `Uthman's family) in favour of Banu Hashim (Hashimites). So the insurgents climbed the back walls of the house and entered the room where Hadrat `Uthman (R.A.) was reciting the Holy Qur'an.

On seeing Hadrat `Uthman, one of the insurgents hit his head with an axe while the next struck him with a sword. His wife, Nailah tried to shield her husband but she also got several wounds and her fingers were chopped off. Chronicles record that Muhammad bin Abi Bakr was the leader of the assassins. He got hold of Hadrat `Uthman's beard and pulled it. On this Hadrat `Uthman remarked, "O my dear nephew if your father (Abu Bakr) were alive you would not have done this." The remarks of Hadrat `Uthman cut him to the quick and he turned back and did not take part in the assassination.

After giving severe injuries to Hadrat `Uthman, one of insurgents, an Egyptian named `Amr bin Hamq cut off *Khalifah*'s head.

Hadrat `Uthman (R.A.) was assassinated on Friday, the 17th Dhul-Hijjah, 35 A.H. (July 17, 656 A.D.).

A great martyr

Hadrat `Uthman was a great martyr as prophesied in the following Hadith quoted by Bukhari and others:

> Hadrat Anas (R.A.) narrated that the Holy Prophet (*Sallallahu `alayhi wa Sallam*), Abu Bakr, `Umar and `Uthman went up Uhud (the mountain near Medina) and when it quivered because of them the Holy Prophet kicked it with his foot and said, "Keep steady,

O Uhud, for there is a Prophet, a *Siddiq* and two martyrs on you."

In the above Hadith, Hadrat Abu Bakr had been said as the *Siddiq* (friend) while `Umar and `Uthman (R.A.) had been prophesied as the martyrs.

The news of martyrdom

The news of Hadrat `Uthman's cruel assassination shocked everybody. Hadrat `Ali (R.A.) received the news when he was returning from Ahjar to see Hadrat `Uthman. He was stunned on hearing the assassination of Hadrat `Uthman and exclaimed, "O Allah, You know it, I am free from any blame." He rebuked his sons Hasan and Husain (R.A.) and others who had stood guard at the gate for not being more alert.

After assassinating the *Khalifah*, the insurgents virtually took over charge of Medina. They also looted the *Baitul Mal*. Medinites were afraid of them and did not come out of their houses. The corpse of the *Khalifah* could not be hurried for two days. At last some Muslims succeeded getting into the house and carried out the burial service. There were only 17 Muslims who participated in the funeral prayer. Hadrat `Uthman (R.A.) was 82 years old at the time of his assassination and remained in the office of *Khilafat* for about 12 years. His words "I do not want to spill Muslim blood to save my own neck", will be remembered forever in the history of Islam. He sacrificed his life to save Muslim blood.

Consequences of assassination

The assassination of Hadrat `Uthman (R.A.) was unparalleled in Islamic history and it had far reaching effects. Hadrat Hudhaifah (R.A.), the secret keeper of the Holy Prophet's prophecies remarked on hearing the assassination of Hadrat `Uthman, "Ah, the assassination of `Uthman has divided the Muslims till resurrection, they would never be united again." It proved to be true because just after the assassination, civil war started and continued upto the tragedy of Karbala. At that time the Muslim community was divided into four groups:

i. `Uthmanis: The Syrians and Basrites were in favour of capital punishment of the assassins. Syrians thought Hadrat Mu`awiyah the most suitable person to punish the assassins while the Basrites wanted the *Khalifah* from any of these two Talha or Zubair, as they were included in the panel appointed by Hadrat `Umar to select the *Khalifah*.

ii. Shi`an-i-`Ali: These people did not think Hadrat `Uthman (R.A.) fit for *Khilafat* and called themselves as the "Shi`an-i-`Ali" i.e., the friends of `Ali. Kufans and some Egyptians were in this group. According to Sunni historians, the assassins were from amongst this group.

iii. Murhibah: These were those people who were busy in Jihad (Holy Wars) at the time when Hadrat `Uthman was assassinated. They said, "Neither we are with `Uthmanis nor with Shi`as. We want to keep aloof from their differences."

iv. Ahl-i-Sunnah wal Jama`ah: These were the bulk of the Companions and the Muslims of various parts of the Islamic state including Mecca, Medina and other parts of Arabia. They said, "We love both `Uthman and `Ali and consider them as righteous and pious Companions. We do not curse any of the Companions and the righteous Muslims. If any of the Companions committed a mistake it was due to his *Ijtihad* (his disciplined verdict based upon the Holy Qur'an and *Sunnah* of the Holy Prophet) and he would not be questioned for it. We follow the *Sunnah* (ways) of the Holy Prophet and the *Sunnah* of his righteous *Jama`ah* (i.e. the group of all the Companions).

The first and the third — `Uthmanis and Murhibah — proved to be temporary political groups but the other two — Shi`as and Ahl-i-Sunnah wal Jama`ah, or Sunnis, took the shape of permanent theological groups and still exist.

Hearing the news of Hadrat `Uthman's assassination Hadrat `Abdullah bin `Abbas (R.A.), a prominent commentator of the Holy Qur'an, remarked, "Allah might have stoned us as He stoned the people of Lot if majority of the Muslims supported the assassination of Hadrat `Uthman."

Thamamah bin `Adi (R.A.), the governor of Yemen started to cry and weep hearing the news of the assassination of Hadrat `Uthman. Hadrat `Abdullah bin Salam (R.A.), well versed in the past scriptures, said, "By Allah, the power of the Arabs has finished now." Hadrat `A'isha (R.A.), the most beloved wife of the Holy Prophet, said, "Ah, `Uthman has been assassinated most cruelly. His record of deeds is shining like a well washed cloth."

Hearing the news of the assassination Hadrat Abu Hurairah and Hadrat Zaid bin Thabit (R.A.) started to weep continuously and their tears did not stop for a long time. The shirt of Hadrat `Uthman, which was spotted with his blood, and the cut fingers of his wife, Nailah, were carried to Hadrat Amir Mu`awiyah (R.A.), the Governor of Syria, in Damascus. When they were shown to the Muslim public the whole gathering started to cry and shouted, "Revenge! Revenge!".

Joseph Hell, a Western historian says, "The assassination of `Uthman was a signal for civil war." Wellhausen, a German historian says, "The murder of `Uthman was more epoch-making than almost any other event of Islamic history." Philip Hitti has remarked, "With `Uthman's death the political unity of Islam came to an end. Soon Islam's religious unity was divided. Islamic society entered upon a period punctuated with schism and civil strife that has not yet ended." A Muslim historian, Prof. K. Ali, writes, "Unity of Islam which was maintained by the first two *Khalifah*s was lost and serious dissensions arose among the Muslims."

The assassination of Hadrat `Uthman was followed by great civil wars and battles between the Muslims, the details of which would come later. The system of centralised government initiated by Hadrat `Umar and developed by Hadrat `Uthman was shattered and a number of internal movements started of which the Kharijite's movement was the most serious.

B. REVIEW OF HADRAT `UTHMAN'S SERVICES TO ISLAM

Victories

Hadrat `Uthman's reign constituted a glorious period in the history of Islam. The territories of the Islamic State (caliphate) were immensely extended. Though the conquests during his time were not so much in number as during the time of `Umar, nevertheless they were not few. He ruled over a vast part of the then known world, right from Kabul (Afghanistan) to Morocco. He put down rebellions with an iron hand.

During Hadrat `Uthman's period Muslim naval force was developed and Muslims started naval victories. The victory over the huge naval force of Byzantine Empire comprising 500 ships has been termed as the Grand Victory.

After the capture of North African territories by Muslims and gaining full control over Mediterranean, the mighty power of Byzantine and Roman Empire had collapsed. Actually Islam was at the zenith of its glory during the period of Hadrat `Uthman.

Official manuscript of the Holy Qur'an

One of the magnificent services to Islam done by Hadrat `Uthman (R.A.) was to safeguard any possible change in the codex of the Holy Qur'an. After the conquests by the Muslims, hundreds of thousands of non-Arabs, whose mother tongue was not Arabic, accepted Islam because of its teachings. Hadrat Hudhaifah (R.A.), one of the prominent Companions of the Holy Prophet (*Sallallahu `alayhi wa Sallam*), went for Jihad (Holy War) during that time and noticed many differences in the manner of recitation (*Qirat*) of the Holy Qur'an. The Syrians recited in a way different from that of Kufis while the Kufis differed from Basris and so on. As a matter of fact these differences were due to the differences in the way of writing Arabic. Seeing this condition Hadrat Hudhaifah reported the matter to the *Khalifah* on his return from the Jihad and suggested that the Medinese codex should be regarded as authentic, i.e. the Holy Qur'an which was written and compiled in Book form during the time of Hadrat Abu Bakr (R.A.) and was kept with *Ummul Mu'minin* Hadrat Hafsah (R.A.). Hadrat `Uthman (R.A.) took that Book from Hadrat Hafsah (R.A.) and canonized the Medinese codex. He asked Hadrat Zaid bin Thabit (R.A.), the person who wrote it during the time of Hadrat Abu Bakr, to make copies of the same with the help of some other Companions like `Abdullah bin Zubair and Sa`d bin `As. Then he ordered all other copies, beside the Medinese codex, to be burnt and destroyed throughout the State. Those people who earned their living in the provinces as the receptacles and expositors of the sacred text were not pleased with this act. It has been discussed before that such persons criticised `Uthman for burning unauthentic texts. However for this great service Hadrat `Uthman (R.A.) is famous as the "*Jami`ul-Qur'an*" (the compiler of the Qur'an).

Extension of the Mosque of the Holy Prophet

The Mosque of the Holy Prophet was too small for the increasing Muslim population. He bought a big plot of land in the neighbourhood of the mosque, but some of the persons living in the nearby houses did not want to leave their places even for reasonable compensation. For four years no new construction was built. One day he gave an effective lecture after the Friday *Salat* and the people agree to donate their places. Then the mosque was extended in the year 29 A.H.

Preaching

Hadrat `Uthman (R.A.) spent a lot of his time in preaching to the prisoners of war. Many of them accepted Islam because of his efforts. He also taught Islamic law to the Muslims. Once he himself demonstrated the correct method of making *wudu* before a large gathering of Muslims. He took special care to send missionaries to various places and appointed teachers to teach Islamic law, the Holy Qur'an and Hadith. Persons were appointed to make the rows (*Saff*) of worshippers straight during a congregational *Salat* specially on Fridays when the congregation was quite large.

Construction of buildings, bridges, roads and embankments

A number of new buildings were constructed for offices at various places. Rest houses were constructed on various highways, and guest houses were built in various cities like Kufa. For the welfare of the general public new bridges and roads were constructed, and general condition of various roads was improved. The roads leading to Medina were given special attention. He got tanks made, and wells dug up along many roads to supply water to the travellers.

Medina was not safe from floods. Sometimes the building of the Prophet's mosque was in danger. Hadrat `Uthman constructed a strong embankment along that side of the city which used to get flooded. This was known as the Embarkment of Mahroz.

`Uthman (R.A.) as a great scholar

Hadrat `Uthman had a beautiful handwriting because of which the Holy Prophet (*Sallallahu `alayhi wa Sallam*) appointed him as one of the scribes of the *Wahy* (Revelation).

His style of writing was well recognized among the Companions. Arabic knowing persons can recognize the fluency of his writings specially of the letters and the orders he sent to various officers during his *Khilafat*. Though he was not an orator but his way of lecturing was very effective. His addresses and lectures can be seen in history books.

Hadrat `Uthman was a great scholar of the Holy Qur'an and was a *Hafiz* (i.e. one who commits the whole Holy Book to memory). He was well versed in *Shan-i-Nuzul* (the chronology of revelation of various verses and the chapters of the Holy Qur'an) and was considered an authority in this respect. He was one of the few Companions who excelled in deriving laws from the verses of the Holy Qur'an.

Although he was not a great jurist like `Umar and `Ali (R.A.) nevertheless he was well qualified in this respect. His verdicts and judgements have been mentioned in books. He was considered an authority on the laws of Hajj. Even `Umar (R.A.) asked `Uthman about that during his time.

Character and piety

Hadrat `Uthman (R.A.) was a very pious Companion and a man of high character. He was the most modest of all the Companions. Once the Holy Prophet (*Sallallahu `alayhi wa Sallam*) was sitting with some of his Companions and the shin of his leg was not covered. In the meantime somebody informed him about the arrival of Hadrat `Uthman (R.A.). The Holy Prophet (*Sallallahu `alayhi wa Sallam*) immediately covered it and remarked, "Even the angels have regard for the modesty of `Uthman."

He was a strict follower of the *Sunnah* of the Holy Prophet (*Sallallahu `alayhi wa Sallam*). Somebody asked him the reason for smiling after *wudu*. He replied he had seen the Holy Prophet smiling after making *wudu*, so he smiled to follow him. Once he demonstrated to Muslims the correct way of making *wudu* according to the *Sunnah* of the Holy Prophet (*Sallallahu `alayhi wa Sallam*).

He used to fear Allah very much. Tears used to roll down his face because of Allah's fear. Whenever the consequences to be faced in the grave were described before him, he used to weep so much that his beard could get wet with tears. Sometimes he wept and cried seeing a corpse or a grave because of fear of Allah. He used to say, "Grave is the first stage among all the stages of the Hereafter. If a person is successful there, he would be successful on the Day of Judgement too. If a person faces difficulty in the grave, other stages would also be difficult for him."

He used to do household work although he was one of the wealthiest persons in the whole of Arabia. He would not wake his slave to take any help from him when he got up to perform the *Tahajjud Salat*.

Hadrat `Uthman was very soft spoken. If any person talked to him in a harsh tone he always replied gently. Once he was delivering

Khutbah of the *Jumu`a Salat*, a person shouted during the sermon, "O `Uthman, repent for Allah's sake and keep away from going wrong." He immediately turned his face towards the *Qiblah* and exclaimed, "O Allah, I am the first to repent before Thee and to turn towards Thee."

He never took any allowance from the *Baitul-Mal* for his services as a *Khalifah*. Hadrat `Umar got 5,000 Darhams annually as an allowance from the Public Treasury, thus Hadrat `Uthman contributed 60,000 Darhams after his 12 years' service, towards the Public Fund.

Examples of his generosity have already been given. He was the most generous among all the wealthy Companions and never hesitated to spend his money for the cause of Islam and Muslims. His house was one of the biggest in Medina which he built near the mosque of the Holy Prophet. He established a library in the back of his house for the education of the Muslims.

Wives and children

Hadrat `Uthman was first married to the Holy Prophet's daughter, Hadrat Ruqayyah (R.A.) who died in Medina while the Holy Prophet was away on the expedition of Badr. Then he was married to the younger daughter of the Holy Prophet whose name was Hadrat Ummi Kulthum. She also died in the year 9 A.H. His first wife, Hadrat Ruqayyah bore him a son, `Abdullah, who died at an early age. He had no child from Ummi Kulthum (R.A.).

After the death of his second wife Hadrat Ummi Kulthum, he married the following ladies from time to time: Fakhtah bint Walid; Ummi `Amr bint Jundah; Fatimah bint Shaibah; Ummi Banin bint `Uwainah; Ramlah bint Shaibah; `A'ishah; Ummi Aban; and Nailah bint Farafsah, his last wife whose fingers were chopped by the insurgents.

Eleven sons were born to him from different wives. Some of them died at an early age. One of his sons, Aban became famous and held high positions during the Umayyads. He had six or seven daughters.

C. ADMINISTRATION OF HADRAT 'UTHMAN (R.A.)

Hadrat 'Uthman observed the same principles in his government as were laid down by Hadrat 'Umar (R.A.). In the following lines some of the main features of his government would be described in brief.

Shura (Counsel of Advisers)

He maintained the Council of Advisers (*Shura*) in the same way as was maintained by the first two caliphs. The main members of his *Shura* were Hadrat 'Ali, Zubair and Talha. General councils for consultations were also called from time to time. All the prominent Companions, governors and prominent officers were present in the general council (conference) held in the year 34 A.H. to consider the internal condition of the state.

Administration of the Provinces

Hadrat 'Uthman (R.A.) divided the state into various provinces according to a new plan. Before him, there were three provinces in the region of Syria, viz. Syria, Palestine and Jordan. Hadrat 'Uthman combined all the three provinces into one — Syria — and put it under the control of a single Governor — Mu'awiyah (R.A.). This was necessary and important from the point of view of defense. Hadrat Mu'awiyah (R.A.) was a good and intelligent administrator and was able to control the whole region in a better way. He also separated the post of Governor from that of the commander of the armed forces in various provinces. Separate officers were appointed for both the posts who were under the direct control of the Khalifah. However, in some cases this rule was not observed due to lack of suitable persons.

Though Hadrat 'Uthman was a soft natured gentleman, yet he did not condone the mistakes of his officers including the Governors. The details have already been mentioned in the preceding pages. On various occasions he sent commissions of enquiry.

On Fridays he used to come to the mosque long before the *Khutbah Adhan* to listen to the complaints of Muslims and to remove their difficulties. On the occasion of every Hajj he used to listen to the public about their difficulties and complaints against officers.

Following were the Officers (civil) at the time when Hadrat 'Uthman (R.A.) was assassinated in 36 A.H.

1. **Mecca:** 'Abdullah bin Hadrami
2. **Ta'if:** Qasim bin Rabi'ah Thaqafi
3. **Yemen (with Sana as its capital):** Ya'la bin Munabbah
4. **Syria:** Hadrat Amir Mu'awiyah.

The following places were under the direct control of the governor of Syria. Each place was under the charge of an administrator:

a. **Jordan:** Abul A'war al-Salimi.

b. **Hims (Homs):** 'Abdur Rahman bin Khalid bin Walid, who was also the administrator of Jazirah (Mesopotamia).

c. **Palestine:** 'Alqamah bin Hakim.

5. **Egypt:** Abdullah bin Sa'd, who was also in charge of North African territories each of which was having its own administrative officer, under the governor of Egypt: Tripoli, Algeria and Morocco etc.
6. **Basrah:** Abdullah bin `Amir, who was also in charge of all the territories in Eastern Persia, each of which was having its own administrative officer, under the governor of Basrah: Balkh, Kabul, Herat, Samarkand, Sajistan, Arghiyan and Turkmenistan etc.
7. **Kufa:** Abu Musa Ash`ari, who was also in charge of all the territories in Western Persia, each of which was having its own administrative officer under the governor of Kufa: Khurasan, Tabrastan, Azerbaijan (with Ash`ath bin Qais as the administrative officer), Isfahan (with Sa'ib bin Aqra'y as the administrative officer), Hamdan (with Nasir as the administrative officer).
8. **Qansirin (Asia Minor):** Habib bin Muslimah Fahri, who was also in charge of Armenia, and Antalya etc.

Hadrat Zaid bin Thabit was the Qadi of Medina and Hadrat `Uqbah bin `Amir was the Treasury officer in Medina.

Administration of the armed forces

Hadrat `Uthman (R.A.) kept the armed forces on the same pattern as was laid down by his predecessor. During his time there was a notable increase in the number of armed forces. Not only he increased the military power of the Islamic State (Caliphate) but also connected various military units with each other. For example when Hadrat Mu`awiyah (R.A.) needed reinforcement to face the Romans, the armies in Iran and Armenia were immediately moved to Syria. Hadrat

'Uthman established a number of new cantonments at Tripoli, Cyprus, Armenia and Tabrastan. Besides the central cantonments there were a number of small cantonments as well in various districts.

He had made arrangements for breeding and raising of horses and camels. Large pastures were reserved for the animals used for military purposes. The pasture at Rabdhah, near Medina was ten miles long and about nine miles wide. Another pasture near Medina at Darbah was six miles long. He built ponds near the pastures and houses for the caretakers. Number of camels and horses had immensely increased to meet the needs of the armed forces. There were 40,000 camels in one pasture alone at Darbah. The number of animals kept all over the vast Islamic State was stupendous.

He took special care of military personnels and increased their allowances. The civil departments were separated from the military departments.

One of the remarkable features in the development of military power during the period of Hadrat 'Uthman was the establishment of naval force. The Muslim navy was expanded and very well equipped. Amir Mu'awiyah (R.A.) played a very important role in this respect. He is the man who worked for the development of the Islamic naval force. Under his command the first naval battle took place in the history of Islam.

Administration of Public Treasury and Revenue

During the time of Hadrat 'Uthman the revenue of the State was greatly increased. The *Kharaj* of Egypt alone was two million Dinars annually during the time of Hadrat 'Umar but it increased to four millions annually during 'Uthman's period. Hadrat 'Uthman (R.A.) used the entire public funds for the general welfare of the public. He increased the allowances given to various people and the poor. Not only this he also arranged for free distribution of food stuffs and cooked meals to the poor and disabled persons during the month of Ramadan. He used a major part of the revenue in construction of bridges, roads, barrages and mosques. He also fixed salaries for the *Muadhdhins* (i.e. the persons who call *Adhan*) which had not been done by Hadrat ʿUmar (R.A.).

No use of force against civilians

Hadrat ʿUthman (R.A.) showed an exemplary tolerance against the insurgents. By not using force against the civil public, he set the first example of the highest democratic rule in human civilization. If studied from this point of view, it would be noted that ʿUthman (R.A.) was at the peak of modern democratic principles. It is unfortunate that the masses at that time were not trained for that highest form of democracy. They have had experienced in the past of the tyranny of Persian and Roman Emperors and their officers.

However the base elements took advantage of the Islamic democratic principles and incited some of the Muslim population against the *Khalifah*. Hadrat ʿUthman used all the democratic principles, now prevailing in the modern society, to satisfy the insurgents. He gave before the public full explanation of all the allegations brought against him, and the public was fully satisfied with his explanation. He acceded to the demands of the insurgents by appointing Muhammad bin Abi Bakr as the Governor of Egypt. But he did not resign because the majority of the Muslims were in his favour and only a few were the mischief mongers. His words "I do not want to spill Muslim blood to save my own neck" would be remembered forever.

SECTION IV

`Ali Ibn Abi Talib
35-40 A.H./656-661 A.D.

11
'Ali Ibn Abi Talib: His Early Life

Name and parentage

Hadrat 'Ali (R.A.) was born some thirty years after the birth of the Holy Prophet (*Sallallahu 'alayhi wa Sallam*). He belonged to the most respectable family of Quraish, the Banu Hashim (i.e. Hashimites). His father Abu Talib was the paternal uncle of the Holy Prophet (*Sallallahu 'alayhi wa Sallam*) who brought him up after the death of the Holy Prophet's grandfather. Hadrat 'Ali's mother was Fatimah bint Asad, who belonged to Banu Hashim. Hadrat 'Ali's patronymic name was Abul Hasan. The Holy Prophet gave him another name, Abu Turab, which was most liked by Hadrat 'Ali. The Holy Prophet (*Sallallahu 'alayhi wa Sallam*) took Hadrat 'Ali in his childhood from his father, Abu Talib, and brought up him like his own son.

First youth to accept Islam

When the Holy Prophet (*Sallallahu 'alayhi wa Sallam*) started receiving revelations Hadrat 'Ali (R.A.) was about ten years old. The Holy Prophet disclosed his mission before Hadrat 'Ali and he accepted it immediately, thus he became the first youth to enter the fold of

Islam. When the Holy Prophet started to preach openly, he invited all of his family members to a feast and announced his mission before them. Nobody listened to him, but young `Ali stood up and said, "Though my eyes are sore, my legs are thin and I am the youngest of all those present here, yet I will stand by you, O Messenger of Allah." Hearing this all the leaders of Quraish laughed but `Ali proved his words to be true after supporting the Holy Prophet in his mission from the beginning till the end.

The Holy Prophet (*Sallallahu `alayhi wa Sallam*) loved him very much. The night when the Holy Prophet was migrating to Medina, his house was surrounded by the bloodthirsty tribesmen, who had plotted to assassinate him. They were ready to kill any person who came out of the house. In such a situation, the Holy Prophet (*Sallallahu `alayhi wa Sallam*) asked Hadrat `Ali (R.A.) to sleep in his bed. He followed the command gladly and immediately jumped in the bed.

Although the Meccans did not accept his mission, they considered the Holy Prophet the most trustworthy man of Mecca and continued keeping their trusts (cash and gold etc.) with him. It was `Ali (R.A.) to whom the Holy Prophet gave the deposits to return to the owners, when he was leaving Mecca for Medina. `Ali (R.A.) migrated to Medina after returning the deposits.

Life in Medina

Hadrat `Ali (R.A.) was very close to the Holy Prophet, and the closeness was changed to a permanent relationship when he married his most beloved daughter, Fatimah (R.A.), to `Ali (R.A.).

Hadrat `Ali (R.A.) also had the distinguished honour that the progeny of the Holy Prophet continued through Hadrat `Ali's sons from Fatimah (R.A.), namely Hadrat Hasan and Husain (R.A.). The two children were the most beloved of the Holy Prophet (*Sallallahu `alayhi* *wa Sallam*).

When the Holy Prophet (*Sallallahu 'alayhi wa Sallam*) went to the expedition of Tabuk in 9 A.H., he left Hadrat 'Ali in charge of Medina. On this some hypocrites remarked that the Holy Prophet did not like Hadrat 'Ali. On this the Holy Prophet remarked, "You are in the same position in relation to me as Aaron was with relation to Moses. But the only difference is: there is no prophet after me."

His bravery and the "*Dhulfiqar*"

Hadrat 'Ali (R.A.) was a very brave man. He participated in almost all the battles against the non-believers during the time of the Holy Prophet (*Sallallahu 'alayhi wa Sallam*). The stories of his bravery are famous in history.

In the first battle of Islam at Badr, he was holding the flag of Islamic army. When three famous warriors of Quraish challenged the Muslims, according to Arab tradition, Hadrat 'Ali (R.A.) along with Hadrat Hamzah and Abu 'Ubaidah (R.A.) accepted the challenge. He killed his opponent, Walid, only with one thrust of his sword and cut him in two pieces. Then he helped Hadrat Abu 'Ubaidah (R.A.) to kill the next Quraishi warrior.

In the battle of Uhud when Hadrat Mus'ab bin 'Umair, the bearer of the Islamic standard, was martyred, it was Hadrat 'Ali (R.A.) who held it up. Seeing this one of the non-believers, Abu Sa'd challenged him. Hadrat 'Ali attacked him and he fell down on the ground naked. 'Ali (R.A.) felt pity on him and left him in that condition.

In the battle of the Trench, the all-Arabia fame warrior, 'Abdwood challenged the Muslims after jumping on his horse across the trench. Nobody dared to accept his challenge except 'Ali. The Holy Prophet (*Sallallahu 'alayhi wa Sallam*) warned 'Ali about 'Abdwood but 'Ali insisted on going and fighting with him. Then the Holy Prophet (*Sallallahu `alayhi wa Sallam*) gave him his famous sword "*Dhulfiqar*" and put a turban on his head before he went to fight with `Abdwood. A few minutes later people saw `Abdwood's head was cut off from his body by `Ali.

The title of "*Asadullah*"

Because of his bravery Hadrat `Ali was popularly called "*Asadullah*" ("The Lion of Allah").

In the battle of Khaibar against Jews, the Muslims tried to conquer the strongest Jewish fort, Qumus, but were not successful in the beginning. Then the Holy Prophet (*Sallallahu `alayhi wa Sallam*) said, "I will give the command and the standard tomorrow to such a brave person who loves Allah and His Prophet and whom Allah and His Prophet love." Everybody was desiring to be that fortunate man. The people were rather surprised when the next morning the Holy Prophet (*Sallallahu `alayhi wa Sallam*) called `Ali who was sick and his eyes were sore. The Holy Prophet applied his finger, wet with his saliva, over the eyes of `Ali (R.A.) and they were cured immediately. Then he gave the standard, and advised him, "First of all call them towards Islam. Even if one man is guided towards Islam because of you, it would be better than red camels."

Following the advice of the Holy Prophet Hadrat `Ali invited the Jews towards Islam. Instead of accepting the Right Path they sent their commander Marhab, the great warrior of Arabia and one of the bravest men of his time. He challenged Hadrat `Ali to fight. `Ali (R.A.) accepted the challenge and slew him in one attack. His famous sword cut Marhab's body into two pieces.

He showed great bravery in each and every battle he fought and earned fame. He was counted as one of the great warriors of Arabia.

`Ali (R.A.) the great scholar of Islam

`Ali (R.A.) was not only a great warrior but a great scholar as well. The Holy Prophet (*Sallallahu `alayhi wa Sallam*) said about him, "I am the city of knowledge and `Ali is its gate." He was one of the great jurists among the Companion. The Holy Prophet appointed him as the *Qadi* (Judge) of Yemen during his life time. He was a master of Arabic and his writings were as effective as his speech. More about his scholarly services to Islam would be mentioned at the end.

Special messenger of the Holy Prophet

In 9 A.H., the first Hajj of Islam took place. Hadrat Abu Bakr (R.A.) was appointed as the leader of the Hajj group. After he left Medina revelation came to the Holy Prophet (few verses in the beginning of chapter IX) according to which the treaty with the non-believers had to be dissolved and they were given four months' notice. The announcement was to be made on the great day of Hajj. The Holy Prophet (*Sallallahu `alayhi wa Sallam*) asked Hadrat `Ali to carry the message of Allah on his behalf. He gave Hadrat `Ali (R.A.) his own she-camel, Qaswa, on which Hadrat `Ali rode and went to Mecca to read out the message before the crowd on the occasion of Hajj.

Excellence of `Ali

There are so many virtues and services of `Ali (R.A.) that it is difficult to mention them all in this short book. On many occasions the Holy Prophet (*Sallallahu `alayhi wa Sallam*) had prayed for him. When he sent `Ali to Yemen in Ramadan 10 A.H. he blessed `Ali (R.A.) with the following prayer: "O Allah put truth on his tongue, and enlighten his heart with the light of guidance." Then he himself put a turban on his head and gave the black standard.

On one occasion the Holy Prophet said to `Ali, "You belong to me and I belong to you." He also said, "When I am patron of anyone, `Ali is his patron also." Once the Holy Prophet said, "Only a hypocrite does not love `Ali and a believer does not hate him."

According to a Hadith transmitted by Imam Ahmad the Holy Prophet said to `Ali, "You have a resemblance to Jesus whom the Jews hated so much that they slandered his mother and whom Christians loved so much that they placed him in a position not rightly his." `Ali afterwards said, "Two (types of) people will perish on my account, one who loves me so excessively that he praises me for what I do not possess, and one who hates me so much that he will be impelled by his hatred to slander me."

Shock of the Holy Prophet's death

The death of the Holy Prophet (*Sallallahu `alayhi wa Sallam*) was a great shock to Hadrat `Ali (R.A.). He had attended him day and night during his illness, and after his death he gave bath to the Holy Corpse and enshrouded it.

Pledge of loyalty (*Bai`at*) to the former *Khalifah*s

Hadrat `Ali (R.A.) had taken pledge of loyalty on the hands of all the three past *Khalifah*s. However he was late in taking pledge at the hand of Hadrat Abu Bakr (R.A.). The reason why he was late in taking pledge on the hands of Hadrat Abu Bakr (R.A.) was the serious illness of his beloved wife, Hadrat Fatima (R.A.) and that he was busy in collection of the Holy Qur'an. It is mentioned in the famous history book, *Tabaqat ibn Sa`d*: When Hadrat Abu Bakr (R.A.) enquired of `Ali (R.A.) why he was so late in taking pledge of loyalty and whether he disliked his *Khilafat*, `Ali (R.A.) replied, "I do not dislike your leadership but the fact is that I had taken an oath after the death of the Holy Prophet not to put on my sheet (i.e., not to engage in any work) except for performing *Salat* until I have collected all the parts of the Holy Qur'an."

Then Hadrat `Ali (R.A.) took the pledge of loyalty on the hand of Abu Bakr and helped him throughout his *Khilafat*. He was very active during the time of Hadrat `Umar and also married his daughter Ummi Kulthum to him. In the matter of Hadrat `Uthman's election he voted in his favour as has been mentioned before. Hadrat `Ali (R.A.) was one of the very important members of *Shura* (Advisory Council) during the time of the first three *Khalifah*s. He was also the great jurist (*Mufti*) of Medina during the time of past *Khalifah*s. He was among the panel of six persons who had to select the *Khalifah* amongst themselves after Hadrat `Umar (R.A.). Hadrat `Uthman had great regard for him and consulted him in all the matters. His sons were the main guards at `Uthman's residence when the rebels laid siege to his house.

Thus we conclude that Hadrat `Ali (R.A.) gave his fullest possible support to all of his predecessors.

12
Hadrat `Ali's Caliphate

A. PROBLEMS FACED BY HADRAT `ALI AS A *KHALIFAH*

Hadrat `Ali (R.A.) as the fourth *Khalifah*

The insurgents' shameful act of assassination of the Khalifah could never have been imagined by Hadrat `Ali or any other eminent Companion at Medina. It came as a total surprise to Hadrat `Ali (R.A.) whose two sons, Hasan and Husain (R.A.) were guarding the gate of `Uthman's residence. The insurgents after climbing the back wall of the residence had assassinated the *Khalifah*. The assassination of Hadrat `Uthman was really due to creation of faction among the Muslim community which was the goal of `Abdullah bin Saba' and his followers (the insurgents), and they achieved it.

After the assassination of Hadrat `Uthman, the insurgents virtually controlled the capital, Medina for several days. The Muslims were frightened and sat behind closed doors. After the assassination of Hadrat `Uthman (R.A.) an unprecedented calamity had fallen on the Muslims and for three days, Medina was without any government.

Afterwards the insurgents approached Hadrat `Ali (R.A.) to be the *Khalifah*. Egyptians led by Ibn Saba and Ghafqi were the main group of insurgents behind the proposal for the *Khilafat* of Hadrat `Ali (R.A.). Hadrat `Ali first declined to bear the responsibility of this great office but the insurgents pressed him to accept it. As a matter of fact Hadrat `Ali wanted to approach Hadrat Talha and Hadrat Zubair (R.A.) who were included in the panel of the six persons appointed by Hadrat `Umar (R.A.) to select a *Khalifah*. He wanted to take pledge of loyalty (*Bai`at*) at the hands of any of these two gentlemen. But at the end, pressed by the threats of the regicides he decided to put the matter before the Muslim public in the Mosque of the Holy Prophet (*Sallallahu `alayhi wa Sallam*). Most of the Companions in Medina considered him to be the fittest person for *Khilafat* after Hadrat `Uthman (R.A.). He then agreed to take the responsibility and gave his consent.

On the 21st Dhul-Hijjah 35 A.H., the pledge of loyalty took place at the hands of Hadrat `Ali (R.A.). At first, the leading insurgents took the pledge of loyalty on his hands, followed by the general public, at Medina. Hadrat Talha and Zubair (R.A.) did not want to take a pledge (*Bai`at*) until the case of Hadrat `Uthman's assassination was decided. Before that Hadrat `Ali had offered the office of *Khilafat* to both of them but they had declined. However under the threats of insurgents they took the pledge of loyalty at Hadrat `Ali's hands, on the condition: "You (i.e. `Ali) have to decide matters according to the Holy Qur'an and Sunnah (ways of the Holy Prophet) and would punish the guilty according to Islamic Law." Hadrat `Ali (R.A.) agreed to their conditions. Hadrat Sa`d bin Waqqas said that he would take pledge when all the Muslims had done so. The following Companions did not take pledge at the hands of Hadrat `Ali (R.A.): Muhammad bin Muslimah, Usamah bin Zaid, Hassan bin Thabit. Ka`b bin Malik, Abu Sa`id Khudri, Nu`man bin Bashir, Zaid bin Thabit, Mughirah bin Shu`bah and `Abdullah bin Salam. Most of the members of Banu Umayyah (`Uthman's family) also did not take pledge of loyalty at

Hadrat 'Ali's hands. Some of such persons who did not take *Bai'at* went to Syria.

However the majority of the Muslims in Medina took pledge at the hands of Hadrat 'Ali. According to *Ahli Sunnah wal Jama'ah*, Hadrat 'Ali was the most suitable and the fittest person for *Khilafat* after Hadrat 'Uthman (R.A.). If some of the Companions did not take pledge on his hands, because of the political situation of that time, it did not mean that his *Khilafat* was not accepted by the Muslim majority. Besides Hadrat 'Ali (R.A.), nobody including Hadrat Mu'awiyah (R.A.) claimed to be the *Khalifah* at that time. The difference between them was the question of punishment to the assassins, which took the shape of various battles. As it would be seen afterwards Hadrat Amir Mu'awiyah (R.A.) decided his *Khilafat* only after the death of Hadrat 'Ali (R.A.). Hadrat 'Ali was declared to be the *Khalifah* not only by the insurgents but by the Muslim public as well including the leading Ansar (Helpers) and Muhajirin (Emigrants). This could also be noticed with the fact that in the first battle which took place between Hadrat 'Ali and Hadrat 'A'isha (and her group) about 800 of those Companions who had participated in the Treaty of Hudaibiyah were with Hadrat 'Ali besides other Companions. As a matter of fact Hadrat 'Ali was the most popular figure at that time and was the most appropriate person to be the fourth caliph.

Disobedience of 'Abdullah bin Saba and other Sabaites

On his third day as the *Khalifah*, Hadrat 'Ali asked all the Sabaites (insurgents) to return to their places. Some of them started to go back but a party headed by 'Abdullah bin Saba did not obey the *Khalifah* pretending all the while to be his friends. In the history of Islam this was the first incident of disobedience of a *Khalifah*. Their aim was to be with him in order to create mischief as it would be observed later.

`Ali's Caliphate

Hadrat `Ali (R.A.) faced a very difficult situation. His three main problems were:

i. To establish peace in the State and to set right the deteriorating political situation.

ii. To take action against the assassins of Hadrat `Uthman (R.A.) who had gone underground after he took the office. Actually some of them were among the persons who requested Hadrat `Ali (R.A.) to take office of the *Khilafat*, but neither he nor any other Muslim at that time knew the real assassins. It was the hardest job at that time to find out the real assassins because the persons who recognised them had already left Medina, and those among the Sabaites, who were present there did not tell Hadrat `Ali the truth. All of the Sabaites told `Ali (R.A.) that they did not want to assassinate Hadrat `Uthman, that was done only by some of the wicked persons whom they did not recognise. Some time, therefore, was required to investigate the matter and that was possible only after peaceful atmosphere was restored in the state which, unfortunately, never occurred during the caliphate of Hadrat `Ali as the situation continued to worsen.

iii. The third problem was the attitude to be adopted towards those Companions (R.A.) who would not pledge loyalty at the hands of Hadrat `Ali unless he either handed over the assassins to them or punish them according to Islamic Law. Though we cannot criticise the sincerity of their intention but in fairness to all, it has to be said that it was rather an impossible job for `Ali (R.A.) to fulfil their demands immediately in that situation.

Hadrat `Ali (R.A.) was a very straight-forward man who considered the *Khilafat* (Caliphate) as a great trust. His aim was to establish peace in the State which should be the first aim of every good ruler in such a place where certain elements try to destroy the order. According to leading Islamic jurists it is quite right for a Muslim ruler to delay the cases of murder etc. in order to establish peace in an Islamic State (as mentioned by Qadi Abu Bakr Ibn al-A`rabi in his book *Ahkam-ul-Qur'an*). Hadrat `Ali (R.A.) was quite right in his decision to tackle the assassins on restoration of normality. The majority of the Muslims, specially *Ahli Sunnah wal-Jama`ah* had agreed with him on this point.

The events which took place during the caliphate of Hadrat `Ali in the form of various battles will be discussed in the light of the above facts.

Hadrat `Ali (R.A.) seeks to ascertain the names of Hadrat `Uthman's assassins

After assuming office, Hadrat `Ali (R.A.) tried to find out the assassins of Hadrat `Uthman (R.A.). He called Marwan bin al-Hakam, the chief secretary of Hadrat `Uthman, who was present, in the house at the time of assassination, but he had already left for Damascus along with a number of Banu Umayyads.

The only other witness was Hadrat Nailah, wife of Hadrat `Uthman (R.A.). But she was a housewife who used to live under *Hijab* (*pardah*) in accordance with Islamic custom and as such she could not tell the names of the persons present at that time except the features of some of them. She could only name Muhammad bin Abi Bakr who had entered the house but as stated before he had left the house before Hadrat `Uthman assassination. Moreover Muhammad bin Abi Bakr took an oath (in accordance to Islamic Law) that he was not an assassin and he had left the house as soon as Hadrat `Uthman (R.A.) recognised him and said, "O my dear nephew, if your father (Abu Bakr) were alive you would have not committed this." Hadrat Nailah gave her evidence in favour of Muhammad bin Abi Bakr and had confirmed that he was not one of the assassins. In spite of his efforts Hadrat `Ali could not locate the assassins.

Hadrat `Ali (R.A.) dismisses the governors

In the opinion of Hadrat `Ali (R.A.) the governors appointed by Hadrat `Uthman (R.A.) were basically responsible for all the events. They did not pay much attention to check the subversive activities of the insurgents. So he dismissed all the governors appointed by Hadrat `Uthman (R.A.). Some of the Companions did not agree with Hadrat `Ali (R.A.) on this. Among such persons were Hadrat Mughirah bin Shu`bah and Hadrat Ibn `Abbas (R.A.). They advised Hadrat `Ali not to take such a hasty action. According to them it was not wise to dismiss them unless they pledged loyalty to Hadrat `Ali, because `Uthman's assassination could be an easy excuse for them to refuse the pledge of loyalty to Hadrat `Ali. Hadrat `Ali did not listen to their advice because he believed that expediency should not be the guiding factor. Hadrat Mughirah bin Shu`bah (R.A.) was totally against `Ali's action. He left Medina and went to Mecca.

He appointed Hadrat `Abdullah bin `Abbas as the governor of Yemen; `Uthman bin Hanif as the governor of Basrah; `Ammarah bin Hissan of Kufa, and Qais as the governor of Egypt. Hadrat Sahl bin Hanif was asked to take charge of governorship of Syria from Hadrat Amir Mu`awiyah (R.A.).

When the governors went to take charge they were faced with difficulties. Egypt was one of the provinces in favour of `Ali (R.A.) but when the new governor, Qais reached there the public was divided in three groups. Some of them accepted him but others demanded that the assassins must be punished first. There was a third group, belonging to Sabaites and the insurgents, who demanded that the assassins must not be punished in any case. The same difficulty was faced by the newly appointed governor of Basrah. A group of people was in favour of the insurgents while the other was against them. While the governor of Kufa was on his way a spokesman of Kufis came and asked him to return to Medina because they did not want to change their governor Hadrat Musa Ash'ari (R.A.) in any case. So Hadrat 'Ammarah bin Hissan (R.A.), the governor designate, returned to Medina. The new governor of Yemen, Hadrat 'Abdullah bin 'Abbas did not face any difficulty because Ya'la, the old governor had already left Kufa for Mecca before Hadrat Ibn 'Abbas reached there. When Hadrat Sahl bin Hanif, the governor designate of Syria, reached Tabuk (the out-post of Syria), Amir Mu'awiyah's cavalry men stopped him from proceeding any further and asked him to go back to Medina. Thus Kufa and Syria were the two provinces which had openly flouted Hadrat 'Ali's authority.

Hadrat 'Ali sent his special messengers to Kufa and Syria. The governor of Kufa, Hadrat Abu Musa Ash'ari (R.A.) sent a satisfactory reply and assured Hadrat 'Ali of his loyalty to him. Not only this he also wrote to him that he had already taken pledge of loyalty for him from the people of Kufa.

The case of Hadrat Mu'awiyah (R.A.) was entirely different.

Hadrat Mu'awiyah's demand for assassins

After the assassination of Hadrat 'Uthman (R.A.) his family except his wife Nailah, reached Damascus and told Amir Mu'awiyah (R.A.) the details. They also carried with them the blood stained shirt of Hadrat 'Uthman (R.A.) and the chopped off fingers of his wife Hadrat Nailah. Amir Mu'awiyah, a kinsman of Hadrat 'Uthman (R.A.) was shocked on hearing the news, and when it was made public, all the Muslims of Syria were greatly perturbed. Hadrat Amir Mu'awiyah (R.A.) was a great statesman and was in Syria for about 20 years. He hung the blood stained shirt and the chopped off fingers of Hadrat `Uthman's wife on the *Mimbar* (pulpit) of the Jami` Mosque of Damascus because of which the Syrian Muslims got inflamed. This was the situation of Syria when Sahl bin Hanif, the governor designate of Syria was forced to return to Medina from Tabuk.

On receiving the special messenger from Hadrat `Ali, Amir Mu`awiyah (R.A.) did not reply for about three months and detained the messenger. Then he sent his own messenger to Hadrat `Ali (R.A.) in Rabi`ul Awwal, 36 A.H. The messenger handed over the letter to Hadrat `Ali addressed as "From Mu`awiyah to `Ali". When the letter was opened it was a blank paper on which only "*Bismillahir-rahmanir Rahim*"(In the name of Allah, Most Gracious, Most Merciful) was written. Hadrat `Ali (R.A.) was amazed to see the letter, which was in fact, an insult to the office of the *Khalifah*. The messenger also told `Ali (R.A.) that 50,000 shaikhs of Syria were bemoaning the death of Hadrat `Uthman and were determined to fight until the assassins were handed over to them. Hadrat `Ali replied, "O Allah! You know it well that I am free from any charge of `Uthman's assassination. I swear by Allah that the assassins have escaped."

The Sabaites pretending to be friends of Hadrat `Ali, tried to create another disturbance by trying to kill the messenger, but Hadrat `Ali (R.A.) did not allow it. However exchange of hot words took place between them and the messenger. Amir Mu`awiyah's reply was a clear indication of his intention. The matter was not going to be settled without force. Therefore Hadrat `Ali decided to use force against Mu`awiyah (R.A.) and started preparations for it.

Hadrat Ali's elder son Imam Hasan (R.A.) was a man of rather mild temper. He requested his father to give up the *Khilafat* and not to think of fighting against Muslims (i.e., to start a civil war). But there was no other way and Hadrat `Ali (R.A.) had to handle the situation with an iron hand in order to keep the provinces under the centre as they were since the time of Hadrat Abu Bakr (R.A.).

This was the first time in the history of Islam when the Muslims were preparing to fight against each other. As a *Khalifah* Hadrat `Ali was quite right in his decision. Not to pledge loyalty was an open revolt against his authority and he had to deal boldly with any type of internal rebellion. Amir Mu`awiyah as a matter of fact, was overexcited on the tragic assassination. The family of `Uthman (R.A.) which had reached there after the assassination was also a cause of this attitude. Moreover some of the Sabaites, whose only aim was to divide the Muslim community, had reached Syria and incited the Muslims against Hadrat `Ali (R.A.). They were playing double role. On the one side a group of them was with Hadrat `Ali (R.A.) to stir him up against Mu`awiyah, while on the other side some of them went to Syria only to inflame the feelings of Muslims over there. Under such conditions Mu`awiyah had no alternative but to insist upon his demand for punishment of the assassins before pledging loyalty to Hadrat `Ali (R.A.).

Hadrat `A'isha's demand for chastisement of assassins

While Hadrat `Ali (R.A.) was preparing for war against Amir Mu`awiyah another difficulty arose. After the assassination of Hadrat `Uthman (R.A.) some members of his family went to Hadrat `A'isha (R.A.) who was in Mecca to perform the Hajj. They and a number of Medinites informed her about the tragedy while she was on her way from Mecca to Medina after the Hajj. Hearing the news of the assassination of Hadrat `Uthman she returned to Mecca and appealed to the people over there to avenge the death of Hadrat `Uthman (R.A.). Hundreds of people including the governor of Mecca came out at

`A'isha's call. The governor of Yemen, Ya`la bin Munabbah also joined her in Mecca. Among Banu Ummayyads who joined Hadrat `A'isha in Mecca were Sa`id bin `As, Walid bin `Uqbah and Marwan bin Hakam.

In the meantime Hadrat Talha and Zubair (R.A.) demanded Hadrat `Ali to punish the assassins. He told them, "Please wait. I will do my duty as soon as conditions allow me." Hadrat Talha and Zubair were not satisfied with Hadrat `Ali's reply and left Medina for Mecca to join Hadrat `A'isha (R.A.). They had not correctly assessed the delicate situation in Medina. The city was not free from the grip of Sabaites and there was a general feeling against Umayyads in the public. Hadrat `Ali (R.A.) was anxious to restore peace first so that the assassins could be punished.

In Mecca Hadrat `A'isha (R.A.) started to march to Medina at the head of about two thousand men with the object of dealing with the assassins. Hadrat `Abdullah bin Zubair was also there. They also asked him to join but he declined to do so and remained neutral.

When Hadrat `A'isha was about to march to Medina, proposals came to visit Basrah first to collect more supporters. She decided to go to Basrah.

Hadrat `A'isha goes to Basrah

While Hadrat `A'isha was on her way to Basrah more people joined her in the way. By the time she reached Basrah, there were three thousand men under her flag.

The governor of Basrah, `Uthman bin Hanif (appointed by Hadrat `Ali), sent some men to find out the object of her visit. She and other Muslims told them that they wanted to tell people of their duty towards the late *Khalifah* so that proper action would be taken to punish the assassins. The messenger of the governor asked Hadrat Talha and

Zubair for what reason they were breaking the *Bai`at* on the hands of Hadrat `Ali. They told them that the pledge (*Bai`at*) was taken from them at the point of sword, and that they would have kept the pledge if Hadrat `Ali had avenged `Uthman's assassination.

The governor of Basra decided not to allow them to enter the city till he got help from Hadrat `Ali. He called a public meeting and asked people to fight against them. In the meeting some people favoured the governor while some of them supported Hadrat `A'isha, Talha and Zubair. The supporters of Hadrat `Ali (R.A.) and the governor came out to fight.

Hadrat `A'isha takes over Basra

Hadrat `A'isha gave a stirring speech before the Muslims. It was so impressive that half of the supporters of the governor left him and joined Hadrat `A'isha. Seeing this she tried to settle the matter peacefully instead of fighting. But there were some agents of `Abdullah bin Saba (Sabaites) especially his famous disciple, Hakim bin Hublah, who did not allow any settlement. He attacked Hadrat `A'isha's army before the governor gave him permission to do so.

The fight took place but no result came out till the evening. In the meantime the governor got instructions from Hadrat `Ali to resist Hadrat `A'isha's army if they did not agree to pledge loyalty to him. Then a furious battle took place in which `Uthman bin Hanif, the governor, was defeated and captured. Hakim bin Hublah and some of his followers were killed, and Basra was occupied by Hadrat `A'isha and her supporters.

B. CIVIL WAR

March to Basrah

The capture of Basrah by Hadrat `A'isha (R.A.) made the situation very grave. The Islamic state was really on the verge of serious civil war. Hadrat `Ali (R.A.) never wanted to start war against the Muslims but the internal situation at that time compelled him to do so. War was unavoidable.

The *Khalifah*, therefore, postponed his march to Syria for the time being in order to set things right in Iraq. He decided to march on to Basrah. A number of Ansar and other Companions were not in favour of Hadrat `Ali (R.A.) leaving Medina, instead they asked him to send his army. When Hadrat `Ali (R.A.) was leaving Medina, `Abdullah bin Salam (R.A.) took hold of his camel and said, "O *Amirul-Mu'minin* (Leader of the Believers), don't leave Medina. If you leave it at this moment, you would never come back and the capital would be changed." But he decided to go ahead with his mission because of the seriousness of the situation.

Some of the Companions remained neutral and did not join Hadrat `Ali (R.A.) even though he asked them to do so. Among such persons were: `Abdullah bin `Umar, Muhammad bin Muslimah, Sa`d bin Waqqas and Usamah bin Zaid (R.A.).

Hadrat `Ali started for Basrah towards the end of Rabi`ul Awwal, 36 A.H. i.e., November 656 A.D. `Abdullah bin Saba and his followers were accompanying Hadrat `Ali.

Help from Basrah

Hadrat `Ali (R.A.) asked Abu Musa Ash`ari to send help but he got no response because Hadrat Abu Musa (R.A.) dreaded a civil war.

Therefore Hadrat `Ali (R.A.) sent his eldest son, Hasan (R.A.) to Kufa who addressed the people and pleaded for `Ali (R.A.). The people were stirred on the appeal and about nine thousand men marched on to join `Ali (R.A.).

`Ali (R.A.) seeks peace

Hadrat `Ali (R.A.) assured all the people accompanying him that he would try his best to avoid bloodshed and to set things right peacefully. On reaching Dhi Qar, a place near Basrah, Hadrat `Ali, with his characteristic aversion to bloodshed sent his cousin `Abdullah bin `Abbas and Qa`qa bin `Amr (R.A.) to negotiate peacefully with Hadrat `A'isha, Talha, and Zubair (R.A.) who were preparing to face Hadrat `Ali (R.A.) with a big army.

The messengers of Hadrat `Ali (R.A.) assured Hadrat `A'isha, Talha, and Zubair (R.A.) that Hadrat `Ali would avenge the assassins of Hadrat `Uthman (R.A.) as soon as peace was established in the state. Hearing this they were satisfied and there were hopes for a peaceful settlement.

But in the army of `Ali (R.A.) there were `Abdullah bin Saba and his henchmen to whom peace was fatal. At the possibility of peaceful settlement they were much disturbed. They met in a secret council and whispered to each other that `Ali (R.A.) was prepared to avenge the death of Hadrat `Uthman (R.A.). They were determined to make the peaceful settlement a total failure. They sent their agents to Basrah to incite the Muslim population by saying that if `Ali (R.A.) entered Basrah he would enslave all the inhabitants and would kill all the youths. The Basrites, therefore, must check and fight him back.

Hadrat `Ali (R.A.) hoping for a peaceful settlement, marched towards Basrah to talk personally with Hadrat Talha and Zubair (R.A.). The two armies were facing each other. Hadrat `Ali gave an address to

Basrites in which he said, "I am but your brother . . . I will avenge `Uthman's assassins." Hadrat Talha, Zubair and the Basrites were fully satisfied with what Hadrat `Ali (R.A.) told them. `Ali (R.A.) also returned to his camp very satisfied. He gave strict orders to his men not to fight in any case, and prayed all the night to Allah.

But Ibn Saba and his henchmen had planned otherwise. In the darkness of night they made a sudden attack on Hadrat `A'isha's army. Hadrat Talha and Zubair were startled by the sudden attack and said that `Ali (R.A.) could not desist from shedding Muslim blood and he has ordered a night attack. On the other hand Hadrat `Ali (R.A.) was shocked when he was told by Sabaites that Talha and Zubair had taken them by surprise. He also remarked in the same way that they did not stop from taking the blood of Muslims. According to Tabari the following Sabaites were the leaders behind this plan: Ashtar Nakh`i Ibn Sauda, Khalid bin Muljam, `Alba bin Haitham and Shuraib bin Aufa. Ibn Saba was the ring leader.

The Battle of Camel (Jamal)

Soon a full scale war started. Hundreds of Muslims fell on each side. Hadrat `Ali (R.A.) was greatly pained at the situation. He tried to stop the battle but the battle had already flared up.

In the dawn the troops of Hadrat `A'isha (R.A.) apprised her of the situation and suggested that she should mount on a camel in *Hijab* (*Pardah*) so that the situation might ease. But it worked the other way and the Basrites thought that Hadrat `A'isha came in the field to fight with them. During the fight Hadrat `Ali reminded Talha and Zubair (R.A.) the words of the Holy Prophet: "One day you (Talha and Zubair) will fight `Ali wrongly." They remembered the saying and left the battlefield but when Talha was leaving the field somebody rained arrows on him and he was killed.

When the fight did not come to an end Hadrat `Ali (R.A.) ordered one of his men to cut the hind legs of the camel on which Hadrat `A'isha was mounting in a *howdah*. The order of Hadrat `Ali was carried out and the camel fell on its forelegs. Hadrat `A'isha was taken out of the *howdah* with due respect. The battle came to an end in favour of Hadrat `Ali (R.A.). Hadrat `A'isha (R.A.) was sent with due respect to Medina escorted by her own brother, Muhammad bin Abi Bakr. In this battle about ten thousand Muslims on both sides lost their lives. Hadrat `Ali (R.A.) felt deeply moved because of the loss of Muslim blood. Hadrat Zubair who had already left the field after remembering the Holy Prophet's saying was going to Mecca. He stopped in a valley to perform his *Salat*, but was slain by a man, named `Amr bin Jarmoz while he was busy in his *Salat*. When Hadrat `Ali came to know, he rebuked the murderer by saying, "I have seen him fight for the Prophet of Allah several times. I give the murderer the news of hell-fire."

After the battle he took pledge of loyalty from the people of Basrah and appointed Hadrat `Abdullah bin `Abbas as the governor of Basrah. He gave general amnesty to all those who fought against him including Marwan bin Hakam and other persons of Banu Umayyah's family. The address which Hadrat `Ali (R.A.) gave at Jami` Mosque of Basrah before the *Bai`at* (pledge of loyalty) moved the Muslims, and they were convinced that `Ali (R.A.) was a just *Khalifah*.

Change of capital

Hadrat `Ali (R.A.) was very much grieved on seeing the disrespect of the *Haram* (Forbidden Place) of Medina when the insurgents laid siege to the late *Khalifah*'s house and then assassinated him. He wanted to change the capital to save Medina from future political disturbance. After staying for a few days at Basrah, Hadrat `Ali (R.A.) went to

Kufa. There he was given a warm welcome. He got more supporters at Kufa and thought it to be a more suitable place as the capital of his *Khilafat*. Therefore in Rajab 36 A.H., he decided to transfer the capital from Medina to Kufa.

Hadrat `Ali's final invitation to Hadrat Mu`awiyah

Hadrat `Ali (R.A.) now turned his attention towards Hadrat Mu`awiyah (R.A.). He was then ruling over the whole Islamic State with the exception of Syria. The peace-minded Hadrat `Ali (R.A.) wanted a peaceful settlement. He, therefore, wrote a letter to Hadrat Mu`awiyah (R.A.) asking him to take pledge of loyalty at his hand in the interest of Islam and the unity of the Muslims. But Hadrat Mu`awiyah again demanded of him to avenge Hadrat `Uthman's assassins first.

The show of Hadrat `Uthman's blood-stained shirt and the chopped-off fingers of his wife, Hadrat Nailah, was still going on in the Jami` Masjid of Damascus. The powerful Syrians had rallied round Hadrat Mu`awiyah. On the other hand Hadrat `Ali (R.A.) was still unable to overcome the insurgents. When Hadrat Amir Mu`awiyah's messenger came to Hadrat `Ali to put the demand to hand over the assassins, 10,000 men of Hadrat `Ali's army said with one voice, "All of us are the assassins of `Uthman (R.A.)." Hadrat `Ali (R.A.) then said to the messenger, Hadrat Muslimah, "You can see for yourself the situation. I am still unable to find out the real assassins." But Hadrat Mu`awiyah was determined not to give up his demand. Hadrat `Ali (R.A.), finding no other way, was compelled to declare war against Hadrat Mu`awiyah (R.A.).

The Battle of Siffin

The above situation forced Hadrat `Ali (R.A.) to march out against Syria. In the beginning there was not much response for Hadrat `Ali's call. But when Hadrat `Ali explained the position to the Muslims, a large army gathered around Hadrat `Ali and 50,000 Muslims came out under his banner to fight the Syrians. When Mu`awiyah (R.A.) came to know about Hadrat `Ali's advance, he too proceeded with a vast army and occupied a better position in the field. Hadrat `Ali (R.A.) encamped at Siffin, and Amir Mu`awiyah on the other side of Siffin.

Hadrat `Ali's intention was not to shed Muslim blood in vain. He therefore again tried and sent a deputation of three men on a peace mission to Amir Mu`awiyah (R.A.). Amir Mu`awiyah (R.A.) again demanded that the assassins of Hadrat `Uthman must be slain before any compromise can be reached and that he was demanding this as a *Wali* (next of kin of a murdered person) of Hadrat `Uthman. The demand was again refused by Hadrat `Ali (R.A.) on the ground that he was not able to find the real assassins and it would need some time, and that the pledge of loyalty must be taken without any condition.

In the month of Dhul Hijjah 36 A.H., Hadrat `Ali (R.A.) ordered his troops to take positions. But there seemed unwillingness to fight on both the sides. Muslims were facing Muslims. However in the beginning fighting began with single combats followed by light encounters of single battalions. Thus the whole month of Dhul Hijjah ended without any big fight. When the moon of Muharram appeared Hadrat `Ali and Mu`awiyah made a truce for one month. During this time he again got an opportunity for renewed peace talks. Hadrat `Ali (R.A.) sent another mission led by `Adi bin Hatim Tai to Amir Mu`awiyah (R.A.). But this time Amir Mu`awiyah (R.A.) took it as a threat and refused to recognize Hadrat `Ali (R.A.) as the *Khalifah* unless he avenged Hadrat `Uthman's assassination. In this way the last attempt proved to be fruitless.

`Ali's Caliphate

On the evening of the last day of Muharram 37 A.H., Hadrat `Ali (R.A.) gave orders to his army to attack the Syrian forces because they had been given enough time to think. The war started the following morning. Hadrat `Ali (R.A.) gave strict orders that no person should be killed if he left the field or ran away. Women and old people would be secure. Hadrat Amir Mu`awiyah (R.A.) also gave the same order to his army.

The war started on Tuesday 1 Safar, 37 A.H. On the first day a battalion of Hadrat `Ali's army, led by Ushtar fought with the Syrians led by Habib bin Muslimah. On the second day another battalion led by Hashim bin `Utbah from Hadrat `Ali's side fought with the Syrians led by Abul A`war Salama. On the third day the battalion from Hadrat `Ali side was led by Hadrat `Ammar bin Yasir and the Syrians were led by `Amr bin `As (R.A.). During the battle Hadrat `Ammar bin Yasir (R.A.) was martyred but no result came out. The martyrdom of Hadrat `Ammar bin Yasir, however, proved that Hadrat `Ali (R.A.) was right because of the Hadith mentioned in Bukhari, Muslim, Tirmidhi and other authentic books of Hadith. According to this Hadith the Holy Prophet (*Sallallahu `alayhi wa Sallam*) said, "`Ammar bin Yasir would be killed by a group of rebels." Since Hadrat `Ammar (R.A.) was fighting in favour of Hadrat `Ali, and was killed by the army of Hadrat Amir Mu`awiyah (R.A.) Hadrat `Ali (R.A.) was in the right and his opponents were the rebels.

For seven days the battle continued in this way. A new battalion used to fight from each side under a new commander. On the eighth day the whole army of Hadrat `Ali (R.A.) clashed with that of Amir Mu`awiyah (R.A.). A fierce battle was fought but with no end in sight. According to most historians, Hadrat `Ammar bin Yasir was martyred on that day. However no result came out till the evening. The death of Hadrat `Ammar bin Yasir was a shock to Hadrat `Ali (R.A.). The battle went on the whole night. At one time Hadrat `Ali reached the tent of

Hadrat Mu'awiyah and challenged him to fight personally with him instead of shedding Muslim blood, the winner would be the *Khalifah*. But Hadrat Mu'awiyah (R.A.) did not accept the challenge because Hadrat 'Ali was a noted warrior of Arabia.

On the second day of the battle Amir Mu'awiyah (R.A.) was about to lose the battle. But Amir Mu'awiyah was a shrewd person and had been the governor of Syria from Hadrat 'Umar's time. He had with him Hadrat 'Amr bin 'As (R.A.), the conqueror of Egypt and a recognised statesman of Arabia. Seeing the impending defeat he consulted Hadrat 'Amr bin 'As (R.A.) who advised Amir Mu'awiyah to give orders to the troops of the front ranks to fasten the Holy Qur'an to their lances as a sign that war would cease and that the decision would be referred to the Holy Book.

Seeing copies of the Holy Qur'an on lances, Hadrat 'Ali (R.A.) recognised it as a clever move of the enemy but a good many men of his army did not share his view and stopped fighting. Being helpless he ordered his troops to stop fighting.

Arbitration

Hadrat 'Ali (R.A.) sent his envoy to Hadrat Mu'awiyah (R.A.) to find out what he meant by making the Holy Qur'an a judge. Hadrat Amir Mu'awiyah told him that he wanted an arbitration through judges, one from his side and the other from Hadrat 'Ali's side, and that both the parties should abide by the decision of the judges. Hadrat 'Ali accepted it. He tried to make Hadrat 'Abdullah bin 'Abbas as the arbitrator from his side, but some of his followers objected to it on the ground that he was related to Hadrat 'Ali. They proposed the name of Hadrat Musa Ash'ari (R.A.). Hadrat 'Ali accepted their proposal and he was appointed as the arbitrator of 'Ali's (R.A.) side. Hadrat Mu'awiyah appointed 'Amr bin 'As (R.A.) as the arbitrator from his side, and none of his followers questioned his choice although he was related to Amir Mu`awiyah. This shows that the followers of Hadrat Mu`awiyah were more united than the followers of Hadrat `Ali. There were many Sabaites in Hadrat `Ali's camp and they were the real cause of such differences. Whenever they saw the Muslims uniting they tried to create confusion with the aim of disuniting them.

In case the two arbitrators could not come to an agreement, the decision was to lie with eight hundred men (400 from Hadrat `Ali's camp and 400 from Hadrat Mu`awiyah camp) and it would be settled by the majority. A place named Dumatul-Jandal, in between Syria and Iraq, was proposed for the talks. Both the judges with 800 men would go there to finalise their award by the month of Ramadan, and to make it public. A temporary agreement was signed on 13th Safar, 37 A.H. between Hadrat `Ali and Hadrat Mu`awiyah. The two armies then left for their homes leaving about 90,000 men dead in the field of Siffin, which number exceeded the total Muslim casualties in all the Islamic battles against the non-Muslims by the time.

Khawarij or **Dissenters**

Hadrat `Ali (R.A.) who was almost winning the battle against Amir Mu`awiyah (R.A.) marched back from Siffin with a sense of loss. There was a tremendous loss of Muslim lives in Siffin. Never before in the history of Islam had the loss of Muslim blood been so heavy. Hadrat `Ali after all wanted a peaceful solution, although the price was heavy.

When Hadrat `Ali announced the agreement before his troops, formed of various tribes, two brothers of the tribe of `Anza stood up and opposed the appointment of arbitrator (*Hakam* or Judge) between the two parties, for Allah's commandments were with them in the form of the Holy Qur'an which is the best *Hakam*. Others also followed this example and a good many people were against the arbitration. According to them the arbitration was against the spirit of Islam. Some of these men requested Hadrat `Ali to throw away the agreement but he said, "I did not want any agreement at that stage but you forced me to do so. When I gave my word of honour, you are forcing me to give them up. I would never do it." The followers of Hadrat `Ali split into two groups. One group stood by the agreement while for the other the arbitration was un-Islamic.

The second group, which was opposing arbitration, was known as Kharijites (*Khawarij* in Arabic). By the time Hadrat `Ali returned to Kufa, their number reached 12,000. They did not stay with other Muslims in Kufa; instead, they encamped at Harorah and appointed Sheith bin Rabi`i as their commander-in-chief, and `Abdullah bin Kawa as their Imam to lead *Salat*s. They announced their policy which was as follows:

> "The *Bai`at* (Pledge of Loyalty) is only for Allah, and He alone is to be obeyed. To spread good and forbid evil according to the Holy Qur'an and the *Sunnah* is our foremost duty. There exists neither a *Khalifah* nor an *Amir*. Both `Ali and Mu`awiyah are in error. Mu`awiyah in error because he did not accept `Ali while `Ali is in error because he agreed on arbitration. After gaining power, we will set up a social order based on Allah's Book (i.e. the Holy Qur'an)."

`Ali (R.A.) sends his emissary to *Khawarij*

After returning to Kufa, Hadrat `Ali sent `Abdullah bin `Abbas to remove the misunderstanding of the *Khawarij* (Dissenters). Instead of returning to the right belief, they started a lengthy argument with him. Seeing this Hadrat `Ali himself went to them. He gave them all the assurances that the arbitration would only be accepted if it was based upon the Holy Qur'an and the *Sunnah*. He was successful in his efforts after a great difficulty, and the *Khawarij* joined him again temporarily.

Verdict of the Arbitrators

The two arbitrators thought over the matter for six months then met at the frontier town of Dumatul-Jandal in Sha`ban, 37 A.H. (January 658 A.D.). Each of them was having four hundred men with him. The commander of men from Hadrat `Ali's side was Shuraih bin Hani, and the Imam Hadrat `Abdullah bin `Abbas. The four hundred men from Mu`awiyah's camp were under Surjil bin Samah. Besides these some neutral Companions like `Abdullah bin `Umar, `Abdullah bin Zubair, and Sa`d bin Waqqas were also present there.

Hadrat `Amr bin `As, the judge appointed by Hadrat Mu`awiyah, was a famous statesman and diplomat of Arabia. On the other hand Abu Musa Ash`ari, the judge from Hadrat `Ali's side, was a simple Muslim, unacquainted with diplomatic tactics. In the beginning a discussion between the two judges took place. A scribe was ordered to write down the points of agreement during the discussion. They reached on the following agreement after a long discussion:

"`Ali and Mu`awiyah both withdraw their right for the *Khilafat*. The Muslims should appoint a third person as their *Khalifah*."

According to some historians the discussion was not recorded and the agreement was reached verbally. However they could not reach an agreement, on the choice of the most suitable person to be approved as the *Khalifah* in place of Hadrat `Ali or Hadrat Mu`awiyah.

After the agreement Hadrat `Amr bin `As asked Hadrat Abu Musa Ash`ari to make it public by announcing it in the mosque before the Muslims. Hadrat Abu Musa (R.A.) announced, "We have agreed that neither `Ali nor Mu`awiyah would be considered as the *Khalifah*. You may elect any other man you think fit." After this Hadrat `Amr bin `As (R.A.) stood up and said, "I do not consider `Ali fit for the *Khilafat*, but in my opinion Mu`awiyah is fit for it." The statement of Hadrat `Amr not only showed the split of opinion between the arbitrators but also meant one sided decision according to which Hadrat `Ali (R.A.) was supposed to lose his power but not Amir Mu`awiyah (R.A.).

Hearing the statement of `Amr ibn `As (R.A.) there was a big uproar. The result of the arbitration was a mere confusion. In this way the arbitration proved to be futile and the hopes of peace were gone. Both the parties left the place in great disgust. The acceptance of such arbitration, really proved to be disastrous to `Ali. Hadrat `Ali lost the case before it opened.

When `Ali (R.A.) heard the result of the arbitration he said, "The judgement is not based upon the Holy Qur'an and the *Sunnah* which was the condition for arbitration. Therefore it cannot be accepted." He then delivered a lecture in the Jami` *Masjid* of Kufa and asked the Muslims to prepare to attack Syria.

Split in Muslim community

As soon as the *Khawarij* knew the result of arbitration they again separated and this time rose in an open revolt. A new group was thus created in the history of Islam which proved to be more dangerous than any other group existing before then.

As it has been discussed in connection with the assassination of Hadrat `Uthman (R.A.), the Muslim community was divided into four main groups *viz.*, `Uthmanis, Shi`an-i-`Ali, Marhabah and Ahl Sunnah wal Jama`ah. Marhabis were absorbed in other groups. The remaining three groups were still existing. Now the fourth group of Kharijites was formed. Before proceeding further let us see the main beliefs of these groups:

i. *'Uthmanis:*

They were now confined to Syria under the banner of Amir Mu'awiyah (R.A.). They demanded that until the assassins of Hadrat 'Uthman were punished or handed over to them, they would not accept the *Khilafat* of Hadrat 'Ali. But after the so called judgment of the arbitrators, they totally rejected the *Khilafat* of Hadrat 'Ali and took *Bai'at* (Pledge of Loyalty) at the hand of Amir Mu'awiyah after declaring him as the *Khalifah*. It would be discussed in more detail later on.

ii. *Shi'an-i-'Ali (or Shias)*:

They called themselves the friends of 'Ali (R.A.) in the beginning but later on they developed their own beliefs and considered Hadrat 'Ali as *Wasi* i.e., Administrator of the Holy Prophet (*Sallallahu 'alayhi wa Sallam*), and the only fit person for the *Khilafat*. They not only criticised and condemned Amir Mu'awiyah (R.A.) but also 'Umar, Abu Bakr, and 'Uthman (R.A.) and discarded the authority of the first three *Khalifah*s. However they did not criticise the first two *Khalifah*s openly during the time of Hadrat 'Ali (R.A.). As years passed this group became an exponent of a separate school of thought in Islamic Law and Jurisprudence and they wrote their own books of Hadith, history of Islam and commentaries of the Holy Qur'an based upon their beliefs. They disagreed with most of the works produced by Sunni scholars.

iii. *Ahl Sunnah wal-Jama'ah*:

The majority of the Companions, and Muslims at the time were not only in favour of Hadrat 'Ali but all the preceding *Khalifah*s i.e. Abu Bakr, 'Umar and 'Uthman (R.A.). They believed that the "Right Path" was to follow the *Sunnah* of the Holy Prophet (*Sallallahu 'alayhi wa*

THE PIOUS CALIPHS

Sallam) and the traditions of his pious Jama'ah (i.e., all the Companions), especially the first four *Khalifah*s who set examples to solve various problems according to the Holy Qur'an and the *Sunnah*. This group was in great majority not only at that time but in all the periods of Islamic history.

They fully supported Hadrat `Ali (R.A.) during his *Khilafat*. According to them Amir Mu`awiyah (R.A.) was not right in not accepting Hadrat `Ali's authority. But they considered that mistake based upon *Ijtihad*. After all, he was a pious Companion and the sincerity of a Companion must not be questioned. Hadrat Shah Waliullah, in his famous book, *Izalat-ul-Khafa* writes, "Amir Mu`awiyah (R.A.) was an excellent Companion of the Holy Prophet (*Sallallahu `alayhi wa Sallam*). Do not criticise or condemn him otherwise you would be committing a *Haram* (unlawful) act because in a Hadith the Holy Prophet (*Sallallahu `alayhi wa Sallam*) said: Do not criticise and condemn my Companions. I swear by Allah, Who holds my life, gold equal to mountain Uhud spent by you for the sake of Allah, cannot be equal even to the handful of grains spent by a Companion (Abu Da'ud)." According to a number of *Ahadith*, it is forbidden for a Muslim to criticise a Companion. In a number of *Ahadith* the virtues of Hadrat Mu`awiyah (R.A.) have been mentioned.

Once the Holy Prophet (*Sallallahu `alayhi wa Sallam*) prayed for Amir Mu`awiyah as follows, "O Allah, make him a Muslim who would be on Your Guidance and such a Muslim who may guide others." Ibn Sa`d says that the Holy Prophet (*Sallallahu `alayhi wa Sallam*) prayed for Amir Mu`awiyah as follows, "O Allah, give him the knowledge of the Book (i.e., the Holy Qur'an) and make him ruler (king) of the countries, and save him from the punishment (of the Hereafter)." Moreover Amir Mu`awiyah (R.A.) was one of the scribes of the Revelation (i.e., the Holy Qur'an) during the time of the Holy Prophet. It is necessary, therefore, that we must not question his sincerity. Due to political conditions at that time, he was strict in his demand of chastisement of the assassins of Hadrat `Uthman (R.A.). Most of the historians agree on this point that he did not declare himself a *Khalifah* during the life of Hadrat `Ali although people took *Bai`at* on his hand.

iv. The *Khawarij*:

The *Khawarij* were more a political group than theological. They accepted the authority of Hadrat Abu Bakr and `Umar (R.A.) but denounced Hadrat `Uthman, `Ali, and Mu`awiyah (R.A.). They said that the *Hakam* (Arbitrator or Judge for the dispute between Hadrat `Ali and Mu`awiyah) was against the principles of Islam. Only Allah had to be obeyed through the Holy Qur'an and not the *Hakam*. They also formulated a number of other beliefs as well. In the later period of Islamic history this group became almost extinct.

The Kharijite trouble

The *Khawarij* set up their centre at Nahrwan and began to preach their cult. Many people gathered around them and they gained sufficient strength. They were very harsh to those who differed from them and regarded such Muslims as rebels against Islam and murdered them. Loyalty to the *Khalifah* was a great crime in their eyes and they called it "the cult of personality".

The Kharijites seemed to be very pious as far as their appearance was concerned. They used to offer long *Salats*, wore simple dress and were honest in their dealings. But they were misguided in beliefs and killed all those who said that they were the followers of the *Khalifah*.

After the failure of arbitration Hadrat `Ali (R.A.) wanted to march to Syria but the Kharijite movement diverted his attention. It was a great danger not only to the Muslim unity but to the Islamic beliefs and practices as a whole. It was an urgent need to wipe out such a movement in its early stage. Therefore he set out for Nahrwan, the centre of *Khawarij* instead of Syria.

Reaching there Hadrat `Ali tried to negotiate with them peacefully. He sent some prominent Companions to persuade Khariji leaders but they did not listen to them. Then Hadrat `Ali asked them to hand over such people who have murdered innocent Muslims. He told them that he would leave the rest if they handed over the murderers. To this he replied to the *Khalifah*, "All of us are murderers and we want to murder all of your followers. We would never stop from this."

The stage reached when there was no other way than to fight with them. Before declaring war against them Hadrat `Ali declared that those who would be loyal to him or those who left Nahrwan and did not fight would be given amnesty. On his appeal 3,000 Kharijites repented and again took *Bai`at* at his hands. The rest did not move from their position.

The battle began. A fierce fight took place. Kharijites fought desperately but were defeated. Most of their leaders were slain. After the battle Hadrat `Ali searched the slain body of the man about whom the Holy Prophet had prophesied, and had given some of the signs which were really the forecast of Kharijite trouble. Hadrat `Ali (R.A.) found the body with all the signs told by the Holy Prophet (*Sallallahu `alayhi wa Sallam*) and remarked, "The Holy Prophet was very true in his prophecy."

Unwillingness to march to Syria

After the battle at Nahrwan Hadrat `Ali (R.A.) wanted to march on to Syria but his men were in no mood for that. They asked for some rest when he was encamping at Nakhila, some miles away from the capital. Hadrat `Ali (R.A.) allowed them to take some rest over there but they started to slip away to their homes and only a few of them were left with him. Seeing the situation Hadrat `Ali was also forced to return to Kufa.

After some time Hadrat `Ali again asked the Kufis to march on to Syria. He gave a stirring address in the Jami` *Masjid* of the capital but the leaders of Kufa did not show any inclination. Despite many efforts Hadrat `Ali was not successful in raising another army against the Syrians.

Loss of Egypt

Hadrat `Ali (R.A.) appointed Qais bin Sa`d (R.A.) as the governor of Egypt. He took pledge of loyalty from the Egyptians for Hadrat `Ali (R.A.). The inhabitants of the town of Khartaba were not loyal to Hadrat `Ali. He left them alone on the condition of a peaceful conduct. Some friends of Hadrat `Ali, who were having an eye on the governorship of Egypt, started to doubt loyalty of Qais to Hadrat `Ali. They told Hadrat `Ali that Qais was more sympathetic to Hadrat Mu`awiyah and must be sacked.

When Hadrat Mu`awiyah noticed that the position of Qais was doubtful in the eyes of Hadrat `Ali, he declared him as his man. Hearing this Hadrat `Ali (R.A.) dismissed him and appointed Muhammad bin Abi Bakr as the governor of Egypt. Muhammad bin Abi Bakr was a young man and was not able to control the Egyptians in a tactful way. He forced the people of Khartaba to pledge loyalty for Hadrat `Ali and remained busy with them for a long time. In the meantime the battle of Siffin took place but he was so busy with the internal affairs of Egypt that he could not send any army to help Hadrat `Ali (R.A.).

After the battle of Siffin Hadrat `Ali appointed Malik bin Ushtar as the governor of Egypt. Ibn Ushtar was a strong man, but he could not join his duty and passed away. Muhammad bin Abi Bakr, therefore, continued as the governor of Egypt.

After the award of the arbitration, the Syrians declared Hadrat Mu`awiyah as their *Khalifah* and took *Bai`at* on his hands. According to a number of historians, Amir Mu`awiyah did not declare himself as the *Khalifah* during the life of Hadrat `Ali (R.A.). However he tried to extend his control over the Islamic state after the award. The first step was to send his army under the command of Hadrat `Amr ibn `As to attack Egypt. Muhammad bin Abi Bakr, the governor of Egypt wrote to Hadrat `Ali for help. But before he got any help `Amr ibn `As (R.A.) reached Egypt with six thousand men. Ten thousand inhabitants of Khartaba also joined his army. They easily beat back two thousand men of Muhammad bin Abi Bakr. He himself took shelter in a house but was caught and slain. In 38 A.H. Hadrat Amir Mu`awiyah (R.A.) became the master of Egypt. He appointed Hadrat `Amr ibn `As as the governor.

Unrest in Basrah and Iran

Hadrat `Abdullah ibn `Abbas (R.A.) was the governor of Basrah controlling the whole of Persia and other parts of the Islamic State in the East. Basrites were pro-`Ali but there were `Uthmani (pro-Mu`awiyah) elements as well over there.

In 38 A.H. Hadrat `Abdullah ibn `Abbas went to Kufa to pay a visit to the *Khalifah*. `Abdullah ibn Hadrami, an `Uthmani (pro-Mu`awiyah) was in Basrah in those days. In the absence of Ibn `Abbas he saw his chance and incited the people to avenge the assassination of Hadrat `Uthman. He got support and was able to raise an army which invaded Basrah. The governor's deputy, Ziyad ibn Abi Sufyan, could not face him and fled. Hearing the uprising Hadrat `Ali sent Jariah ibn Qudamah who belonged to Bani Tamim tribe. He went to Basrah with fifty people and negotiated with Basrites, most of whom were from

'Ali's Caliphate

Bani Tamim tribe. He was successful in his mission and the rebellion was put down. Ibn Hadrami and seventy of his followers shut themselves in a house which was burnt by pro-'Ali Basrites.

When the people of Eastern Persia and Kirman heard the burning of Ibn Hadrami they refused to pay *Kharaj* revenue in protest. However their uprising was put down by police action.

After consulting with 'Abdullah ibn 'Abbas (R.A.), Hadrat 'Ali appointed Ziyad ibn Abi Sufyan as the governor of Basrah to control Persia and other Eastern parts of the State.

Pro-Muawiyan parties invade various parts

After the award, 'Uthmanis tried to create general unrest in the country. During the year 39 A.H. strong parties were set out from Syria. Hadrat 'Ali (R.A.) tried to stir his friends in Kufa but they would never come out at 'Ali's call. Neither they were prepared to fight the Syrians again nor they tried seriously to check the invading parties of 'Uthmanis.

One of such parties went to 'Ain al-Tamr under the command of Nu'man ibn Bashir but he was defeated by 'Ali's governor, Malik ibn Ka'b. Another party of six thousand men under Sufyan ibn 'Auf went to Ambar and Mada'in (Midian). They killed the officer in charge of Ambar. Hadrat 'Ali sent Sa'id ibn 'Auf with an army but they ran away. Another party of three thousand men under Dahak ibn Qais came as far east as the neighbourhood of Basrah. Hadrat 'Ali sent four thousand men under Hajar ibn 'Adi. A fight took place in which 19 Syrians ('Uthmanis) were killed. The rest of them ran away in the darkness of the night.

In the same year (i.e., 39 A.H.) Hadrat 'Ali sent his deputy Ibn 'Abbas to lead the Hajj. Amir Mu'awiyah also sent his deputy, Yazid ibn Sanjar to lead the Hajj. A tussle between the two men took place. At the end it was settled that a third person, Shaibah ibn `Uthman ibn Abi Talha, would lead the Hajj. In this way Hadrat `Ali lost this symbol of *Khilafat* as well.

Hadrat `Ali's hold weakened day by day. His most effective and eloquent speeches could not arouse his friends to action. Each day that passed witnessed the *Khalifah* becoming more and more helpless.

A number of other incidents between pro-Mu`awiyans and pro-`Alis also took place in the same year the details of which are ignored here.

Loss of Hijaz and Yemen

Hijaz and Yemen were still under the control of Hadrat `Ali (R.A.). In the year 40 A.H., Amir Mu`awiyah sent Busr ibn Abi Artat with three thousand men to Hijaz. First of all he went to Medina. The governor of Medina, Abu Ayyub was not able to check the Syrians and he left for Kufa. Busr took pledge of loyalty from the Medinites forcibly for Amir Mu`awiyah (R.A.), and exclaimed, "Had Mu`awiyah not forbidden me, I would not have left a single adult in Medina alive."

After taking over Medina, Busr reached Mecca and occupied it unopposed. There too he took the pledge of loyalty from the Meccans for Amir Mu`awiyah forcibly.

From Mecca Busr went to Yemen. At that time Hadrat `Ubaidullah ibn `Abbas was the governor of Yemen. Hearing of the Syrian army he fled to Kufa. Busr occupied San`a, the capital of Yemen and killed two little sons of `Ubaidullah. He also slew a number of `Ali's supporters in Yemen. Hearing the cruelty of Busr Hadrat `Ali sent Jariah ibn Qudamah with two thousand men. But before he reached Yemen, Busr fled to Syria. He also sent Wahb ibn Mas'ud with another two thousand men to Hijaz. Jariah ibn Qudamah, after establishing `Ali's rule in Yemen, was advancing to Mecca. As soon as he reached the Holy city, he received the news of Hadrat `Ali's assassination which ended his campaign.

According to Ibn Jarir at the end of the year 40 A.H. a treaty was signed between Amir Mu`awiyah and Hadrat `Ali, on the request of Amir Mu`awiyah to avoid bloodshed among the Muslims. Under that treaty Syria and Egypt remained under the control of Amir Mu`awiyah and the rest of the state under the control of Hadrat `Ali. Thus the conflict between the two parties ended. This civil war which ended to the detriment of Hadrat `Ali was the end of Islamic democratic rule.

But according to some other historians, no treaty took place between Hadrat `Ali and Mu`awiyah. While Hadrat `Ali (R.A.) was preparing to attack Syria (for which he had issued an ordinance compelling each and everyone under him to march to Syria) he was assassinated.

Victories

The civil war did not allow Hadrat `Ali (R.A.) to launch Jihad (Holy War) and the Islamic Empire saw no further extension. However some parts of Sistan (near Kabul) were conquered during this period. According to some historians Muslims made a naval attack on Kohan (near Bombay, India) in the year 38 A.H.

13
Hadrat 'Ali's Martyrdom and Review of His Works

A. MARTYRDOM

Assassination of Hadrat 'Ali (R.A.)

After the battle of Nahrwan the *Khawarij* had gone underground. As a matter of fact they were as much against Hadrat 'Ali (R.A.) as they were against Hadrat Mu'awiyah (R.A.). They were still working against the *Khilafat* and they were greatly disgusted with the civil war that seemed endless.

To end this state of affairs, they worked out a dangerous plot. According to them Muslims were divided because of differences between Hadrat 'Ali and Amir Mu'awiyah. They also disliked 'Amr ibn 'As and considered him as chief planner for Amir Mu'awiyah. They decided, therefore, to assassinate all the three of them. It was planned that the three personalities would be struck at the same time on the same day.

Three persons, appointed to assassinate 'Ali, Mu'awiyah and 'Amr ibn 'As (R.A.) were Abdur Rahman Muljam, Bark ibn 'Abdullah and 'Amr ibn Bark respectively. Early hours of the 17th of Ramadan,

40 A.H., was fixed for the assassination.

After the *Fajr Salat* of the 17th Ramadan in the year 40 A.H. (661 A.D.) the three appointed Kharijis struck the three men. Amir Mu`awiyah escaped with a scratch, Hadrat `Amr ibn `As did not turn out for the *Imamat* because he was sick that day, thus was unhurt, but Hadrat `Ali (R.A.) was mortally wounded with the poisoned sword of Ibn Muljam. He passed away in the evening of Ramadan 20, 40 A.H.

Ibn Muljam was caught by the people after he had struck Hadrat `Ali. Hadrat `Ali asked the Muslims to slay him if he died. At the same time of his death Hadrat `Ali called his sons and advised them to serve Islam and to be good with the Muslims. When somebody asked him if the Muslims should take pledge of loyalty at the hands of his elder son Hadrat Hassan, he replied, "I leave this decision to the Muslims." He also advised people not to kill any person other than the assassin to avenge him.

He was sixty three years old at the time of his death and had ruled for four years and nine months as the *Khalifah*. According to a number of historians his real grave is not known because his son Hadrat Hasan took out his body from the grave after he was buried because of the fear of Kharijis and buried him at an unknown place.

B. REVIEW OF HADRAT `ALI'S SERVICES TO ISLAM

Period of his *Khilafat*

The period of Hadrat `Ali's *Khilafat* extending to four years and about nine months was marked by civil war. His rule was characterised by a series of revolts for the first time in the history of Islam. He was elected as the *Khalifah* in the most critical period of Islamic history. The martyrdom of Hadrat `Uthman was an extraordinary event about which the Holy Prophet (*Sallallahu `alayhi wa Sallam*) had already prophesised. Hadrat `Ali was in a very difficult situation. On the one hand the assassins and the insurgents were creating endless trouble for him, and on the other hand Banu Umayyah (`Uthman's family) fled to Syria and incited Amir Mu`awiyah to stick to his demand for avenging Hadrat `Uthman's asassins. Hadrat `Ali faced these problems and difficulties with extraordinary courage and presented before us an exemplary character. He never had full support even from his friends in Kufa but still remained firm in his position.

As it has been described before, he could never locate the real assassins of Hadrat `Uthman and this could not be achieved until peace was established. Therefore his first task was to create an atmosphere of peace in the state. But the Sabaites (insurgents) never wanted peace. They worked on both sides. On the one side they made it difficult for Hadrat `Ali to find out the assassins, and on the other hand they sent their agents to Syria to incite the people (especially Umayyads) against Hadrat `Ali. Their main aim was to let the Muslims fight among themselves so that they might prosper. Although Hadrat `Ali knew all this but he was unable to take any firm action because of the civil war.

The third problem faced by Hadrat `Ali (R.A.) was the Kharijite movement. They were extremists and misled a number of innocent Muslims. They did not hesitate to use sword against persons who do not agree with them. They developed many beliefs foreign to Islam, although they appeared to be very pious but politically, they were corrupt. Hadrat `Ali dealt with them with an iron hand. He realised that if they were not wiped out in the beginning they would mislead future generations. He was successful in destroying their strong hold. However some of them who escaped went underground but they were never in a strong position.

Hadrat `Ali (R.A.) tried his utmost to unite the Muslims and bring them back on one platform but he was not successful. The tragic death of Hadrat `Uthman (R.A.) was a signal for bloodshed among the Muslims. The Companions were not to be blamed for it at all. This was caused by anti-Islamic elements in the form of Sabaites (`Abdullah ibn Saba and his followers). Historical facts bear it out that `Abdullah ibn Saba became the greatest enemy of Islam. It was he who shattered the unity of Muslims forever. After completing their mission the Sabaites made a pretence of being `Ali's friends but they never helped him nor the cause of Muslim unity. No sooner had Hadrat `Ali assumed *Khilafat* than a group of the same miscreant Sabaites who had brought about the cold-blooded assassination of Hadrat `Uthman (R.A.) began to demand due retribution for the murder of the *Khalifah* and started to incite Muslims only to create division among them. Thus they played a double role. A group of them showed themselves as friends of `Ali and another group (much smaller than the first) went to Syria and other parts of Islamic State to incite the Muslims against Hadrat `Ali (R.A.).

Hadrat `Ali (R.A.) faced all these problems with courage and never lost heart. He was a man of strong will power and determination and was quite right in his decisions.

Character, piety and excellence

Hadrat `Ali (R.A.) was a model of simplicity and self denial. He led a simple life from the cradle to the grave, and was a true representative of the Holy Prophet (*Sallallahu `alayhi wa Sallam*). `Ali (R.A.) had neither a servant nor a maid when Fatima (R.A.) the most beloved daughter of the Holy Prophet was married to him. She would grind corn with her own hands. Purity of motives and selflessness were the keynote of his life. He was a wise counsellor, a true friend and a generous foe. He did not have a desire for the *Khilafat* after Hadrat `Uthman's assassination, but when he was selected he tried his best to fulfil his responsibility.

He was very honest and trustworthy. His trustworthiness can well be imagined from the fact that the Holy Prophet entrusted to him all the cash and other things he was having in his trust, at the time of his migration to Medina, so that `Ali (R.A.) would return them to the owners. Once some oranges came to *Baitul-Mal* (Public Treasury), Hadrat Hasan and Husain took one orange each. When Hadrat `Ali saw them having the oranges he took the fruit away from them and distributed them among the poor. Whenever any booty came to be distributed according to the Islamic law, he distributed it very honestly. Once he distributed all the revenue of the *Baitul-Mal*, then broomed it and offered two *rak`at* of *Salat* in the room.

He did not leave his simplicity even though he was the *Khalifah* and the ruler of a vast state. Once a person named `Abdullah ibn Zarir had an opportunity to take meals with him. The meal was very simple. `Abdullah asked, "O *Amirul Mu'minin*, don't you like the meat of birds?" Hadrat `Ali replied, "The *Khalifah* has a right in Muslim (public) property only to the extent sufficient for him and his family."

Hadrat `Ali was a very generous Muslim. He never refused a beggar. Sometimes he gave all of his property to the poor and sold his arms to get food. Once he said during his lecture, "I went to sell my sword. I swear Allah, had I only that amount of money for which I could buy a *Sirwal* (i.e. trousers), I would never have sold my sword." Hearing this one person stood up and said, "I give you a loan."

There are many stories about his generosity which for lack of space are not being mentioned. Hadrat `Ali (R.A.) was a great worshipper and used to offer long *Salat*s. He was *Hafiz* of the Holy Qur'an. He was so punctual for the *Tasbih* (the famous *Tasbih-i-Fatima* i.e., remembrance of Allah) that he never left it, even during battles.

He was very kind to others. He showed his kindness even to his enemies. Once one of his enemies fell down naked because of his attack. Seeing his condition he did not kill him and left him so that he might not be ashamed of his nakedness. After the battle of *Jamal* against lady `A'isha, he treated lady `A'isha (R.A.) very respectfully. He himself went to see her and when she told him that she would like to go to Medina he asked her brother Muhammad ibn Abi Bakr to escort her. He never mistreated his enemies. During the time of the Holy Prophet (*Sallallahu `alayhi wa Sallam*) once he overcame a Jew in a fight, and sat on his chest to kill him. The Jew spat at his face. Hadrat `Ali at once left him. Seeing this the Jew was very much surprised and asked the reason. `Ali (R.A.) said, "I was killing you for Allah's sake but when you spat on my face, my sincerity was endangered because of the personal feelings." Hearing this the Jew immediately accepted Islam.

His character and morals were so high that even Amir Mu`awiyah praised them. Once Amir Mu`awiyah asked Dirar Asadi, one of his friends, to tell some of `Ali's high quality. Dirar Asadi refused first but when Amir Mu`awiyah insisted Dirar said, "He was a man of strong will power and determination. He always gave a just judgement, and was a fountain of knowledge. His speech was full of wisdom. He hated the pleasure of this world and loved the darkness of night to cry before Allah. His dress was most simple and he liked simple meals. He lived like a common man and when anybody put anv question before him, he replied with outmost politeness. Whenever we asked him to wait for us he waited like a common man. Although he was very near to us because of his high morals, we were afraid of him sometimes of his grandeur and eminence due to his nearness to Allah. He always respected a pious man and a scholar. He was nearest to the poor. He never allowed a powerful man to take advantage of his power. The weak were never disappointed of his justice. I bear witness that in many battles he woke up during the night and took hold of his beard and started to cry and weep before Allah as though he was in a state of commotion and exclaimed: O world! do not try to betray me. I have divorced (left) you long ago. Do not have any desire for me. I hate you. Your age is short and your end is despised. 0! the provision is very little and the journey is too long (i.e., the journey to hereafter), and the way is full of danger . . ."

Hearing this Hadrat Amir Mu'awiyah started to weep and cry and said, "May Allah bless Abul Hasan (ie. `Ali). I swear by Allah he was a person of the character you described."

At this point it should be noted that the differences of the Companions were not like that of us. They differed with each other for the sake of Allah but always admired each other's good habits. Although Amir Mu'awiyah was having differences with Hadrat `Ali, he admired the excellence of `Ali throughout his life and often said that he could never be equal to `Ali (R.A.). As a matter of fact the degree of their sincerity could not be imagined. We think everything in terms of wordly benefit, they considered every matter in terms of love with Allah, love with the Prophet of Allah and the success in the hereafter.

Tasawwuf (Mysticism or spiritual science) and Hadrat `Ali

The genealogical chain of Sufis (Islamic mystics) ends at Hadrat `Ali (R.A.) and through him it is linked to the Holy Prophet (*Sallallahu `alayhi wa Sallam*) in most of the orders. Thus Hadrat `Ali (R.A.) has been considered as the great Imam of *Tasawwuf* (spiritual science or mysticism).

As it has been mentioned in the Urdu book of the author, *Tasaisulat-i-Imdadiah*, Hadrat Shah Walliyullah of Delhi holds the view that the genealogical chain of the great Sufis is linked to the Holy Prophet through all the first four Caliphs among whom Hadrat `Ali (R.A.) stands like a gateway between the Sufis on the one hand and the first three caliphs and the Holy Prophet on the other hand. Spiritual secrets were transferred by the Holy Prophet (*Sallallahu `alayhi wa Sallam*) to Hadrat Abu Bakr. From Abu Bakr (R.A.) the secrets were transferred to Hadrat `Umar; from Umar (R.A.) to Hadrat `Uthman; from `Uthman (R.A.) to Hadrat `Ali and from Hadrat Ali to Sufis through Imam Hasan Basri (R.A.) as it is believed in most of the schools of thoughts of *Tasawwuf*.

Historically there are not enough proofs that Hadrat Hasan Basri had only tutelage under Hadrat `Ali. However it has been confirmed that Hasan Basri met Hadrat `Ali at the age of 15. In the science of *Tasawwuf* training under the Shaikh (*Murshid* or *Pir* or Spiritual Guide) is not necessary and spiritual secrets can be transferred even in a single meeting from the Shaikh to the *Murid* (the spiritual disciple). Therefore the great Sufis do not doubt the fact that Hadrat `Ali (R.A.) transferred spiritual secrets to Hasan Basri (R.A.), from whom they were passed on to the succeeding generations.

Therefore Hadrat `Ali (R.A.) and Imam Hasan Basri are the most important links in the genealogical orders (*Shajrahs*) of most of the Schools of Thought of Tasawwuf.

`Ali (R.A.) "the gate of the City of Knowledge"

The Holy Prophet (*Sallallahu `alayhi wa Sallam*) said, "I am the City of Knowledge and `Ali is its gate." No doubt Hadrat `Ali (R.A.) was a great scholar and jurist of Islam. He had memorised whole of the Holy Qur'an during the time of the Holy Prophet (*Sallallahu `alayhi wa Sallam*) and knew its commentary including the order of descent and the time of revelation of various verses. It is given in *Tabqat Ibn Sa`d* that Hadrat `Ali said, "I could tell for each and every verse of the Holy Qur'an why and when it was revealed." Hadrat `Ali has been counted among the top most commentators of the Holy Qur'an. Nobody among the Companions with the exception of `Abdullah ibn `Abbas was so learned in the Holy Qur'an as Hadrat `Ali (R.A.). His commentaries of various verses of the Holy Qur'an have been given in a number of books like *Ibn-i-Jarir, Ibn Abi Hatim, Ibn Kathir*, etc. He had confined himself to his home for six months after the death of the Holy Prophet *(Sallallahu `alayhi wa Sallam)* only to collect various parts of the Holy Qur'an. He was excellent in deducing law from the verses of the Holy Qur'an. When he argued with *Khawarij* on the question of arbitration, they could not stand before him. He was also very learned in the knowledge of *Nasikh* and *Mansukh* i.e. the knowledge of such verses of the Holy Qur'an outdating the laws given in other verses.

Hadrat `Ali (R.A.) spent thirty years of his life with the Holy Prophet *(Sallallahu `alayhi wa Sallam)* and knew all the manners and practices of the Holy Prophet *(Sallallahu `alayhi wa Sallam)*. He stood next to Abu Bakr (R.A.) as far as the knowledge of sayings, practices and orders of the Holy Prophet *(Sallallahu `alayhi wa Sallam)* were concerned. During the period of the first three caliphs and also during his time he was the great *Mufti* (Jurist) of Islam. He performed this service for about thirty years after the death of the Holy Prophet *(Sallallahu `alayhi wa Sallam)*. In the narration of Hadith he was very cautious like three of his predecessors. For this reason only 586 *Ahadith*, narrated by Hadrat `Ali (R.A.) have been mentioned in the books of Hadith. He has also mentioned a number of sayings of various Companions as well. Hadrat Shah Waliyullah of Delhi says, "Most of the *Ahadith* in connection with the appearance of the Holy Prophet, his method of offering *Salat* and praying to Allah etc., have been mentioned by Hadrat `Ali (R.A.) because of the fact that he was with him not only in his public but also in the private life." `Ali (R.A.) was one of the few Companions who were having collections of Hadith recorded during the time of the Holy Prophet *(Sallallahu `alayhi wa Sallam)*.

Hadrat `Ali (R.A.) was not only a great scholar but a great Jurist as well. He was famous for giving correct verdicts of different problems very quickly which were based upon the Holy Qur'an and the *Sunnah* of the Holy Prophet (*Sallallahu `alayhi wa Sallam*). Great Companions used to visit him for seeking solution of different problems of Islamic law and jurisprudence. Hadrat `Umar remarked, "`Ali is the greatest jurist and judge among all of us". Hadrat `Abdullah ibn Mas`ud said,"`Ali's decision is the most authentic." Because of his vast knowledge of the Holy Qur'an and Hadith, he became the greatest jurist of his time, as Islamic jurisprudence requires knowledge of the Holy Qur'an and Hadith to the fullest possible extent. On many occasions he corrected the decisions given by great Companions like `Umar and `Uthman (R.A.). Even though Amir Mu`awiyah was having differences with `Ali, he sometimes referred some of the complicated problems of Islamic law to Hadrat `Ali (R.A.) and admitted his profoundity in this field.

Hadrat `Ali (R.A.) was a great orator as well. On many occassions mobs of people were changed because of his effective speeches. Arabic knowing persons can note the beauty of his speeches. He was a wonderful master of the Arabic language. His writings were as effective as his speech. He had also composed a few peoms as well. He also framed rules of Arabic syntax and appointed Abul Aswad to compose a book on the basis of the rules he framed.

No doubt Hadrat `Ali was one of the greatest sons of Islam. Very few Companions equalled him in his closeness to the Holy Prophet (*Sallallahu `alayhi wa Sallam*), which burrished qualities of head and heart. Muslims are forever indebted to him.

Wives and children

1. Hadrat `Ali's first wife was the most beloved daughter of the Holy Prophet, Hadrat Fatimah (R.A.). He got three sons (Hasan, Husain and Muhsin), and two daughters (Zainab and Ummi Kulthum) from her. The youngest son, Muhsin died in childhood. After the death of Hadrat Fatimah he married a number of wives from time to time.

2. Umm al-Banin bint Hizam from whom he got `Abbas, Ja`far, `Abdullah and `Uthman. All of these except `Abbas were martyred at Karbala.

3. Laila bint Mas`ud who gave birth to `Ubaidullah and Abu Bakr. They were martyred at Karbala.

4. Asma bint Umais who gave birth to Yahya and Muhammad Asghar.

5. Sahba bint Rabi`a who gave birth to `Umar and Ruqayyah.

6. Amamah bint Abil `As: She was daughter of Zainab (R.A.), daughter of the Holy Prophet (*Sallallahu `alayhi wa Sallam*). Hadrat `Ali got Muhammad Aswat from her.

7. Khaulah bint Ja`far who gave birth to Muhammad ibn `Ali.

8. Umm-i-Sa`id who gave birth to Ummul Hasan and Ramiah Kubra.

9. Mahyah bint Ummul Qais, she gave birth to a daughter who died in childhood.

He also had a number of slave girls from whom he bore the following daughters: Umm-i-Hani, Maimunah, Zainab Sughra, Ramlah Sughra, Ummi Kulthum Sughra, Fatimah, Umamah, Khadijah, Umm-i-Salama, Umm-i-Ja`far, Jamanah and Nafisah.

According to Ibn-i-Jarir, Hadrat `Ali had 17 daughters and 14 sons. His family continued through five sons: Imam Hasan, Imam Husain, Muhammad ibn `Ali, `Umar bin `Ali and `Abbas ibn `Ali.

C. ADMINISTRATION OF HADRAT `ALI (R.A.)

General administration

Hadrat `Ali (R.A.) followed the administrative pattern set by Hadrat `Umar (R.A.) and did not make any noticeable changes. He tried to improve the administration of those places where it was not proper during the time of Hadrat `Uthman (R.A.). He usually gave useful advice to his governors at the time of their appointment. When he appointed Hadrat Ka`b ibn Mailk for supervision of various officers in various provinces he gave him the following instructions: "Check officers of each and every distict of Iraq thoroughly so that they may not act wrongly."

Watch for general morals of the officers

Like Hadrat `Umar (R.A.), he was very particular for the standard of morals of his officers. He never allowed his officers to neglect their duties or to behave immorally. Once he found that Mundhar ibn Jarud, governor of Istakhr, spent most of his time hunting instead of giving attention to administration. He wrote to him, "I have been informed that you are spending much of your time in hunting and recreation and neglect your duties. If that is true you would be punished for that." When his negligence was proved, Hadrat `Ali dismissed him. He wrote to another governor for his negligence: "It has come to my notice that you are leading a luxurious life. Your table is provided with different varieties of meals which common people cannot get. You behave un-Islamically while you are alone, but deliver sermons like the most pious people (*Siddiqin*) on pulpits (*Mimbar*). If these complaints are true then remember that you are in loss and I would punish you. You cannot hope for the reward given to righteous people in a position when you have spoiled the wealth of orphans and widows for your pleasure. Repent for your sins and give the right of Allah due upon you."

Besides warning them in writing he also sent various commissions to watch the officers of various provinces.

Baitul-Mal (Public Treasury) and administration of revenue

He took care of *Baltul-Mal* in the same way as was done by Hadrat `Umar (R.A.). Once his cousin Hadrat `Abdullah ibn `Abbas (R.A.) took ten thousand Dirhams from *Baltul-Mal*. When he knew about it, he immediately wrote to Hadrat `Abdullah ibn `Abbas to return it and warned him for future.

He never allowed his family members to take from the *Baltul-Mal* more than what they deserved. Once Hadrat `Amr ibn Salamah brought some fat and honey from Isfahan in *Kharaj* (Land Tax). Hadrat Ummi Kulthum, daughter of Hadrat `Ali took some honey and fat from that. When Hadrat `Ali counted the barrels of honey and fat the next day he found that one barrel of each was missing. Then he was told that his daughter took them. He immediately paid the price of the honey and fat used by his daughter.

Hadrat Abu Rafi`, the slave of the Holy Prophet, once took a pearl from the *Baltul-Mal* for his daughter. When Hadrat `Ali knew about it he not only took it back but also warned him not to do that ever again in future.

Hadrat `Ali (R.A.) was very strict in the matter of public revenues and its administration. Whenever there was delay in receiving the tax he immediately wrote to the officers. Once Yazid ibn Qais was very late in sending the revenue tax, Hadrat `Ali wrote him: "Explain the delay in sending the *Kharaj*. I advise you to fear Allah and warn you not to repeat it in future, otherwise your virtues would be lost and your Jihad (Holy War) for the sake of Allah would be spoiled. Fear Allah, and keep away from unlawful wealth. Don't give me a chance again to warn you for your mistakes . . . "

Once Nu`man ibn `Ujlan, a revenue officer, did not deposit the revenue in time and went to some other place. Hadrat `Ali wrote to him: "One who embezzles the trust cannot be saved from the punishment of Allah. He destroys his worldly interests and the interests of the hereafter both . . . You belong to a righteous family, repent before Allah for your misbehaviour, pay all the revenue you have charged from the public and do not compel me to punish you."

Hadrat `Ali (R.A.) improved the taxation system. He imposed land tax on forests the produce of which was not contributed to meet military expenditure or marketed.

Stipends from the *Baitul-Mal* to the poor

Hadrat `Ali (R.A.) gave stipends to the needy persons and helped the poor from the *Baitul-Mal*. He was very generous in this respect. Even though Persians had revolted against him one time he treated them so generously that they were highly pleased with him and remembered him for a long time, and named him "Arabi Noshairwan" (the Just Arab).

Kindness to non-Muslims

He was very kind to his non-Muslim population (*Dhimmis*). He instructed his officers to treat them well and to take special care of their needs. Once he wrote to one of his officers, `Amr ibn Muslimah: "It has come to my notice that the non-Muslims (*Dhimmis*) of your area are complaining about your strict behaviour. Treat them well and don't be so strict with them. Your strictness may cross limits and can turn into cruelty."

Once a canal for irrigation belonging to non-Muslims was littered with rubbish. When Hadrat `Ali was informed about it, he immediately wrote to the officer-in-charge, Karzah ibn Ka`b Ansari, "The non-Muslims (*Dhimmis*) of your area have complained that one of the irrigation canals belonging to them has been covered with rubbish. It is your duty to get it cleaned. I swear by Allah that it is better for you that the non-Muslims of your place continue living happily than migrating to another place because of difficulties."

Justice

His justice was equal to both the Muslims and the non-Muslims, the poor and the rich, officer and subordinate. He had himself once appeared before the Judge (*Qadi*) and the decision was given against him because of lack of evidence. Once his Armour was lost. After sometime he found it with a Christian man. He filed a suit against him in the court of the famous Judge, Qadi Shuraih. Qadi Shuraih asked him to produce a witness but he could not do so. The Armour was returned to the Christian. The Christian was so impressed that he accepted Islam immediately saying, "This is the example set by Prophets. The Caliph's case has been rejected because he had no evidence for his lawful claim."

Administration of army

Hadrat `Ali (R.A.) was an experienced army general of Islam. He had fought a number of battles in the company of the Holy Prophet (*Sallallahu `alayhi wa Sallam*). During his caliphate he gave a crushing defeat to his opponents in the battle of Jamal (Camel). He also defeated *Khawarij*. As has been said before, he had the upper hand in the battle of Siffin but accepted arbitration only for the sake of Muslim unity.

Hadrat `Ali (R.A.) established a number of new cantonments in the state, and built a number of forts. He built a number of forts in Persia when there was a revolt. Hadrat `Ali took special care of his border with Syria, which was under the control of Hadrat Mu`awiyah (R.A.). He established a number of army posts all along the Syrian border.

He built a bridge over the river Euphrates which was very important from the defence point of view. The fort of Askhar, built in Persia was considered to be one of the strongest forts of his time.

Preaching of Islam

To preach true way of life i.e. Islam, is one of the foremost duties of a *Khalifah*. He paid special attention to it during his caliphate. Although he was not able to conquer many regions during his caliphate because of the civil war, yet a number of people accepted Islam because of the good-treatment meted out to them. In Iran many people accepted Islam due to his kindness with the public. Those who forsook Islam rejoined the Faith because of `Ali's teachings.

Thus we see that Hadrat `Ali was a great administrator. He was one of the closest Companions of the Holy Prophet (*Sallallahu `alayhi wa Sallam*) and possessed unparalleled courage, vigour and faith.

SECTION V

The Downfall of the Pious Caliphate

14

The Downfall of the Pious Caliphate

A. APPRAISAL OF THE PIOUS CALIPHATE

Thirty years of *Khilafat-i-Rashidah*

The decision to abdicate in favour of Amir Mu`awiyah (R.A.) by Hadrat Hasan (R.A.) marked the fall of the *Khilafat-i-Rashidah* (the Pious Caliphate). This marks the 30 years of rule after the Holy Prophet (*Sallallahu `alayhi wa Sallam*). According to a famous Hadith, the Holy Prophet (*Sallallahu `alayhi wa Sallam*) prophesised: "For thirty years after me, there would be *Khilafat* after which it will change to Kingship." The period of thirty years was completed in Rabi`ul Awwal 41 A.H. when Hadrat Hasan abdicated the *Khilafat* in favour of Amir Mu`awiyah (R.A.). In the following lines some salient features of the Pious Caliphate are described briefly in order to prove that Islam is the first way of life to give a practical concept of government of Allah by His servants for His servants i.e. the Islamic Democratic System.

B. ISLAMIC DEMOCRATIC SYSTEM OBSERVED BY *KHULAFA-I-RASHIDIN*

Foundation of *Khilafat*

As described in the beginning *Khalifah* means a vicegerent or a viceroy. Man is the vicegerent of Allah Almighty as described in the Holy Qur'an:

> *"And when thy Lord said unto the angels: Lo! I will create a Vicegerant (viceroy) on earth"* (11:30).

To perfect the trust of Vicegerecy or Viceroyship (*Khilafat*) Allah sent his Last Messenger, Hadrat Muhammad (*Sallallahu `alayhi wa Sallam*), who was fully successful in building a nation, as demanded by Allah, out of the warring tribes of Arabia. He established a community and a State whose foundations were laid on firm faith in Allah and upon the *Sunnah*, of His prophet (*Sallallahu `alayhi wa Sallam*). The Holy Prophet trained the Muslims of his time, known as *Sahabah* (the Companions) for 23 years and aroused and directed their latent forces to observe and preach the Right Way of life. He initiated the best system of government for the human race, which we may call as the "Islamic Democratic System" the full accomplishment of which was left to his successors, who were called his *Khulafa* (Caliphs), the *Khulafa-i-Rashidin* (The Pious Caliphs).

The institution of *Khilafat* therefore came into existence with the accession of Hadrat Abu Bakr who became the first head of the Islamic State better to be called as the Republic of Islam. His appointment was not pre-planned as the Holy Prophet (*Sallallahu `alayhi wa Sallam*) had not nominated him. It was the Ansar who wanted to choose a successor to the Holy Prophet (*Sallallahu `alayhi wa Sallam*) after his death, the details of which have already been mentioned. The Ansar as well as the Muhajirin accepted him as a *Khalifah* in a special gathering and it was approved next day in the general assembly of the Muslims in the Mosque of the Holy Prophet through pledge of loyalty (the *Bai'at*). This became a precedent for the subsequent elections of succeeding *Khulafa*.

Basic features of the Government of *Khulafa-i-Rashidin*

The Government of *Khulafa-i-Rashidin* rightly called as the Islamic Democratic System was based upon the following principles:

i. Election of the *Khalifah* by *Shura* and general consent

The *Khalifah* was never a nominated person during the period of the Pious Caliphs. The election of Hadrat Abu Bakr, as described above, took place after the general consent. It was an exemplary democratic way of election never held before in history. The election of Hadrat `Umar, Hadrat `Uthman and Hadrat `Ali (R.A.) also was in no way undemocratic. If the voting system, as we know today had prevailed in those days, all these three caliphs would had got the largest number of popular votes in their respective times. Although Hadrat Abu Bakr nominated Hadrat `Umar (R.A.) as his successor, nevertheless it had the backing of general consent of the people. At the time of nomination he asked the Muslim public to assemble in the Mosque of the Holy Prophet (*Sallallahu `alayhi wa Sallam*) and told them, "Do you agree on the successor I propose to appoint? I swear by Allah I have not done anything wrong in proposing the name of the person who is not my relative. He is no less a person than `Umar ibn Khattab. I ask you to listen to him and obey him." All the Muslims said with one voice, "We will listen to him and obey him."

The election of Hadrat `Uthman (R.A.) was done by a panel of persons appointed by Hadrat `Umar (R.A.) and then approved by the general public in the Mosque. Hadrat `Ali (R.A.) was also nominated by the public. When insurgents approached him, he clearly said, "I cannot allow you to take pledge secretly. It should be done by the Muslim Republic." His nomination was approved by the Muslims. Hadrat `A'isha (R.A.), who opposed him in the beginning because of the delay in taking avenge from the assassinators, consented to his *Khilafat* later on. All the Muslims, except those who were in Syria, accepted him as the *Khalifah*. Amir Mu`awiyah did not agree on his *Khilafat* due to the political situation at that time but he did not declare himself a *Khalifah* during the lifetime of Hadrat `Ali (R.A.).

This clearly proves that the companions considered the institution of *Khilafat* as a sacred office and believed that a *Khalifah* must be appointed on the basis of *Shura* and general consent. Once Hadrat `Umar, (R.A.) heard a man saying, "I would take pledge at the hand of the person I liked most after `Umar." Hadrat `Umar (R.A.) said, "If a person took pledge on the hand of a person without the *Shura* (here it means the council of advisers and the general consent of the Muslims), then both of them (i.e. the person who took the pledge and the person on whose hand the pledge was taken) should be killed." Hadrat Abu Musa Ash`ari (R.A.) said, "*Khilafat* (or *Imamat*) is established by *Shura* while kingship is established by sword."

ii. The *Khalifah* was bound to follow the Holy Qur'an and the *Sunnah*

Though the *Khalifah* was the head of the State, he was bound by all means to follow the Holy Qur'an and the *Sunnah* of the Holy Prophet (*Sallallahu `alayhi wa Sallam*). He had to exercise his authority according to the injunctions of the Holy Qur'an. If the Qur'an was not explicit in any given matter he was bound to refer to the *Sunnah* of the Holy Prophet *(Sallallahu `alayhi wa Sallam)*. In case there was no clarification in the *Sunnah* it had to be referred to the consent of scholars and he could give his own verdict based upon the Holy Qur'an and the *Sunnah*.

The *Khalifah* had to perform some religious duties. He was the Imam of Holy Prophet's mosque for the daily *Salat*, the Friday *Salat* and the *'Id*. To lead congregational *Salat*s (in the position of an Imam) was regarded at that time as the sign of religious and political leadership in Islam.

The *Khalifah* was also the Commander-in-Chief of the armed forces. He used to appoint generals and send armies for war and at times he also gave instructions to the generals. Usually the *Khalifah* took advice of the *Shura* (the Council of Advisers) in appointment of the generals.

The *Khalifah* was also the final court of appeal and acted in a position similar to that of Chief Justice of today. In the beginning (i.e., during the time of Hadrat Abu Bakr) judges were not appointed and the *Khalifah* used to decide all the cases himself as the Holy Prophet *(Sallallahu `alayhi wa Sallam)* did so. In the provinces the Governors used to perform judicial functions on his behalf. But later on (i.e., during the time of Hadrat `Umar) separate judges were appointed and the judiciary was independent of the executive, but the *Khalifah* was considered as the final court of appeal, because all the *Khulafa-i-Rashidin* were prominent jurists and experts of Islamic law and jurisprudence of their time. It has already been mentioned that Hadrat `Umar (R.A.) separated the executive and the judiciary for the first time in the Islamic history.

iii. The *Majlis Shura* or the Council of Advisers

Although the *Khalifah* was the head of State and the highest authority, he did not generally decide matters without consultation. The Consultative Body or the Council of Advisers was known as the *Shura* or *Majlis Shura*. All the four *Khulafa* consulted it in all the affairs of the State. The *Shura* has its origin in the teachings of the Holy Qur'an and one chapter of the Holy Book is named as *Shura*. The Holy Prophet (*Sallallahu `alayhi wa Sallam*), who was the source of all the Islamic knowledge and who was the sole authority of Islamic laws, himself followed the *Shura* and was commanded by Allah to do so.

Hadrat `Umar (R.A.), the pioneer of the Islamic Democracy had emphasised on several occasions that there can be no *Khilafat* except by consultation.

The number of members of *Shura* was not fixed. The *Shura* consisted of the principal companions of the Holy Prophet (*Sallallahu `alayhi wa Sallam*) who were given preference on the basis of their services to and sacrifices for Islam. The ten companions who had been given the glad tiding of Paradise in this world by the Holy Prophet (*Sallallahu `alayhi wa Sallam*) and were known as Ashrah "*Mubash-Sharah*" were the chief members of the *Shura*. They were: Hadrat Abu Bakr, Hadrat `Umar, Hadrat `Uthman, Hadrat `Ali, Hadrat `Abdur Rahman ibn `Auf, Hadrat Talha, Hadrat Zubair, Hadrat Sa`d ibn Waqqas, Hadrat Abu `Ubaidah ibn Jarrah and Sa`id ibn Zaid. Besides, the leading Muhajirin (the Immigrants) and the leading Ansar (the Medinites) were also included in the *Shura*. On special occasions even common citizens of Medina or visiting dignitaries and chiefs of the tribes of various provinces were also called to attend the meeting of the *Shura*. Usually to call a meeting of the *Shura* a herald used to go round proclaiming "*As-Salatu Jami`ah*" (i.e. "assemble for prayers").

Everybody in the *Shura* was free to express his views whether

The Downfall of the Pious Caliphate

they were in accord with the *Khalifah*'s opinion or not. Once Hadrat `Umar clarified it in a short address given in a meeting of *Shura*, "I have called you to share with me the trust of which I am the trustee. I am an ordinary person amongst you and you are free to claim your rights. Everyone of you is free to oppose me or to agree with me. I will never impose my view upon you" (*Kitab-ul-Kharaj* by Imam Abu Yusuf).

The *Shura* used to advise the *Khalifah* in the performance of various duties. The *Khalifah* also took advice of the *Shura* in appointment of generals for the armies, in the appointment of Governors, in the despatch of armies, in the fixation of salaries, in the appointment of public officers and judges, in assessment of taxes and in creation of new posts, etc.

Neither the *Khalifah* nor the *Shura* was a sovereign legislative body. They did not have any power to change the Islamic law or to modify it or to violate the dictates of the Holy Qur'an and the *Sunnah*. The *Khalifah* used to refer first of all to the Holy Qur'an in case of a new problem, then to the *Sunnah*. In case he did not find any solution in these sources he referred it to the special *Shura* which included the chief Jurists and the Scholars of that time and usually the matters were decided by their unanimity, ie., by the *Ijma`* (or the unanimous consent of the scholars). In absence of all the above three sources, he used to give his own verdict by *Qiyas* or *Ijtihad* based upon the Holy Qur'an and the *Sunnah*. It should also be borne in mind that the *Khalifah* at that time was also an expert of Islamic religion and law (*Shari`a*) and a great jurist, and by all means was authorised to give his verdict by *Qiyas* or *Ijtihad* for every Muslim is not authorised to do so unless he has acquired that standard of knowledge.

iv. Freedom of opinion

At no time in history this rule was observed so completely as during the time of *Khulafa-i-Rashidin*. Every Muslim was free to express his opinion and even to criticize the *Khalifah*. The details have been mentioned before. The *Khalifah* not only met the Muslims during the time of the meeting of the *Shura* but also five times in the congregational *Salat*, once a week in the Friday *Salat*, and once a year at the time of Hajj when the Muslim public from all parts of the State assembled at Mecca.

The *Khulafa* did not live in palaces having big gates. There were no watchmen at their houses which were open to every Muslim. It was the strict order of Hadrat `Umar for the Governors not to keep watchmen at their houses so that everybody could see them freely and could put his problems to them. The houses of Hadrat Abu Bakr and `Umar were below the standard of the houses of most of the Muslims. They were merely mud huts and everyone was free to visit them any time he liked. Freedom of opinion, as observed during the time of *Khulafa-i-Rashidin* is exemplary even for the modern age.

v. *Baitul-Mal* (the Public Treasury) was not considered as personal property of the *Khalifah*

For the first time in history the treasury or the *Baitul-Mal* was considered as public property and not the personal property of the ruler. They considered it as a great trust of the Muslims and never spent even a single Dirham according to their own choice. Hadrat Abu Bakr, Hadrat `Umar and Hadrat `Ali took only that amount of salary from the Baitul-Mal which was sufficient for a common man. Hadrat `Uthman (R.A.) never took anything from the *Baitul-Mal*. Once Hadrat `Umar asked Hadrat Salman Farsi (R.A.), "Tell me whether I am a king or a *Khalifah*." He replied, "If you impose tax of even a single Dirham

THE DOWNFALL OF THE PIOUS CALIPHATE

on a Muslim wrongly and spend it wrongly, you are a king, otherwise you are a *Khalifah*."

Hadrat `Umar (R.A.) clarified on various occasions what a *Khalifah* was entitled to take from the *Baitul-Mal* for his use. He said, "Nothing is *Halal* (lawful) for me and for my family from Allah's money (i.e., the *Baitul-Mal*), except a dress for the summer and a dress for the winter, and a salary equal to the income of an average Qurayshi (Meccan). I am no more than an ordinary Muslim amongst you."

Hadrat Abu Bakr took a small salary from the *Baitul-Mal* which was barely enough for his family. At the time of his death he asked his wife to sell his property and pay back the money he took from the *Baitul-Mal* as his salary.

Hadrat `Ali followed the example of Hadrat Abu Bakr and Hadrat `Umar (R.A.) and took a salary equal to an ordinary Muslim's income. He used to wear a Tahmad having a number of patches on it, and there were a number of patches on his shirt as well. They all treated the *Baitul-Mal* as a trust.

vi. Supremacy of law

In those days the Islamic law was supreme. The *Qadi*s and the courts were never interfered in their proceedings. They were totally free from any kind of pressure. The *Khalifah* did not think of himself as an extraordinary person — independent of the law. In the eyes of law he was just an ordinary Muslim. A *Qadi* was free to give decision against the *Khalifah* as he was free to give it against a common man.

The example of Hadrat `Umar's time has already been mentioned. Here is cited an example of Hadrat `Ali's time. Once Hadrat `Ali saw a Christian selling his lost armour during his caliphate. He did not take it by force but put him in the court. Hadrat `Ali (R.A.) had no evidence to prove that it was his armour and the *Qadi* gave his decision in favour of the Christian. Whenever a *Khalifah* appeared before a *Qadi* he did not allow the *Qadi* to pay to him undue respect and asked him to treat him (the *Khalifah*) like a common Muslim.

vii. The Government (*Khilafat*) was treated as a trust

They did not treat the Government (*Khilafat*) as their inherited right but as a great "trust" and as such they declared themselves as "trustees". The first address of Hadrat Abu Bakr, after he was made the *Khalifah* has already been mentioned in which he said, "I have been appointed as a ruler over you, although I am not the best amongst you, I swear by Allah Who holds my life in His hands that I never wanted it (i.e., the *Khilafat*) and I never prayed to get it . . . Obey me as long as I obey Allah and His Prophet (*Sallallahu `alayhi wa Sallam*)."

Hadrat `Umar (R.A.) declared, "Don't obey me when I am disobeying Allah. I explain to you the rights you have over me and you are free to demand them anytime . . ." Whenever Hadrat `Umar appointed a governor or an officer he advised him, "I am not appointing you to be the master of the public. You have been appointed so that you may establish *Salat*, and observe justice and pay the rights of the people to them."

Hadrat `Uthman (R.A.) said in his first address, "I am to follow my predecessors and not to create anything new in the government. I promise you to obey the Book of Allah, to follow the *Sunnah* of His Prophet and to he observant in three matters: (a) the principles formed on the basis of the consensious opinion of the Muslims will be obeyed; (b) in case I do not find any principle set by my predecessors I will decide a case after due consultation; (c) I will not punish you until it is due in law."

When Hadrat `Ali (R.A.) appointed Hadrat Qais ibn Sa`d (R.A.)

as the Governor of Egypt he sent a communication to the Muslims of Egypt which read: "You have the right to see if we are following the Book of Allah (the Holy Qur'an)and the *Sunnah* of His Holy Prophet *(Sallallahu `alayhi wa Sallam),* and are ruling over you according to the Right Path; and that we may order you according to the ways of the Holy Prophet and be good to you even at your back."

The above examples clearly show that they treated the government as a great trust entrusted by Allah and not an inherited institution like kingship.

C. ADMINISTRATION UNDER THE *KHULAFA-I-RASHIDIN*

i. The Secretariat

During the time of the *Khulafa-i-Rashidin* there was no office for conducting the affairs of the Government. In the beginning the governmental activities were conducted under the direct supervision of the *Khalifah*. But when the work increased and different duties were entrusted to different companions, the courtyard of the Mosque of the Holy Prophet was used as the main office where the secretaries and assistants of the *Khalifah* used to work sitting either on the floor or on mats made of grass. The *Khalifah* himself used to sit either on the floor of the Mosque or on mats made of grass. So the Mosque of the Holy Prophet *(Sallallahu `alayhi wa Sallam)* became the centre of all the religious activities.

ii. Administration of the provinces

During the time of Hadrat `Umar (R.A.), the Islamic State was divided for the first time into eight provinces viz. (1) Mecca, (2) Medina, (3) Syria, (4) Jazirah (Mesopotamia), (5) Basra (Persia or Iran), (6) Kufa

(Iraq), (7) Egypt and (8) Palestine.

Each province was under the administration of an officer named *Wali* or Governor. The *Wali* was supposed to be the representative of the *Khalifah* in the province and was entitled to perform the administrative functions on his behalf. He was also the religious head of the province and used to lead five times *Salat* in the Jami` Mosque of the Capital and also the Friday and `*Id Salat*s. In most of the cases the *Wali*s were also commanders of the provincial army. Besides the *Wali*, there were also the following officers in a province: *Sahib-i-Baitil-Mal* or Treasury Officers; *Shaikh-ul-Kharaj* or Revenue Collector; *Sahib-i-Ahdath* or the Chief Police Officer; *Qadi* or Judge; and Commander of the army if the *Wali* was not the Commander.

The provinces were divided into districts. Each district was under the supervision of a district officer known as *Amil*. In most of the districts there were separate *Qadi*s. The district officers were under the *Wali* (i.e., Governor) of the Province.

At the time of his appointment a *Wali* was given instructions regarding his responsibilities and was advised to conduct himself in accordance with the ways of the Holy Prophet (*Sallallahu `alayhi wa Sallam*). During the time of Hadrat `Umar (R.A.) an officer (*Wali* or *Amil*, etc.) had to furnish a list of his properties and belongings on his appointment. Any extraordinary increase in his property was subject to enquiry. Hadrat `Umar (R.A.) confiscated the properties of some officers like Hadrat Abu Hurairah and Hadrat `Amr ibn `As (R.A.) on this ground.

The officers were paid high salaries so that they might not indulge in corruption.

iii. The revenue administration

There were five main sources of revenue: *Zakat, Jizya, Kharaj, Khums* and *Fay'* (i.e., the income from the State lands). The collection of revenue was not a problem during the days of the Holy Prophet (*Sallallahu `alayhi wa Sallam*) when the State was small and the sources were limited. With the expansion of the Islamic State there arose a need to regularise and control the revenue. Hadrat `Umar (R.A.) was the first *Khalifah* to organize the revenue administration very strictly upon Islamic principles. He also introduced some taxes like `Ushr.

Regarding the expenditure of *Zakat* there are clear instructions in the Holy Qur'an according to which the *Zakat* was spent and a separate account was kept for it. Every Muslim on whom the *Zakat* was compulsory, used to give *Zakat* without any hesitation. The Muslims regarded it a sin to keep wealth without paying the *Zakat*.

Jizya (or the Indemnity Tax) was imposed on the non-Muslims, known as *Dhimmis*. Hadrat `Umar (R.A.) fixed its annual rate which was different for different income groups. *Kharaj* or land tax was charged upon the lands of the non-Muslim owners after conquest by the Muslims. The amount of *Kharaj* was fixed according to the quality of soil. The *Kharaj* was also paid by the Muslims in later days. `Ushr was a tax charged from big estate owners and *Fay'* was a tax upon unclaimed lands or the lands confiscated from rebels, etc. *Khums* was the one-fifth share of the state in the booty (i.e., *Ghanimat*).

All the money was kept in the *Baitul-Mal*. There was no separate building for it during the days of the Holy Prophet (*Sallallahu `alayhi wa Sallam*) and Hadrat Abu Bakr (R.A.), because the income was limited and was distributed among the deserving people as soon as it was received. Realising the need of a building Hadrat `Umar (R.A.)

constructed the building of the *Baitul-Mal* in the form of a mud house in Medina. *Baitul-Mal* buildings were also constructed in various provinces. In the provinces the *Baitul-Mal* was under the supervision of a Treasury Officer known as *Sahib-i-Baitil-Mal*. After the provincial expenses, the surplus money of various provinces was sent to the Central Treasury in Medina.

iv. The police

Police was appointed in various provinces. Hadrat `Umar (R.A.) the second Caliph, introduced night watches and patrol. He himself used to go round the city at night. Hadrat `Ali (R.A.) introduced a regular police force.

v. The army

The *Khalifah* was Commander-in-Chief of the armed forces who appointed commanders in various provinces. There were a number of ranks in the army. On every ten soldiers there was an officer, known as `*Arief*, and on every hundred soldiers a *Qaid* or Lieutenent. There were also spies, doctors and other civilian posts in the army. The army was raised on a regular basis during the time of Hadrat `Umar (R.A.) and cantonments were built. Each army had a cavalry, which used shields, swords and long lances; and an infantry which had shields and helmets for defence and wore trousers and boots.

vi. The naval force

Since Arabia is surrounded on three sides by water (on the east by the Arabian Gulf, on the South by the Indian Ocean and on the west by the Red Sea), a naval force was created during Hadrat `Uthman's period, and in 28 A.H. the first naval battle took place under the command of

Hadrat Mu`awiyah (R.A.) who invaded Cyprus.

The Muslims, at that time were great traders and used to sail across the Red Sea to Abyssinia (Ethiopia) and other African territories. They also went to India and China. The main port of export to these countries at that time was Oballah, an old port of the Persian Gulf.

vii. Non-Muslims (*Dhimmis*)

The non-Muslims, known as *Dhimmi*s enjoyed protection and all basic rights. They were exempted from service in the Muslim army and in lieu of military service they had to pay a tax, named *Jizya* or Indemnity Tax, for their protection. They were entitled to enjoy all other rights and privileges in the state. The main groups of non-Muslims were Christians, Jews and Sabians. Mr. Welhausen, a historian says, "Umar had a keen eye over the advantage of non-Muslims and spared no pains to promote their welfare." Special pensions and stipends were given to non-Muslims from the *Baitul-Mal*. Prof. P.K. Hitti says, "Being outside the pale of Muslim law, they were allowed to adjudication of their own laws as administered by the respective heads of their religious communities."

This clearly shows that the non-Muslims were never forced to repudiate their faith. They entered the fold of Islam because of their own choice. They were given full security of their honour, lives and property and the policy of the Muslims towards them was very generous.

D. SOCIAL LIFE

The *Khulafa-i-Rashidin* led a very pious and simple life. It was quite different from that of Persian and Roman monarchs. They did not build palaces, big residential quarters and big buildings for their courts and offices. Their own residences were mud huts or cottages. They worked like ordinary Muslims and did not feel any shame in doing their household works. Although they could have amassed plenty of wealth and had all the means at their disposal, they led a humble and most simple life, because their supreme aim was the welfare of the people to seek Allah's pleasure. Their doors were open to the poor and they listened to the complaints of the people. They used to serve the people during the day and worshipped during most part of the night. Their hearts were dedicated to the love of Allah and they were the most pious and God-fearing Muslims of their times. The *Khalifah*'s dress was no better than that of the common Muslims. Sometimes they had a number of patches on their dresses.

i. Dress

The dress consisted of a long shirt reaching up to the knees and trousers (*Salwar*) or a Tahmad. A loose fitting tunic-like garment was also used for shirt over which a robe or *Jubbah* (gown) or a cloak called "Iba" was worn. Turban was used as a head dress by the Arabs. It differed according to age, position and learning. Sandals and shoes were used as foot wear.

The female dress was loose trousers (*Salwar*) and a shirt with full and loose sleeves. The head was covered by a handkerchief. Before the caliphate of Hadrat `Umar, women used to attend congregational prayers in mosque but he placed restrictions on it. They used to travel on camels in *Hijab* (or *Pardah*). Women were given full privileges in the society and if a Muslim was having more than one wife (which was a common feature) he was asked by law to treat them equally. For the first time in human history women were allowed equality in the society. They used to teach girls and also boys but under *Hijab*. Hadrat `A'isha (R.A.) was a great scholar of Hadith and Islamic law (especially that law which pertained to ladies). The ladies attended the *Khutbat* (addresses) of the *Khalifah* in *Hijab* (i.e., veiled).

ii. Education

Education took the shape of mass education during the time of Hadrat `Umar (R.A.). He built mosques in various districts which were used for religious education as well. Besides the mosques, special schools were also built in which the Holy Qur'an, Hadith and Theology were taught. Teachers were appointed to impart knowledge and education was free. In a school in Syria about 1,600 students received higher education.

During the time of Hadrat `Ali, Kufa and Basrah were the main centres of religious education, comparable to universities of the modern age. In such schools, higher education in Arabic language and grammar, the Qur'an and Islamic Law and jurisprudence were given. The *Khalifah*s were themselves great scholars and used to educate their people. Poetry was also common in those days.

iii. Slaves

Slavery as understood and practised in the west for centuries was totally banned by the Holy Prophet (*Sallallahu `alayhi wa Sallam*). However, the prisoners of war were made captives and sold to Muslims, and were known as slaves. Such slaves were treated most humanely. To free a slave is a very pious act in Islam and as such their emancipation was well practised during those days. Slaves and servants could reach high position. Moreover, before law in the social life a slave and a master were placed on an equal footing. To buy and sell a free man (whether Muslim or non-Muslim) was a great criminal act and was punishable under law. If a man bore a child from his slave woman or slave girl he was not allowed to sell her again and the child was treated his child in all respects and was entitled to all the privileges of children by a free woman.

Bibliography

1. `Abdul Malik Ibn Hisham, *al-Sirat al-Nabawijyah*, Cairo, 1375 H/1955.
2. `Abdur Rahman Ibn Khaldun, *Tarikh*, Beirut, 1966.
3. Abu Yusuf Ya`qub, *Kitab al-Kharaj*.
4. Ahmad ibn Hanbal, *al-Musnad*.
5. Ahmad ibn `Ali Sha`ib al-Nasaiy, *al-Sunan*.
6. Ahmad ibn Muhammad Ibn `Abd Rabbih, *al-`Iqd al-Farid*, Cairo 1372 H/1953.
7. Ahmad ibn `Ali Ibn Hajar al-`Asqalani, *al-Isabah fi Tamyizil Sahabah*.
8. *Fathul Bari*, Egypt 1301.
9. Akberabadi, Maulana Saeed Ahmad, *Siddiq-e-Akbar*.
10. `Ali, `Abdullah Yusuf, *The Meaning and the Commentary of the Holy Qur'an*, U.S.A., 1946.
11. `Ali ibn Hasan Ibn `Asakir, *al-Tarikh al-Kabir*.
12. `All K., *A Study of Islamic History*, Dacca, 1968.
13. Al-Azdi, *Futuh-ush-Sham*.
14. Bladhuri, *Futuh-ul-Buldan*.
15. Bosworth, C.E., *The Islamic Dinasties*, Edinburg, 1967.
16. Brockelmann, Carl, *History of the Islamic People*, New York 1947.
17. *Encyclopaedia Americana*, New York, 1964.
18. *Encyclopaedia Britannica*, U.S.A., 1966.
19. *The Encyclopaedia of Islam*, Lelden & London, 1913-1938.
20. Grunebaun G. E., *Classical Islam — A History (600-1258)*, Tr. by K. Waston, London, 1970.
21. Hamidullah, Muhammad, *Muslim Conduct of State*, Hyderabad

(India), IVth Edition, 1961.
22. Hitti, Philip K., *The Near East in History (A 5000 Year Story)*, New York, 1961.
23. *History of the Arabs*, London, 1958.
24. Izaduddin Abul Hasan Ali Ibn al-Athir, *al-Kamil fil Tarikh*, 12 vols., Beirut, 1385 H/1965.
25. Lewis, Bernard, *The Arabs in History*, London, 1950.
26. Malik ibn Anas, *Muwatta*.
27. al-Mas`udi, Abul Hasan `Ali ibn Husain, *Muruj al-Dhahab wa Ma`adin al-Jauhar fil Tarikh*, Egypt, 1346 H.
28. Mawdudi, Syed Abul A`la, *Khilafat wa Mulukiyyat*, Delhi, 1969.
29. Mawdudi, Syed Abul A`la, *Tafhimul-Qur'an"*, Delhi.
30. Muhammad ibn `Abd al-Baqi al-Zurqani, *Sharh al-Mawahib al-Ladunniyah*, 8 vols., Egypt, 1327.
31. Muhammad ibn Jarir Abi Ja`far al-Tabari, *Tarikh al-Rusul wal-Muluk*, Egypt, 1961.
32. Muhammad ibn Ismail al-Bukhari, *al-Jami` al-Sahih*.
33. Muhammad ibn Ismail al-Bukhari, *Adab al-Mufrad*.
34. Muhammad ibn `Isa al-Tirmidhi, *al-Jami` al-Sahih*.
35. Muhammad ibn Sa`d, *al-Tabaqat al-Kubra*, 8 vols., Beirut, 1385 H/1965.
36. Muhammad ibn Yazid Ibn Majah, *al-Sunan*.
37. Muhammad Yusuf Khandhalwi, *Hayatus Sahabah*, 3 vols., Hyderabad (India), 1383-86 H/1964.
38. Muslim ibn al-Hajjaj Abul Husain al-Qashiri al-Nishapuri, *al-Sahih*.
39. Nadwi, Shah Mu`innuddin, *Khulafa-i-Rashidin*, Azamgarh (India), 1346 H/1927.
40. Nadwi, Syed Sulaiman, *Siratun Nabi*, Azamgarh, 1372 H/1955.
41. Nadwi, Abu Hasan `Ali, *Islam and the World*, Lucknow, 1973.
42. Najibabadi, Akbar Shah Khan, *Tarikh-i-Islam*, Karachi, 1970.
43. Nooruddin `Ali ibn Jamaluddin al-Shafi, *Wafa-ul-Wafa*, 4 vols., Egypt, 1326 H.
44. Nu`mani, Shibli, *Siratun Nabi*, Azamgarh. (India), 1375 H.

45. Nu'mani, Shibli, *al-Faruq*.
46. Shihabuddin ibn 'Abdullah al-Baghdadi, *Mu'jim al-Buldan*, Beirut, 1376 H/1957.
47. Shihabuddin Fadaluddin ibn Husain Turbashti al-Hanafi, *Mishkat al-Masabih* (Sharah: *Masabih al-Sunnah* by Muhammad al-Husain ibn Mas'ud al-Baghawi).
48. Siddiqi, Dr. Amir Hasan, *Studies in Islamic History*, Karachi, 1967.
49. (Abu Dawud) Sulaiman ibn al-Ash'ath al-Sijistani, *al-Sunan*.
50. Suyuti, Shaikh Jalaluddin, *Tarikh-ul-Khula*, Lahore, 1870.
51. Suyuti, Shaikh Jalaluddin, *Husnal-Muhadara*, 1321 H.
52. Waliyullah, Shah, *Izalatul Khafa 'An Khilafatul Khulafa*.
53. Ya'qubi, *Kitabul-Buldan*.
54. Yusuf ibn 'Abd al-Barr al-Namri al-Qurtubi, *Kitab al-Isti'ab fi Ma'rifatil Ashab*, 2 vols., Hyderabad (India), 1318 H.
55. Zakariya, Maulana Muhammad, *Hikayat-i-Sahabah*, Delhi.